DUEL
PERSONALITIES

James Stuart

versus

Sir Alexander Boswell

by John Chalmers

To Betty Borthwick
with many thanks

John Chalmers

Published by
Newbattle Publishing
12 Hope Street
Edinburgh
EH2 4DB

ISBN: 978-0-9928676-0-7

Publication layout and design by Lynne Reilly.
Cover artwork by Lynne Reilly.
Cover images:
    (front) The flintlock pistols believed to be the
    pair used in the duel. (Courtesy of the
    Kirkcaldy Museum); (back) Poster distrib-
    uted by Duncan Stevenson in response to
    James Stuart's refusal to accept his challenge
    to a duel. (Courtesy of the National Library
    of Scotland).

Printed and distributed by
Witley Press Ltd
26 Greevegate
Hunstanton
Norfolk
PE36 6AD

Other books by the author:
Audubon in Edinburgh
ISBN-10: 1-901663-79-5
ISBN-13: 978-1-901663-79-2

Andrew Duncan Senior, Physician of the Enlightenment
ISBN: 978-1-905267-30-9

Published by:
NMS Enterprises Limited – Publishing
a division of NMS Enterprises Limited
National Museums Scotland

Contents

List of illustrations

Foreword

by

The Rt Hon. Lord Ross

ALTHOUGH MANY people know that Sir Alexander Boswell, son of James Boswell, the biographer of Dr Samuel Johnson, was killed in a duel; not many know any of the details surrounding the affair. In particular, the events leading up to the duel, the details of the duel and its aftermath are not well known. John Chalmers has researched all these matters and has produced a highly readable account of the circumstances surrounding the deadly event.

He makes clear in this work that the duel was a consequence of the bitter antagonism between the Whigs and the Tories at the time, and many of the judges and lawyers involved in the legal proceedings arising from the affair were themselves ardent supporters of one or other of these political parties. It is interesting to learn of the part played in these events by these well known legal figures, some of whose reputations are not enhanced.

The surviving duellist, James Stuart, was tried and acquitted on a charge of murder. John Chalmers tells us that two accounts of the trial appeared shortly after its conclusion, and that he has also relied on papers prepared by Henry Cockburn, one of James Stuart's counsel at the trial. As Cockburn was a Whig and one of the defence counsel, he can hardly be regarded as objective, but Cockburn's account is probably the best, and the reader is left to make up his own mind on any disputed issues. Although in fatal duels, juries appear to have been reluctant to convict the surviving duellist of murder, according to *Hume on Crimes*, it is murder to kill in a fair duel, and meeting to fight in a duel excludes a plea of self defence. That being so, it is surprising to see what the Lord Justice Clerk said to the jury in his charge at the trial of James Stuart, it would not, I think, be acceptable nowadays for a judge to encourage a jury to return a verdict which was contrary to law.

I had not previously been aware that, subsequent to the trial, debates had taken place in the House of Commons regarding the actions of the Lord Advocate, and I found this part of the book of special interest.

John Chalmers has obviously conducted a great deal of careful research in preparation for writing this book, and he has shone a clear light on a subject that was not well known. The account he has written is of great interest, and I commend his work to those who enjoy reading about events in Scotland in the early nineteenth century.

Acknowledgements

I AM greatly indebted to many individuals and organisations who have helped me gather material for this book. In particular, the librarians and curators of the following institutions have given invaluable advice and assistance – National Library of Scotland, Edinburgh University Library, Libraries of the Edinburgh Royal Colleges of Physicians and Surgeons, Edinburgh City Library, National Archives of Scotland, British Library, Library of University College London, Mitchell Library of Glasgow, Houghton Library of Harvard University, the British Museum and the Museums of Kirkcaldy and Burntisland.

The WS Society kindly allowed me access to their old Minute and Letter books and the librarian James Hamilton was most helpful in guiding me through them.

My friend Peter Abernethy introduced me to Marjorie Appleton who, with her husband Ian, were the architects responsible for the splendid restoration of Balmuto Castle. Marjorie introduced me to Bruce Boswell, who kindly showed me around the castle, pointing out the room in which Sir Alexander Boswell died, and took me to the probable site of the duel itself.

Vanessa Prosser allowed me to see her remarkable Erskine family tree which showed the distant relationship of many of the individuals mentioned in the book including Boswell and Stuart.

To Lord Ross and Ian Macleod, I am greatly indebted for reading the manuscript and making useful comments and corrections relating to the legal content. Lord Ross has kindly contributed the Foreword to the book.

Margaret Elliot of Redhaugh, a descendent of Sir Alexander, gave helpful information regarding the portraits of her forebears.

Ann Carson, a descendant of William Borthwick, generously allowed me to quote and use the illustrations from her excellent website on William Borthwick which can be found at:

http://freepages.genealogy.rootsweb.ancestry.com/~anncarson/Borthwick/wm binverell.htm

Anna Stone, group archivist of Aviva, provided information on Stuart's involvement with the insurance industry.

Thanks are due to Betty Borthwick who identified the Shakespearian quotations, to John Forrester who translated and identified the Latin quotes and to Peter

Clarke for advice regarding inflation price conversion.

Lynne Reilly has been invaluable in helping me prepare the text for publication.

My wife, Gwyneth, suggested the title and she and my daughter Alison and my granddaughter Shona spent many hours correcting proofs and making suggestions for improvement. I cannot thank them sufficiently for their encouragement and assistance.

Preface

WHILE RESEARCHING an earlier book on Dr Andrew Duncan senior, I became intrigued by a reference to a duel between James Stuart and Sir Alexander Boswell, at which Boswell was killed. I thought that the duel, resulting from an offensive newspaper item, might make a short article. The more I researched the background however, it became apparent that the duel was merely an incident in a period of intense social unrest and political discord fomented by partisan newspapers and journals.

The duel and the subsequent trial of James Stuart during this disturbed time attracted intense national attention. Such was the public interest that two accounts of the trial were published within two weeks of its conclusion. The circumstances of the duel and the subsequent legal shenanigans were hotly debated in Parliament resulting in threats of further duels and accusations of breach of parliamentary privilege. Many distinguished individuals were drawn into the affray including lawyers, authors and politicians such as Sir Walter Scott, Henry Cockburn, Francis Jeffrey, Henry and James Brougham, Lord Rosslyn, James Abercromby and Sir William Rae. Some reputations were enhanced while others emerged with little credit. Several lesser mortals including the printers and publishers, Duncan Stevenson, William Borthwick and Robert Alexander had their lives changed by the events.

The duel and the related events had two unexpected beneficial consequences – a move toward more responsible journalism and a contribution towards the popular demand for parliamentary reform.

The intended short article has expanded against my original intentions into something larger. I empathise with Alexander Boswell when he wrote:

> I cannot, however, repress my rising apprehension, that I shall be unable
> to swell my pages, so as to make a book: for, notwithstanding all my projected notes,
> I fear I shall cut but a pitiful figure in print, and be consigned to the pedlar's basket.
> Yet, as my ambition is not overweening, my disappointment must be correspondent. I throw myself with all my faults on the mercy of the Reader.[1]

Notes

1   Alexander Boswell's 'Advertisement' for *Edinburgh, or, The Ancient Royalty: A Sketch of Former Manners.* Cited in Boswell, A. (1871): *The Poetical Works of Sir Alexander Boswell,* pp. 42–3.

CHAPTER 1

The protagonists

There was a natural demand for libel at this period. The human mind had made a great advance, and the pressure of war being removed, new opinions were coming everywhere into collision with the old ones; so that there was a general shock between those who wished to perpetuate old systems, and those who wished to destroy or reform them … a war of opinion is a condition of which libel is one of the natural products.

Henry Cockburn, *Memorials of his Time*, p. 300

THE DUEL between Sir Alexander Boswell and James Stuart of Dunearn was a consequence of the bitter antagonism between Whigs and Tories which prevailed in the early years of the nineteenth century. Newspapers played a prominent part by supporting one or other side. Public figures including the eminent lawyers and authors Sir Walter Scott, Sir William Rae, Francis Jeffrey, Henry Cockburn, John Hope and James Gibson, and humble printers Duncan Stevenson and William Borthwick, became major participants. The duel attracted enormous public interest at the time and subsequent accounts of the events gained ever increasing embellishment and conflicting detail. Distinguishing fact from folklore has been difficult but here the sources are given and the reader can make up his/her mind.

The two protagonists were born in same year, were distantly related and from similar backgrounds. Both had eccentric fathers and had forebears who became presidents of the Royal College of Physicians of Edinburgh.[1] They studied law at University of Edinburgh at the same time; both had country estates and got heavily into debt by making ill-advised land purchases.

Both Boswell and Stuart were keen collectors of antiquarian books and took an active part in their local communities as justices of the peace and officers in the yeomanry. Each was active in politics and this was to be the source of their dispute, for at a period of intense political unrest when feelings ran high, one was an ardent Whig and the other a dedicated Tory. Although the two men were well acquainted with each other, perhaps because of their differing politics, they were only 'half friends' according to Cockburn.

James Stuart of Dunearn (1775–1849)

James Stuart of Dunearn (Fig. 1), commonly spelt Stewart in legal documents, had an aristocratic pedigree. He was descended from James, 3rd Earl of Moray, and his grandfather, also James Stuart of Dunearn, was Lord Provost of Edinburgh for two terms from 1764–66 and 1768–70.[2] James was the eldest son of Charles Stuart (1745–1826), who was licensed as a Presbyterian minister in 1772 and served for three years at Cramond Kirk before he become disillusioned with the established church and left to join an Anabaptist congregation. When this church was dissolved he decided to study medicine in Edinburgh, graduating MD in 1781. Sir Walter Scott was rather scornful of Charles, describing him as:

> A foolish old man who has spent his whole life in finding a north-west passage to heaven, and after trying many sects, has settled in what he calls the Universal Church, which consists of himself, his housekeeper, one of the maids, and the foot-boy. The butler is said to be in a hopeful way but is not yet converted. All this argues a touch of madness, which, as they come of a very respectable family in Fife (where all the gentry are a little crazy), is not improbable.[3]

Charles can't have been quite as ineffective as Scott painted him for he is recognised as the father of the Society for the Support of Gaelic Schools, founded in 1810,[4] and was elected to the prestigious Speculative Society as well as becoming President of the Royal College of Physicians of Edinburgh from 1806–09.

His son James was brought up in Edinburgh where he attended the High School, before studying law at University of Edinburgh, becoming WS (Writer to the Signet or solicitor) in 1798. Stuart practiced law in partnership with Hay Donaldson WS from 1804–16 and was elected collector of the Widows' Fund of the WS Society from 1818–28, for which he received £200 annually. He became a founding director and co-partner of the North British Fire & Life Insurance Company[5] in 1809. His friends Henry Brougham[6] and the Earl of Rosslyn also became subscribers to the company. On 19 May 1817 he obtained a loan of £1,000 from the company for the purchase of the land of Bolton in East Lothian. Stuart indulged in speculative land and property purchases on a massive scale which led to his bankruptcy in later life. His main interest, however, lay in managing the family estate of Dunearn, near Aberdour, in Fife.

In his youth, Stuart joined a number of clubs. While at University he was a member of the Logical Society and the Juvenile Literary Society founded in 1792 by Henry Brougham, in company with Francis Horner,[7] William Fraser Tytler, James Reay, Alexander Monypenny and others who were to become prominent citizens. The Staffa Club was composed of 16 advocates and lawyers who met monthly while the Court was in session. The meetings seem to have been jolly occasions with much banter and raillery to which Stuart contributed. His friend Alexander Maconochie, who became Lord Meadowbank, was one of its members. At the Chicken Pye Club, Stuart was noted for his excellent temper which was often tried at its meetings.[8]

Stuart took an active part in county affairs, acting as justice of the peace. As a Trustee for Roads, Bridges and Ferries he played a large part in carrying out the improvements of the Forth Ferries and the roads leading to the north from these ferries in accordance with an Act of Parliament of 1809 for the improvement of Queensferry. The road from Burntisland to Perth became known as the Dunearn Road towards which he advanced £2,000 of his own funds.[9] The Rt Hon. William Adam wrote: 'We and ... the whole country are under the greatest obligations to you ... for the great aid you have given us – indeed without your supports both road and ferry must have gone to the Dogs'.[10] As secretary of the Edinburgh Joint Stock Water Company he played a part in improving the water supply to Edinburgh.

Stuart became much involved in politics and was described as, 'a zealous and an uncompromising Whig. No man ever existed more completely devoted to his party.'[11] Walter Scott said of him that:

> He ... was in early life refused something or other which set him up of course as a violent Foxite making speeches at dinners, county meetings and so forth and lately he made himself more conspicuously ridiculous by proposing himself with his own vote and no other to support him as the County Member [of Parliament]. This made him the subject of ridicule to the tories here.[12]

Stuart's politics were to land him into bitter disagreements, notably with George Douglas, the 16th Earl of Morton (1761–1827). The Earl – a Tory – was the owner of an estate which adjoined Stuart's property of Dunearn. Between 1804–08, the two men had fallen out over boundary disputes in the village of Aberdour and the right of Stuart to extract seaweed and carry out oyster fishing from the shore. These led to legal action in the Court of Session in Edinburgh and then an appeal to the House of Lords. No doubt these quarrels coupled with their conflicting political beliefs provoked the Earl into using his influence to try to discredit him.

Stuart wrote to a friend in October 1807:

> With respect to the reflexions on my character which you have heard from the Noble Lord, I treat them with the contempt they deserve. Those who are acquainted with the multiplied acts of aggression toward me, of which he has been guilty, must

be satisfied that I consider his censure, as the highest praise. I know as well as any man, the respect which is due to rank and power when joined with virtue, but when united with vice and ignoble passions, they only render their possessor more despicable.[13]

Stuart had served as a justice of the peace with diligence for 15 years when in 1815 the Earl of Morton, with his authority as Lord Lieutenant of the County of Fife, suddenly removed his name from the list of justices without the courtesy of informing Stuart. He refused to give a reason when approached by Stuart. This provoked an outcry from the local gentry, who held Stuart in high regard. A general meeting of noblemen and gentlemen assembled in Dunfermline to protest. Among them were Francis Stuart, the 10th Earl of Moray (a relation of Stuart), the Earl of Elgin, the Lord Chief Commissioner and 27 other landed gentlemen. Stuart's record of dedicated service was noted. He had never permitted his business in Edinburgh, his necessary residence there during the greatest part of the year, on his numerous and important occupations to interfere with his attendances or his duty as a magistrate – he was distinguished for his knowledge, ability and integrity, etc. A unanimous agreement of the meeting requested the Earl of Moray to convey the minute of the meeting to the Earl of Morton, 'not doubting that when these things are brought thus distinctly to his Lordship's knowledge and observation, that he will adopt the proper course for having the name of James Stuart Esq. Younger of Dunearn inserted in the New Commission of Peace for Fifeshire'.[14]

Morton was forced to yield, but did so without grace or apology and retaliated in a petty manner by removing the name of Stuart's father, Charles, from the list of justices of the peace in Fife – again refusing any explanation. Charles had been a JP since 1787 when he inherited the estate of Dunearn from his uncle. James tried to have his father's name restored. He sent letters to several Fife worthies trying to gain their support saying: 'it is *my duty* to resist the attempt to fix on my father a mark of degradation which I know to be unwarranted'[15] without success. His father, aged 67 and living in Edinburgh, was unable to attract sufficient local support.

Relationships between Stuart and Morton seemed to improve for a time; a letter from the Earl of Kellie, the Vice Lord Lieutenant of Fife, dated 1 December 1819 read '… it gives me great pleasure to understand that you and Lord Morton have shacken [*sic*] hands so that all unpleasant byegones will be forgot … . Tho' you and I differ somewhat in politics yet I am sure we will never differ in matters that regard the good of our country'.[16]

Alas, this reconciliation did not last. Stuart had served as an officer in the Fife Yeomanry for 20 years, at first as a cornet and later as lieutenant in charge. In

1821 he held an exercise of his troop of lancers without notifying his superior officer. This was contrary to an order which had been issued, but which Stuart had not seen. For this seemingly trivial offence, Stuart received harsh criticism from the Earl of Morton among others. There can be little doubt that the reprimand of Stuart, who by all accounts had been an exemplary commander of his troop, was linked with accusations of cowardice when he declined the challenge to a duel, described in Chapter 4.

Stuart consulted James St Clair-Erskine, the 2nd Earl of Rosslyn, (1762–1837)[17] – another distant relative and a nearby landowner – on whose advice he tendered his resignation. Characteristically, he followed up his resignation with a tirade of letters of protest and self justification to those who had criticised him. Many of the letters were addressed to the Earl of Morton, who became exasperated by them. On 9 February 1822, in reply to a letter from Stuart, he wrote:

> On my arrival here late last night, I found on my table your communication of yesterday's date, <u>demanding</u> an answer to your letter of the 5th of this month, which was delivered at Dalmahoy[18] late in the evening of that day. That answer, which must have reached you ere now, you would have received sooner had I not bestowed on the twenty nine documents, occupying thirty four folio pages by which your letter was accompanied, more time and consideration than perhaps I ought, or than perhaps the subject required. I shall endeavour to avoid falling into a similar error in future, and begging to decline all further correspondence on this matter,
>
> I have the honour, etc.[19]

Stuart subsequently published all the correspondence relating to his censure.[20] His father wrote:

> My dear James
> I have read over your correspondence with Lord Morton and Lord Kellie and am of opinion that you have been exceedingly ill used … I am agitated beyond what I can express. I see the underhand dealing of one Lord and the mean and dastardly conduct of another … . I have lived in this world long enough to know that these things correspond with what the word of God says of it – If you would embrace it now upon its own evidence, you would find yourself raised above all that the world can inflict … . Will you see me any evening soon … [or] write a few lines to relieve my anxiety which I feel on your account …[21]

A rather sad letter suggesting that James was inclined to neglect his father who lived only a few miles away at 41 George Square in Edinburgh.

Stuart's command of his troop had received much praise over the years and his lancers were much upset at the enforced resignation of their popular officer. Under his leadership the strength of his troop had increased from 20 to 80 members. At a meeting of the gentlemen of his troop on 26 January 1822, Stuart was presented with a silver plate as a mark of their esteem.[22] The local gentry recognised that the Earl's attack on Stuart was due to personal animosity rather than to the trivial offence which scarcely merited notice. His resignation was, however regarded in the Tory newspapers as a victory of Toryism over the Whigs and became a source of mocking derision of Stuart (see pp. 65–6). Despite this, his standing in his local community was such that he was elected Provost of Inverkeithing in October of that year. Even this honour became yet another subject for scorn to the warped prejudice of the *Sentinel* newspaper which reported it as 'an attempt to bring Mr Stuart from under the shade'. This was one of the many insults suffered by Stuart in the Tory press which led eventually to the duel.

Stuart married Eleanor Maria Anna, daughter of Dr Robert Moubray of Cockairnie, but had no children.

Sir Alexander Boswell (1775–1822)

Alexander Boswell (Fig. 2) was the elder son of James Boswell, the chronicler of Dr Samuel Johnson. Boswell promptly sent a letter to Johnson announcing the birth of his son '… I have named him Alexander after my father'.[23]
Johnson wrote a year later to Boswell:

> I wish you, my dearest friend, and your haughty lady (for I know she does not love me,) and the young ladies, and the young laird, all happiness. Teach the young gentleman, in spite of his mamma, to think and speak well of.
>
> Sir, Your affectionate and humble servant Sam Johnson[24]

Soon after his birth the family moved to London where Alexander was privately tutored until 1786, when he was sent to Dr Barrow's academy in Soho Square.[25] In 1789, aged 13, Alexander entered Eton College where he spent three years. He did not enjoy the experience at first. His father wrote: 'you cannot imagine how miserable he has been. He wrote to me for some time as if from the galleys, and intreated me to come to him'.[26] His advice to Alexander was to 'think and act like a gentleman and not like a spoiled child'. Alexander was proud of his father's literary achievements and while at Eton wrote Latin verses[27] to commemorate the publication of the *Life of Johnson* which his father thought were truly wonderful. At the same time he was ashamed of the accounts of his father's dissolute behaviour and wrote to tell him so. Later he was to change his opinion about his father's association with Johnson. Sir Walter Scott commented that Alexander was:

> ... a proud man and, like his grandfather, thought that his father had lowered himself by his deferential suit and service to Johnson. I have observed he disliked any allusion to the book or to Johnson himself, and I have heard that Johnson's fine picture by Sir Joshua [Reynolds] was sent upstairs out of the sitting apartments at Auchinleck.[28]

In fact the true explanation is contained in a letter from Alexander to his brother James: 'I would fain Johnson a place but he is so unmanageable in size.'[29]

Despite his English education, Alexander retained the local broad Ayrshire accent emulating his grandfather, Lord Auchinleck, a Scottish judge who was noted for his broad Scottish accent. It was quite fashionable for the Scottish upper classes to speak with a Doric accent at that time. Cockburn, renowned for his oratory, spoke in that fashion 'untinged ... by ... vulgar affectation of the language of the South'.[30] James Boswell, who had been brought up and educated in Scotland, much preferred the sophistications of London to things Scottish. When he first met Samuel Johnson on 16 May 1763, he confessed 'indeed I come from Scotland, but I cannot help it'. In a letter to William Temple dated 20 July 1784 he states:

> ... how unfortunate is it that in this my *native city* my *countrymen* should affect me with such wretchedness ... What of my love of England, where I am *absolutely certain* that I *enjoy life*, whereas *here* it is *insipid*, nay, *disgusting*.[31]

And to his friend Temple on 3 July 1789, he wrote: 'But were my daughters to be *Edinburgh mannered girls*, I could have no satisfaction in their company'.[32] He planned to have then educated in London or the Continent.

Alexander in contrast to his father loved his native country. In 1792 he matriculated at University of Edinburgh for three years to study law but left without a degree. (Stuart was studying law in Edinburgh at the same time.) After university, Alexander went on the grand tour from May 1795 to June 1796 visiting Leipzig, Dresden and Berlin. He wrote from Dessau that he was:

> ... now at the court where my father was betwixt thirty and forty years ago, and of which I had heard so much when sitting on his knee and listening to the stories which he told of the old princes and their hospitable splendour.[33]

In 1795 his father died, and Alexander became the 10th laird of the family estate of Auchinleck, which he referred to as Affleck (the name by which his grandfather, Lord Auchinleck, had been known). The estate was heavily burdened with debts, the result of his father's extravagance – a trait which Alexander inherited. In his turn he was to leave the estate to his son James with increasing encumbrance.[34] Despite the chronic shortage of funds Boswell entered into the life of a country laird with great enthusiasm. He claimed to have planted 30,000 trees in the property with his own hands. He lived in considerable style with a carriage and four, hounds and racehorses. Euphemia Boswell made a very sisterly observation when she described him living 'in very favourable manner as having abilities risen superior to what was expected from him'.[35] An acquaintance described Alexander as:

> ... no great beauty ... he had not one real good feature in his whole face, taken singly; but all blended together, and lighted up with his spirit and vivacity, there was a fascination about it that I never saw in any other ... I would say he was upwards of six feet, with a broad chest, a head well set on his shoulders ... . At ploughing matches, shootings, ice-playings, &c, he mingled freely with the tenantry and villagers around, and imparted life and good humour to whatever was going on.[36]

Walter Scott, who knew Boswell well, described him as 'a most high-spirited joyous fellow with no small share of humour, and a ready composer of songs which he sang himself very well. Very hardy and resolved too, in short a man of a gallant and determined character ...'.[37]

On 26 November 1799, Alexander married Grisel Cumming, usually styled Grace Cuming (Fig. 3). They had two daughters, Janet Theresa and Margaret Amelia, and a son James. Grace was born into the family of wealthy Edinburgh bankers. The firm Cumming and Son was founded by her grandfather William Cumming, one of the few private bankers in Edinburgh to survive the financial crash of 1772. He was described as immensely rich and extremely penurious. 'He never allowed his servant to brush his clothes, lest the process should wear off the pile; but made him place them on the back of a chair, and blow the dust off with a pair of bellows.'[38] As an agent of the State Lottery he accidentally retained the winning ticket for which the prize was £10,000 (about £1 million today). His son, Thomas Cumming, Grace's father, was partner in the family business. As a result of her inheritance Grace was able to assist in paying off some of the family debts inherited by her son James (see p. 139).

Alexander played an important part in Ayrshire affairs acting as a Road Trustee, Commissioner of Supply, justice of the peace, and rose to high rank in masonry. In 1816 he became a Member of Parliament having purchased the seat of Plympton Erle at a cost of £1,000. During his time as an MP from 1816–21, he diligently supported the Tory party. In his maiden speech in 1817 he argued that the land owners of Scotland had no desire for parliamentary reform. He introduced only one bill, on 31 March 1819 – ironically about duelling. This was an appeal to have Scottish laws, which had fallen into disuse for many years, struck out of the Statute Book. Two statutes were singled out for particular notice; one decreed that a person challenging another to fight a duel, forfeited all his moveable property and suffered banishment; the other, that if two individuals quarrelled to the effusion of blood, the party who provoked the quarrel should be considered to have lost his cause. In the subsequent debate several speakers were opposed on the grounds that removing ancient statutes opened a dangerous precedent, nevertheless the 'Scotch Duelling Acts Repeal Bill' was passed into law on 3 July 1819.[39] Cockburn wrote:

> He was a short time in parliament; and it is curious that it was he who introduced, or at least took charge of, and carried the act [59th George III. c.70], which abolishes our two old Scotch statutes against fighting a duel, or sending a challenge … . This was his solitary piece of legislation, I believe.[40]

In his capacity as Colonel of the Ayrshire Yeomanry, Boswell took an active part in the suppression of local civic unrest in 1820, for which he was given a gold snuff-box by his corps. Boswell hoped for greater recognition of his services to his party, which he had faithfully supported. His approaches to the Prime Minister, Lord Liverpool, in this regard were ignored, 'no answer could be given by Lord Liverpool to an independent man who conscientiously supported the administration with more persevering punctuality than any paid man in office'. This rejection coupled with financial difficulties led him to vacate his parliamentary seat on 7 February 1821. The day before he took the Chiltern Hundreds,[41] his last parliamentary activity was to vote in support of the Ministers conduct towards Queen Caroline which was to become a defining issue between the Whigs and Tories (see pp. 24–5). Boswell wrote to Sir Walter Scott:

> After having the satisfaction of giving aid in countering the hopes and endeavours of a most anomalous opposition, I have for the moment retired from Parliament to look after my own estate, which needs a master's eye.[42]

The Home Secretary, Lord Sidmouth, 'the only one of his Majesties Ministers who has treated me with attention' redeemed the situation by obtaining a baronetcy for Boswell. His letter of 13 July 1821 stated that this mark of royal favour was:

... attributed not merely to the just view which has been taken by His Majesty of those fair pretentions which arise from your station in life, your property, and character; but also, in a high degree, to those principles of loyalty, and of attachment to the constitution of your country which you have invariably manifested ... [43]

Alexander had obtained, by various means, two distinctions – a parliamentary seat and a baronetcy – which his father had much desired but never achieved. Unlike his father he was proud of his Scottish heritage. He had a great admiration for Robert Burns and many of his own poems and songs were written in Scots dialect. Some of these were published in 1803 under the heading *'nulla venenato litra mixta joco'*. This quotation is a line from a verse in Ovid's poem *Tristia* (line 566, book II). The verse translated reads:

I've never hurt anyone with caustic verse,
My poetry has never accused anyone.
I've openly avoided wit steeped in venom,
Not a single letter is stained with poisonous jest.

If only he had adhered to this precept, the duel would never have taken place.

His admiration for Burns' poetry clearly overcame any feelings which Boswell may have had about Burns' Whig leanings, for he proposed and raised the necessary funds (£3,300) for the erection of the Burns' Monument in Alloway (Fig. 4). On 25 January 1820 – the anniversary of Burn's birth – Boswell as Depute-Grand-Master of Ayrshire,[44] laid the foundation stone and gave an address to a vast concourse of spectators. A plaque at the monument reads that:

It was at his suggestion, and mainly through his instrumentality, that Scotland thus did homage to the genius of her peerless poet ... the enthusiasm, perseverance, liberality, and personal attention of Mr. Boswell of Auchinleck have been so marked and so excessive, and his nature evidently was so congenial to the task, that he falls unquestionably to be characterised as its first, best, and most steadfast friend.

Alexander was renowned for his sociability and was a welcome guest at social functions. He and his brother James were elected members of the exclusive and prestigious Roxburghe Club, founded in 1812, the oldest society of bibliophiles in the world, which flourishes to this day. Boswell was well qualified to join this, for he had established the Auchinleck Press in a cottage on his estate, publishing rare historical works and his own compositions. In 1817 he presented Walter Scott with a volume 'written, printed, and bound by himself'. (Scott was elected to the Roxburghe Club three years after Boswell.)

The Harveian Society had been founded in Edinburgh by Dr Andrew Duncan in 1778 in honour of William Harvey, the discoverer of the circulation of the blood. The Society, which survives to this day, is a dining club which was created to promote harmony and good will between physicians and surgeons who, at that time, formed two opposing branches of the medical profession. Duncan allowed a few non-medical individuals of a genial disposition to become members and Alexander Boswell was elected in 1810. He was appointed poet laureate and entertained the Society with his songs and poems.[45] This extract from his Harveian Ode, was his last work, read at the Society after his death:

> Hail! To immortal Harvey hail!
> Thine inspiration breathed upon his soul,
> And to his ken the hidden truth unfurled;
> That as the seasons change, the planets roll,
> As from the eastern wave to western flood,
> Thy course revolving animates the world,
> So circling moves the current of the blood.[46]

After the recitation of the Ode, a bumper was quaffed to the memory of Sir Alexander, the toast being introduced by some elegiac verses, no doubt written by Duncan who also fancied himself as a poet. The first verse reads:

> Lo! behold us here assembled,
> After death has thrown a dart,
> Which deprived us of a Poet
> Who possess'd a noble heart.[47]

Boswell was a great friend and frequent guest of Sir Walter Scott. On Sunday evenings Scott had informal dinners at home with a few friends, 'never any person with whom he stood on ceremony'. At these 'dinners without silver dishes' as Scott called them, 'I may mention … Sir Alexander Boswell of Auchinleck, who had all his father Bozzy's cleverness, good humour, and joviality without one touch of his meaner qualities, … sang capitally – and was moreover a thorough bibliomaniac'.[48]

Henry Brougham described Boswell as being 'a very clever man, of violent Tory prejudices, as might be expected of a son of James Boswell, – and of some eccentricity'.[49] Cockburn described him as:

> … able and literary; and when in the humour of being quiet, he was agreeable and
> kind. But in general he was boisterous and overbearing, and addicted to coarse

personal ridicule. With many respectable friends, his natural place was at the head of a jovial board, where every one laughed at his exhaustless spirits, but each trembled lest he should be the subject of the next story or song.[50]

Other important participants

Before leaving the account of the two principal characters of this book, it is appropriate to give brief biographies of the six lawyers who are to be met repeatedly in subsequent chapters as major participants in the events. James Gibson, Sir William Rae, Sir Walter Scott, Francis Jeffrey, Henry Cockburn and John Hope had much in common; all were educated at the High School in Edinburgh and studied law at University of Edinburgh; each achieved distinction in the legal profession and four are remembered in the City of Edinburgh by having streets named after them or statues erected. They differed fundamentally in their political beliefs: Scott, Rae and Hope being ardent Tories, while Cockburn, Jeffrey and Gibson were staunch Whigs. It was their politics which led to their involvement with the duel which is the subject of this book.

James Gibson – later Sir James Gibson-Craig of Riccarton (1765–1850)

James Gibson (Fig. 5) was the oldest of the sextet of lawyers. He became a WS in 1786 and established a successful practice in Edinburgh. He was a fervent Whig and was regarded as one of the founders of the Liberal party in Scotland. Cockburn wrote that:

> … his whole life was spent in fearless usefulness. He was so prominent in our worst times, that it is difficult to understand how Thomas Muir, advocate, could be transported in 1793, and James Gibson not even tried! No private individual out of Parliament … did so much to uphold the popular cause.[51]

In 1844, Gibson played a prominent role in the erection of the monument on Calton Hill to Muir and his fellow martyrs. In 1823 he inherited the estate of Riccarton and adopted the name of Craig; in 1831 he was awarded a Baronetcy by the First Reform Ministry for his services to the Whig cause, although he had never held parliamentary office. He was one of the Whigs, who, like Stuart, was pilloried by the *Beacon* newspaper, which he successfully sued for libel.

A keen bibliophile, he left a large library which was sold at an auction in London lasting several days. Cockburn said of him that he was 'the last of the gallant old Edinburgh party who stood out for freedom during the perilous times' and added that his death 'left nothing to be regretted, unless it be that man is mortal'.[52]

Sir William Rae (1769–1842)

Sir William Rae was a contemporary and lifelong friend of Scott who referred to him as his 'dear loved Rae' in the introduction to the fourth canto of *Marmion*. His father, Sir David Rae (1724–1804) had been a successful advocate, who was appointed to the bench in 1782 in succession to Alexander Boswell (Lord Auchinleck), the grandfather of Sir Alexander. Sir David adopted the title Lord Eskgrove and, as a judge, was noted for his eccentricities and for his curious accent. He became Lord Justice Clerk in 1799. Cockburn said of him that 'never once did he do or say anything which had the slightest claim to be remembered for any intrinsic merit. The value of all his words and actions consisted in their absurdity'.[53] His son, William, followed his father, becoming an advocate in 1791 and was appointed Sheriff of Orkney in 1801 and of Midlothian in 1810. He inherited his baronetcy from his brother in 1815. In 1819 he was appointed Lord Advocate, a government appointment which gave him considerable power as chief advisor to the government on legal matters relating to Scotland. Indeed the Lord Advocate of Scotland was described as having:

> … more ample power than the king has by the law of England … . Without necessary consultation with any one, [he is] not only the public prosecutor in all cases of trial, but the arbiter who decides who shall or shall not be tried; and, in the latter capacity, he, of the plenitude of his own power, performs all the functions of an English grand jury.[54]

As the chief prosecutor in Scotland, Rae had the responsibility of trying to maintain order during the civil unrest of 1820 and was generally regarded as having shown good judgement. As a Tory he resisted the attempts of the Scottish Whigs to introduce parliamentary reform but did introduce a number of measures designed to improve the organisation of the Scottish courts.

Like Scott, Rae was a financial backer of the *Beacon* newspaper, and thus had a share in the events leading to the duel. Chapter 9 details the strong criticism of him in Parliament in 1822 and 1823 for his involvement with the Tory press and his role in the prosecutions which followed the duel, but he managed to survive the storm by a narrow margin of votes, although with considerable damage to his reputation.

In 1830, Rae (as Lord Advocate) and Hope (as Solicitor General) were replaced by Jeffrey and Cockburn respectively when a Whig government under Earl Grey was elected. However, Rae was reinstated in 1834 and again in 1841 with changes in government.

During the Great Fire of 1824 (15–17 November) which destroyed much of the High Street in the vicinity of Parliament Square, Rae distinguished himself by joining the crew of one of the fire engines in his efforts to subdue the blaze, while Scott, Cockburn and Hope were ineffectual onlookers in the confusion.[55]

One of Rae's most celebrated cases was that of William Burke and William Hare, who murdered at least 16 individuals to provide subjects for Robert Knox's anatomy school in Edinburgh. Rae was the prosecutor of Burke and his partner Helen Macdougal and obtained a guilty verdict on 25 December 1828 for Burke who was subsequently hanged and publicly dissected. Cockburn defended Macdougal and succeeded in obtaining a 'not proven' verdict, which was not popular with the masses. Hare turned King's evidence and was spared prosecution.

In March 1841, one of Rae's last Parliamentary contributions was the introduction of a bill for the erection of a monument to Sir Walter Scott on Edinburgh's Princes Street which was completed in 1846.

Sir Walter Scott (1771–1832)

Sir Walter Scott (Fig. 6) is so well known as an author and poet as to need little introduction. He was born in Edinburgh and suffered from poliomyelitis as a child leaving him permanently lame. He was sent to live with an aunt in the Borders to help with his recuperation and from her acquired his love of Scottish history and folklore. He was educated at the High School in Edinburgh, which he disliked and left to enter University of Edinburgh at the age of 12 to study classics, and later law. He was admitted to the Faculty of Advocates in 1792 and in 1799 was appointed Sheriff-Depute for the County of Selkirk. He subsequently became one of the Principal Clerks of Session. Writing however, became his major preoccupation and source of income. His fame and popularity as an author spread throughout the English speaking world and his books were widely translated. Cockburn described the impact of the publication of Scott's first novel *Waverley*:

> ... no work that has appeared in my time made such an instant and universal impression ... the profusion of original characters, the Scotch language, Scotch scenery, Scotch men and women, the simplicity of the writing, and the graphic force of the descriptions, all struck us with an electric shock of delight.[56]

The Prince Regent was one of Scott's admirers and gave him permission to search for the 'Honours of Scotland', the Royal crown jewels, which had not been seen since the Union in 1707. These were found – unsurprisingly – in the Crown Room of Edinburgh Castle and their discovery caused great excitement. The Prince Regent awarded Scott a Baronetcy in 1820. When, as George IV, he visited Edinburgh in 1822, Scott was entrusted with the stage management of the pageantry which he did with enormous success.

Scott had entered into business partnership with his childhood friends and publishers and printers of his works, the brothers James and John Ballantyne and also invested in the publishing firm of Constable & Co. In the financial crash of 1825, both publishing businesses collapsed and Scott lost all his wealth. He had to sell his Edinburgh home in North Castle Street and spent his last years writing with increased intensity to pay off his debts, but it was not until after his death that these were finally cleared from the continuing income from the sales of his books.

Scott's involvement with this book arose out of his friendship with Alexander Boswell and his strong Tory leanings which persuaded him to support the *Beacon* newspaper. An article in this paper lit the fuse that eventually led to the duel. Scott himself was challenged to a duel by James Gibson in connection with his involvement with the *Beacon*.

Francis Jeffrey (1773–1850)

Francis Jeffrey (Fig. 7) attended the Universities of Glasgow, Oxford and Edinburgh where he acquired a law degree. He became a member of the Faculty of Advocates in 1794. In 1802 he was a founder member of the *Edinburgh Review*, which was conceived in his flat in Buccleuch Place and became its editor for 26 years (see pp. 28–29). The students of the University of Glasgow elected Jeffrey as their rector for two terms in 1820 and 1822.

In 1829 Jeffrey was elected Dean of the Faculty of Advocates and gave up his editorship in order to devote his time solely to legal affairs. When the Whigs came into power in 1830, Jeffrey was made Lord Advocate in succession to Sir William Rae. In order to fulfil this office it was necessary that he should be a Member of Parliament and Jeffrey spent £10,000 in his efforts to buy a seat. Cockburn was very critical of this requirement:

> The condition of the Lord Advocate's office in relation to Parliament must be changed, unless it be intended to keep it for men of fortune who are barristers only in name. He must get a Government seat free of expense, …. . At present,

15

for £2,500 a year, he is expected to lay out that money, at the least, on a seat, and then to extinguish his practice by being in London.[57]

Jeffrey's main contribution during his short Parliamentary career was his introduction of the Scottish Reform Bill, which had been largely drawn up by Henry Cockburn and himself. This was passed in 1832 and the resulting increased franchise from 5,000 to 65,000 and the added number of seats largely did away with the corruption which had enabled members to buy their way into Parliament.[58] Edinburgh's Parliamentary representation was increased from one to two members and the wider electorate elected Jeffrey as a member for Edinburgh without cost.[59] The Tory government was returned in 1834 and Jeffrey was replaced as Lord Advocate by the reappointment of Sir William Rae. He was promoted to the Bench with the title of Lord Jeffrey and spent the rest of his life with distinction as a judge, first as a Lord Ordinary and later as a judge of the First Division.

Jeffrey was renowned for his wit and wisdom. His friend and biographer Cockburn said of him:

> … his was the finest nature I have ever known … . In him intuitive quickness of intellect was combined with almost unerring soundness, and the highest condition of reasoning powers with the richest embellishment of fancy. His moral taste was so elevated and so pure, that life with all its interest and honours contained nothing that could be even felt as temptation.[60]

Parties at Jeffrey's summer retreat of Craigcrook Castle on the outskirts of Edinburgh were memorable occasions. 'The Craigcrook Saturdays during the summer session! Escape from the court and the town, scenery, evergreens, bowls, talk, mirth, friendship, and wine inspire better luxury than that of the Castle of Indolence, without any of its dulness [sic].'[61]

Jeffrey acted as counsel for James Stuart together with Henry Cockburn.

Henry Cockburn (1779–1854)

Henry Cockburn (Fig. 8) is a central figure in this book, personally acquainted with many of the individuals connected with the duel. His *Memorials of his Time*, published posthumously, gives a vivid account of contemporary events and personalities and is much quoted and referred to here. His career followed closely that of Jeffrey, his senior by six years, who became his closest colleague. Like Jeffrey he became an ardent Whig despite an upbringing in a Tory family and being a nephew (by marriage[62]) of Henry Dundas, the 1st Viscount Melville, leader of the Scottish Tories. He joined the Faculty of Advocates in 1800 and became one of the leaders of the Scottish Bar. He was described as being a:

> … sure type of an orator, he seemed to feel himself all the emotions which he was anxious to inspire. Before a Scottish jury he was all but irresistible, and the vigorous logic of Moncreiff, or the eloquent versatility of Jeffrey, his chief rivals in that field, suffered frequent discomfiture at this hands. He presented himself…with such an air of simplicity and innocence, a plain man like themselves, speaking a language they could understand … . His most celebrated efforts of which a record is preserved are his speech for Stuart of Dunearn … and that for Helen Macdougal in the trial of the murderer Burke.[63]

In 1830 during the Whig administration of Lord Grey, he was made Solicitor General and assisted Jeffrey in drawing up the Scottish Reform Bill, 'seeing his country freed for ever from the bonds against which he and his friends had so bravely and successfully struggled'.[64] In 1831 he, as Jeffrey before him, was elected Rector of Glasgow University for three consecutive years. In 1834 he was appointed a judge in the Court of Session with the title of Lord Cockburn. On the Bench 'his reputation and efficiency were unequal[led]. In the Criminal Court he was one of the most distinguished of its occupants, master of the criminal law in all its branches, and a model of judicial clearness, quick apprehension, and capacity for elucidating truth'.[65]

Outside the law he was celebrated for his friendship and hospitality both at his country seat of Bonaly, where he had built a tower on an old ruin, and at his town house, 14 Charlotte Square. He was keen to preserve the beauty of his beloved city of Edinburgh and resisted developments which might block the view of Edinburgh Castle from Princes Street, in which campaign he was supported by James Stuart. His name is commemorated to this day in the Cockburn Association, which was founded in 1875 to continue the legacy of his ideals. He married Elizabeth Macdowell in 1811 and they had 11 children. Cockburn's *Memorials*, which ended in 1830, was followed by his *Journal* which covered the period 1831–54 and his *Life of Lord Jeffrey* (1852).

Despite their sharply divided political opinions Scott, Cockburn and Jeffrey respected each other, and frequently met socially. All were members of the Speculative Society where they honed their debating skills. All three played an important part in founding The Edinburgh Academy which opened on 1 October 1824. Scott wrote in his *Journal* on 9 December 1826:

> I do not know why it is that when I am with a party of my Opposition friends the

day is often merrier than when with our own set. Is it because they are cleverer? Jeffrey and Harry Cockburn are, to be sure, very extraordinary men, yet it is not owing to that entirely. I believe both parties meet with a feeling of novelty.

Cockburn visited Scott at his home in Abbotsford in 1828 and wrote that his 'simplicity and naturalness after all his fame are absolutely incredible'. His conversation was 'a joyous flow of anecdote, story, character and scene, mostly humorous, always graphic, and never personal or ill-natured'.[66]

John Hope (1794–1858)

John Hope was much the youngest of the sextet. He was born into a legal family his father, Charles Hope (1763–1851), being Lord President of the Court of Session. He was admitted as an advocate in 1816 and was soon appointed Advocate Depute by his fellow Tory, the Lord Advocate, Sir William Rae. Like Rae, he was one of the backers of the *Beacon* newspaper. He enters this book in connection with his arrest of William Borthwick, which led to him being criticised in the Parliamentary debate of 1822, detailed in Chapter 9. His reaction to the criticism was so vehement that he was threatened with a duel and brought before the House on the charge of breach of parliamentary privilege. Despite this, he was appointed Solicitor General for Scotland later the same year and held this post until 1830 when, with the change of government, he was succeeded by Henry Cockburn. Later that year he was elected Dean of the Faculty of Advocates in succession to Francis Jeffrey.

As an advocate he had a reputation for verbosity. Henry Cockburn comparing him with the conduct of the barristers of the English Bar wrote: 'I heard no voice strained, and did not see a drop of sweat at the [English] Bar .... Our high-pressure Dean screams and gesticulates and perspires more in any forenoon than the whole bar of England ... in a reign'.[67] Scott, however, regarded Hope as:

> ... the most hopeful young man of his time; high connections – great talent – spirited ambition – a ready and prompt elocution with good voice and dignified manner ... will, if I mistake not, carry him as high as any man .... He is hot though, and rather hasty, – this should be amended – they who ply at single stick must bear ... a rap over the knuckles'.[68]

On 1841, when Lord Justice Clerk Boyle became Lord President, John Hope was appointed in his place and served in that office until his death in 1858. He presided over the famous trial of Madeleine Smith.[69] In his later years he was renowned for his opposition to the Disruption of the Scottish Church. He died in his home, 20 Moray Place, which 40 years earlier had been the home of James Stuart. The tradition of legal service continues in the Hope family to the present day.

Notes

1 Alexander Boswell's presidential forebear was a great uncle, John Boswell (1707–80), president of the Royal College of Physicians from 1770–72. Boswell's Court off the Royal Mile in Edinburgh is named after him. James Stuart's presidential forebear was his father Charles Stuart (1745–1826), president from 1806–09.

2 During his first term in office he was responsible for commissioning the North Bridge from 'Cap and Feather Close to Multrees Hill' which linked the developing New Town with the Old Town.

3 Letter to J. B. S. Morritt, 25 June 1822 in Scott (1932–37): *The Letters of Sir Walter Scott*, **VII**, pp. 194–5.

4 Harding (1992): *Transactions of the Gaelic Society of Inverness*, **56**, pp. 365–76.

5 Later the North British and Mercantile Insurance Co., now after various mergers, part of Aviva.

6 Henry Brougham (1778–1868) was the eldest of three brothers who became friends with Stuart and appear in subsequent chapters. Henry was the most eminent. He was one of the founders of the *Edinburgh Review* and contributed many articles to it throughout his life. He became a Whig Member of Parliament in 1810 and was prominent in the opposition to the slave trade. He was called to the English Bar and became the advocate-general to the Princess of Wales. He was appointed Lord Chancellor in 1830 with the title of Lord Brougham and Vaux. During his term in office the Reform Act was passed in 1832 and the Slavery Abolition Act in 1833 with his support. He is remembered as the owner of the two-seater carriage which bears his name. In 1859 he was appointed Chancellor of University of Edinburgh.

7 Francis Horner (1778–1815) was a lawyer and a Whig member of Parliament. Like Henry Brougham and Francis Jeffrey he was a founder of the *Edinburgh Review* and a member of the Speculative Society. He acted as Jeffrey's second in his duel with Moore (see Chapter 3). He was an effective parliamentarian, supporting the Whig cause and gaining a reputation as an expert in financial affairs. His statue by Chantry is in Westminster Abbey. His younger brother, Leonard, also a friend of Stuart, features in Chapter 10 and another brother, John, in Chapter 5.

8 These accounts of Stuarts's club memberships are contained in Cockburn (c. 1822a): *Trial 3*, Precognitions, pp. 129–45.

9 Ibid, pp. 14–9

10 Letter of 25 April 1811 quoted in Cockburn (c. 1822a): *Trial 3*, p. 10. William Adam (1751–1839) was the son of architect John Adam. He was a Tory MP and once fought a duel with Charles James Fox. He wrote this letter in his capacity as Lord Lieutenant of Kinross.

11 Obituary in *Gentleman's Magazine* (1849), new series **XXXII**, p. 659.

12 Scott (1932–37): *Letters*, **VII**, p. 195.

13 Letter book of James Stuart, National Archives of Scotland GD1/555/1. This collection of correspondence is concerned mostly with Stuart's conflicts with the Earls of Morton and Kellie. It ends in 1822. The letters are unnumbered and many are undated.

14 Anon (1822): *Trial 1*, p. xi.

15 Letter to Hon. Robert Lindsay of Balcarres et al. 10 January 1816 in Letter Book of James Stuart.

16 Letter book of James Stuart.

17 Rosslyn was active in politics, firstly as a Whig member of the House of Commons but veering towards Toryism on his translation to the House of Lords when he inherited his title as second Earl in 1805. He inherited the estates of Rosslyn to the south of Edinburgh, and Dysart beside

the town of Kirkcaldy in Fife and close to Stuart's estate of Dunearn. He and Stuart were distant cousins as most of the landed gentry in Scotland at that time seem to have been.

18   The Earl's estate in West Lothian. He had extensive properties there as well as his estate in Fife.

19   Letter book of James Stuart.

20   *Correspondence between James Stuart Esq. Younger of Dunearn and the Earl of Morton, Lord Lt. of the County of Fife relative to Mr Stuart's resignation of his commission in the Royal Fifeshire Yeomanry Cavalry*, Edinburgh (1822). Ref Ry 1.4.284. National Library of Scotland.

21   Letter book of James Stuart.

22   *Caledonian Mercury*, 26 January 1822.

23   Boswell to Johnson, 24 October 1775 in Boswell (1964): *Life of Johnson*, **II**, p. 386. His father, Alexander Boswell, became a judge in the Court of Session with the title Lord Auchinleck.

24   Ibid, p. 412.

25   His father had preferred Charterhouse as being the best for his morals but there was no vacancy in the school.

26   Boswell to W. J. Temple, 30 November 1789 in Boswell (1964), **III**, fn p.12.

27   The opening lines of the poem in schoolboy Latin read: *Adveniit tempus jamjam, quae musa tacebit, Quae non cantabit gloria magna modis?* Roughly translated: Now the time approaches, what muse will be silent, What muse will not sing your great glory in its measures?

28   Crocker, J. W. (1885): *The Croker Papers 1808–1857*, **2**, p. 32.

29   Boswell (1964), **V**, p. 385, fn. In 1825 Alexander's widow sold the portrait of Johnson by Reynolds at Sotheby's. It realised only £76.13 shillings which disappointed Lady Boswell who had been led to believe that it might fetch £1,000. She would not have sold it if she had known, Buchanan (1975): *The Treasure of Auchinleck. The Story of the Boswell Papers*, pp. 14–5.

30   *Edinburgh Review* (1857), **105**, p. 220.

31   Lustig, I. S. (1981): B*oswell: The Applause of the Jury*, p. 261.

32   Lustig, I. S. (1986): B*oswell: The English Experiment*, p. 286.

33   Brady (1984): *James Boswell, the Later Years 1769–1795*, p. 487.

34   Buchanan (1975): pp. 193–5 & pp. 204–5.

35   Farington (1922): *The Farington Diary*, I, p.131, 4 January 1796.

36   Boswell (1871): *The Poetical Works of Sir Alexander Boswell*, pp. lv–lix.

37   Letter to Byron, 26 June 1822 in Scott (1932–37): *Letters*, **VII**, p. 198.

38   Kay (1837–38): *A series of original Portraits and Caricature Etchings with Biographical Sketches and Illustrative Anecdotes*, **II**, p. 157.

39   *Hansard*, 31 March 1819, **39**, pp. 1266–9.

40   Cockburn (1909): *Memorials of his time*, p. 374.

41   The name, applied to this day, to the process of an MP resigning his seat.

42   Partington (1932): *Sir Walter's Post-bag*, p. 152.

43   An account of Boswell's Parliamentary activities and his quest for a baronetcy are given in Thorne (1986): *History of Parliament: The House of Commons 1790–1820*, **III**, p. 229–30. A baronetcy at that time was a much sought after status symbol for country gentleman and social climbers; 152 were created during the period 1790–1820.

44   The Boswell family were keen masons. Alexander was a member of the Ayrshire Kilwinning Lodge, to which Burns had also belonged. As holder of the chair of that Lodge, Boswell was *ex officio* Provincial Grand Master of Ayrshire.

45   Chalmers (2010): *Andrew Duncan Senior: Physician of the Enlightenment*, pp. 122–3. Boswell had other links with the Royal College of Physicians of Edinburgh. His cousin, also Alexander Boswell, was Clerk of the College from 1800–36, and his great uncle, Dr John Boswell, had been President (see note 1). Read also Hale-White (1930), pp. 281–4.

46   Boswell (1871): p. 171–2.

47   Boswell (1871): p. 172.

48   Lockhart (1902): *Life of Sir Walter Scott*, **5**, p. 306.

49   Brougham (1871): *The Life and Times of Henry Lord Brougham*, **2**, p. 503.

50   Cockburn (1909): *Memorials*, p. 373.

52   Quoted in Crombie (1882): *Modern Athenians*, p. 57.

52   Cockburn (1874a): *Journal of Henry Cockburn 1831–1854*, **II**, pp. 261–2.

53   Cockburn (1909): *Memorials*, p. 109.

54   Mudie (1825): *The Modern Athens*, p. 176.

55   Grant (1881–83): *Old and New Edinburgh*, **I**, p. 190 and Cockburn (1909): *Memorials*, pp. 395–6.

56   Cockburn (1909): *Memorials*, p. 270.

57   Cockburn (1874a): *Journal*, **I**, p. 2.

58   The Scottish Reform Act gave the vote to householders who paid an annual rent of £10 or more. Walter Scott, who died two months after the passing of the Act, was bitterly opposed to the franchise reform. His friend James Hogg, the 'Ettrick Shepherd' wrote 'I am certain of it, that the democratic ascendancy … broke the heart of and killed the greatest man that country ever contained'.

59   The other elected member was James Abercromby, also a staunch Whig, who figures prominently in Chapter 9. He became Speaker of the House of Commons.

60   Cockburn (1874a): *Journal*, **II**, pp. 254–5.

61   Cockburn (1909): *Memorials*, p. 282.

62   Dundas' first wife was Cockburn's aunt, Elizabeth Rannie, whom Dundas divorced on the grounds of her adultery, while retaining the considerable wealth which she had brought to the marriage. The relationship between the two families was probably not cordial.

63   *Edinburgh Review* (1857), **105**, p. 224.

64   Ibid, p. 227.

65   Cockburn (1909): *Memorials*, Introduction, p. xxiii.

66   Ibid, p. 423.

67   Cockburn (1874a): *Journal*, **I**, p. 114.

68   Scott (1972): *The Journal of Sir Walter Scott*, 13 December 1825, pp. 36–7.

69   Madeleine Smith the daughter of a wealthy Glasgow family who poisoned her lover, Pierre Emile L'Angelier, with arsenic. The jury at her trial found the case against her 'not proven'. It became a *cause célèbre*.

CHAPTER 2
Turbulant times

O mighty Lord and Governor of the universe! Preserve this kingdom we humbly beseech
thee, from the horrors of civil war, apparently approaching us in this city.[1]

Prayer of the Rev. Dr Thomas Chalmers
in St John's church in Glasgow 1820

THE EARLY nineteenth century was a period of intense political turmoil. In the
aftermath of the Napoleonic wars, financial depression and unemployment
caused distress and hardship among the working classes. The Corn Laws, which
imposed a heavy duty on imported wheat in order to maintain the price of the
home produced product, put the price of bread beyond the reach of many and
caused much unrest. A contemporary account of the troublesome times was
written by Robert Alexander, who is to figure in the later chapters of this book.
He wrote:

> The greater part of 1819 was a season of much mercantile suffering. Capital had
> sustained a deterioration, the manufacturer was embarrassed, wages were conse-
> quently low, and employment scarce; and, worse of all the mechanic and his family
> were doomed to fare scantily, betimes necessitated to stretch out the reluctant hand,
> to crave the pittance of benevolence. With the empty meal barrel, the spirits droop,
> and the poor man's judgement is easily bewildered [by] his children's raggedness,
> and their hungry looks, and their ill concealed sorrows.[2]

He blamed the Whig party for 'sounding the shrill pipe of rebellion among our
heretofore peaceful and laborious population' by introducing ideas of Reform
and overthrow of the Constitution at the 'desperate cost of a hopeless civil war'.

At that time the country Members of Parliament were elected by a handful of
landed gentry or the nominees of a few intriguing peers, only two per cent of the
population had a vote. Seats were advertised and could be purchased for a few
thousand pounds. Town (Borough) members were elected in various ways established by tradition. Thus the village of Old Sarum sent two members from an
electorate of seven, while 'new' towns like Manchester, Birmingham and Leeds
had no representatives. In Scotland, Burgh Members were elected by the town
councillors; Edinburgh, for example, with a population of 150,000 had only one

Member selected by the 33 councillors. Corruption was widespread.

The movement for parliamentary reform gained increasing currency among the masses and was strongly resisted by the Tory dominated government, fearful of an uprising akin to the French 'reign of terror'. A number of stringent measures were introduced. The Habeas Corpus Act was suspended in 1817. Paid spies and government agents reported such activities as distributing seditious pamphlets like Thomas Paine's *Rights of Man* and *Age of Reason* or causing public agitation. Thomas Muir and his fellow 'martyrs' who urged Parliamentary reform at a public convention were transported to Botany Bay. A gathering of 60,000 malcontents in Manchester in 1819 led to the Peterloo massacre in which 11 people were killed and 400 injured by the mounted yeomanry. In December of that year the Tory government introduced the 'Six Acts' designed to curb public unrest and freedom. Amongst these was a ban on holding public meetings of more than 50 people, weapons could be seized, military training was banned and publishing seditious papers could lead to transportation.

Henry Cockburn, reflecting on this period, wrote that the Tory party:

> … engrossed almost the whole wealth, and rank, and public office, of the country, and at least three-fourths of the population. They could have afforded, therefore, to be just and well-tempered. But this, as it appeared to them, would have endangered their supremacy … . Hence the great Tory object was, to abuse everybody but themselves, and in particular to ascribe a thirst for bloodshed and anarchy, not merely to their avowed public opponents, but to the whole body of the people. It is frightful even to recollect the ferocious bitterness and systematic zeal with which this principle was acted upon; and this under the direct sanction of Government.[3]

The 'Radical War'

Glasgow was regarded as a hot bed of radicals. On 1 April 1820 an address was posted on the walls of the city calling for militancy. It read:

> Friends and Countrymen! Roused from the state in which we have been sunk for so many years, we are at length compelled from the extremity of our sufferings, and the contempt heaped upon our Petitions for Redress to assert our right *at the hazard of our lives.*

A general strike was called to pressurise the government into giving some electoral rights to the working classes. Thousands responded and stopped work. The government ordered 5,000 regular troops and yeomanry to enter, guard and occupy the city. A curfew was called by the Provost and Magistrates on 3 April. On 8 April a reward of £500 was offered for information on authors and printers of the seditious document, although it was believed by many to be the work of agents provocateurs, intending to promote unrest and allow the government forces to subdue the masses. A small group of about 40 radicals marched to Falkirk with the objective of seizing some cannons at the Carron iron works. They were met by the Yeomanry Cavalry who killed nine and wounded many. Fifteen were taken prisoner and the three leaders were executed by hanging following which they were beheaded. The episode, which became known as the Battle of Bonnymuir, marked the end of the violent protest and the civil war, feared by Chalmers, failed to materialise although peaceful protests continued.

Alexander Boswell in his capacity as justice of the peace tried to maintain order in his own community by printing and distributing a conciliatory letter to the 'Deluded Operatives' which concluded:

> Much has been done to alleviate distress by the sympathy of those who, under Providence, have inherited wealth, or who have acquired it by honest industry. Ingratitude has too often been the requital. If, however, there is a prompt return to duty we trust that the influence of our blessed religion will operate on all, and that while on one hand there is submission to the laws and contrition for the past. on the other there may be no lack of forgiveness, brotherly love, and charity.[4]

Queen Caroline, martyr of the Whigs

One of the causes which had assumed great importance with the Whigs, who represented the disaffected and disenfranchised masses, was what they regarded as the unfair treatment of Queen Caroline by King George IV and his ministers. The King – as Prince of Wales – married his German cousin, Caroline, for political reasons in 1795, and rejected her soon after the birth of their daughter, Charlotte a year later. The Princess, allowed only limited access to her child, went to live abroad in Italy. On the accession of her husband to the throne in 1820, she indicated that she would like to return and resume her royal status. The King tried to obtain a divorce and have her stripped of her royal title on the grounds of adultery. Henry Brougham, who had been the Princess' legal advisor for many years, acted as her Attorney General and by his eloquence managed to have the Bill of Pains and Penalties quashed in the House of Lords. His speech lasted two days and was so eloquent that it reduced Lord Erskine to tears. The masses were delighted, but Brougham was unable to prevent the Queen's name being removed from the liturgy or allow her access to Westminster Abbey at the coronation. As the King had no authority over the Church of Scotland, the removal of the Queen's name from the liturgy did not apply there and the Scottish clergy prayed for her with increasing fervour.

Brougham had advised Caroline to remain abroad in return for a generous allowance, but she insisted on returning to Britain on 6 June 1821 against his advice, in order to assume her position as Queen. Despite the prohibition on her attending the coronation she turned up at Westminster and was banned from entry at each of its doors. The harsh treatment of the Queen by her profligate husband and his ministers so antagonised the populace that she became a national heroine. To the Whigs, her exclusion from the coronation was the final insult. According to Cockburn 'they were the sentiments of a large portion of the nation, and fixed on the Government a more intense feeling of hostility than is usually produced by ordinary party differences'.[5] The Queen had become a symbol in the conflict between reaction and reform and as will be seen later she became a key figure in the events leading up to the duel. Much to the King's relief, the poor Queen died of obstruction of the bowel a month after the coronation. According to Henry Brougham, the obstruction resisted treatment despite – or perhaps because of – the administration of 35 grains of calomel, castor oil and jalap, and blood letting to the extent of 64 ounces.[6]

The Pantheon meeting

In Edinburgh, feelings against the King and his ministers ran high, largely because of their treatment of the Queen even before the coronation took place. The citizens proposed to hold a meeting with a view to petitioning the King to dismiss his ministers. Assemblies in the open air had been banned by the Seditious Meeting Act of 1819 and the Lord Provost and the Lord Advocate, both Tories, denied the protestors access to any building within their control. The Pantheon in Broughton Street was however in private ownership, and the meeting was held there on 16 December 1820. The place was crammed and many were unable to get in. James Moncreiff (1776–1851), a dedicated Whig, presided over the meeting. Moncreiff was a much respected advocate who became Dean of the Faculty in 1826 and a judge in 1829.[7] The meeting was addressed by Francis Jeffrey, among others, and a petition demanding government reform – signed by 17,000 out of a population of 20,000 eligible males in Edinburgh – was inaugurated. An opposing petition mounted by the Tories only obtained about 1,600 signatures. Animosities between Whigs and Tories became intense. Cockburn wrote: 'The influence of all this can scarcely be overstated. Old Edinburgh was no more'.[8] The publisher Adam Black, who had helped to organise the meeting wrote: 'I date the complete emancipation of the citizens of Edinburgh from political thraldom from the Pantheon meeting'.[9]

Political dinners

The Edinburgh Whigs developed the custom of celebrating the Whig statesman Charles James Fox (1749–1806), by a holding a dinner on his birthday, 24th January. These started in a small way after his death but became enormously popular as Whig influence and power increased. Cockburn wrote that, 'These Fox Dinners did incalculable good. They animated, and instructed and consolidated the Whig party with less trouble and more effect than anything else that could have been devised'.[10] The dinner of 1821 in Oman's Hotel in Waterloo Place was held on 12 January rather than the 24th for the convenience of the members of Parliament. It was a splendid affair with about 500 diners who were addressed by the Earl of Rosslyn, Francis Jeffery and Henry Cockburn and many others. The Whig-aligned *Scotsman* of 13 January gave a glowing account of the occasion.

> No man was there whose heart was not elated with the display of genius, eloquence, talents, and manly independence which took place at the meeting. The tide of patriotic feeling was full ... It was the filling up – the matter and manner of the speakers – the delight and enthusiasm of the hearers, which, filling the heart, and satisfying the judgement, gave more than fascination to the scene ...

The Tories, not to be outdone, decided to hold a Pitt Dinner in the Assembly Rooms on the same date, although they usually held their triennial dinners in memory of their hero William Pitt Jr (1759–1806) on his birthday; 28th May. They claimed to have even more diners than the Foxites – about 700. *The Scotsman* of 13 January gave a very critical account of this event. It suggested that the numbers had been inflated by the provision of subsidised food and drink and the issue of free tickets. The speeches were dull heavy and obscene:

> The seventeenth toast will not be printed, we should think, in any Journal, and we are sure it would not have been given in any other company of gentlemen assembled for a public purpose ... . The Whig meeting was distinguished by a great accession of rank, property, and talent. The Pitt meeting was remarkable for a secession of rank and a want of talent ... . The leaden dulness which settled upon them defied even the powers of song. Mr Boswell [Alexander Boswell] strained his epiglottis, and almost rent his frontal sinuses, without raising the tone of the company.

The Scotsman continued its attack on the Pittites in its next issue of 20 January:

> But, whatever difference of opinion may exist on this point, (i.e. the presence of
> ministers of religion at the dinner) there can be none as to the flagrant indecency
> and impropriety of their being present at a drunken and obscene carnival … many
> of the songs and toasts would have reflected disgrace on the inmates of a brothel!

The visit of King George IV

An anomaly of this period was the surprisingly enthusiastic welcome which the
dissolute King received during his visit to Edinburgh in August 1822. The WS
Society sent an address to the King which stated, '… the presence of the Sovereign
is an event which will form an epoch in our domestic annals, and which has
excited, the liveliest emotions of joy and gratitude, throughout this part of your
Majesty's dominions …' and the Society donated 300 guineas towards the statue
of the King in George Street. Dr Andrew Duncan, President of the Harveian
Society, published the following verse:

> Rejoice, Edina, now rejoice,
> Let acclamations fill the gale;
> Shout all, with loud and joyful voice,
> Hail, to our Monarch! Hail, all hail![11]

Boswell, as poet laureate of the Harveian Society, may well have written this verse
for he wrote others in similar vein including:

> Then long live George the Fourth our King,
> And happy be his reign!
> May we, beneath his watchful wing,
> Our laws and rights maintain!
> May halcyon hours revolving come!
> In peace forget the rolling drum.[12]

The Scotsman, in an editorial on 24 August 1822, gave perhaps a more objective view. While being careful to avoid insulting the King, it did not hesitate to
criticise his courtiers and ministers:

> We know nothing at once so mean and impudent as for selfishness to put on
> sycophancy – as for creatures who, having abandoned all principle and lost all

character, would prostitute the powers and authority of Majesty for the worst of their own corrupt and selfish purposes, … .We believe that nine-tenths of those who crowded from all parts of the city and country to see the King, disapproved of and deplored the measures adopted in his Majesty's Councils; … curiosity, unquestionably has been the great operating principle in drawing company to Edinburgh – curiosity to see a King, … a Court, or a Royal Procession.

The war of words

The political unrest of the time was fostered in newspapers, journals and broadsheets. In Edinburgh the war of words was waged with particular intensity. The quarterly *Edinburgh Review,* was founded in 1802, by Sydney Smith, Henry Brougham and Francis Horner, with Francis Jeffrey its editor for 26 years. The *Review*, a Whig-orientated quarterly magazine of literary and political criticism, became an enormously successful publication with a circulation of over 13,000 throughout the English-speaking world, continued publication until 1929. The *Review* was partly counterbalanced by the appearance of the Tory, *Blackwood's Magazine*, which was founded by 'a considerable body of rebels to the long undisputed tyrannical sway of Mr Jeffrey and his friends; and it was necessary that the sentiments of this class should find some vehicle of convenient expression'.[13] *Blackwood's Magazine*, a monthly, was founded in 1817, with John Wilson, writing under the pen name of Christopher North, Walter Scott's son-in-law, John Gibson Lockhart and James Hogg, the Ettrick shepherd, among its main contributors. It, like its rival the *Review*, developed a wide readership and survived until 1980.

Also in 1817, *The Scotsman* weekly newspaper commenced publication in support of the liberal reforming cause. Its immediate success prompted the following comment:

The Scotsman … professedly attached to the Whig, or Opposition interest, had for some time been established in this city, and the keenness with which it was sought for, and the extensive circulation it had consequently obtained, created so great an alarm in the minds of the leaders of the Tory or Ministerial party, that it was determined in order to avert the consequences dreaded from the uncontrolled circulation of the principles it disseminated, to commence a publication decidedly supporting the other side of the question.[14]

Adam Black, the publisher, wrote:

The year 1817 was memorable for Edinburgh as that which saw the birth of the two chief organs of public opinion it has produced after the Edinburgh Review, the Scotsman and Blackwood's Magazine. Each was hailed by the party it represented as a refreshing novelty and a wholesome power, denounced by the opposite side as an engine of mischief and an offence to all the right minded. The struggle between the dominant but waning [Tories], and the young but growing powers [Whigs], was gradually reaching a crisis and the passions of the combatants became more intense as it drew near. The bitterness of animosity displayed in those days is repulsive now to look back on and difficult to realise … the party represented by Blackwood's Magazine was most to blame. They had more wit on their side but also more venom.[15] (Black was a leading Whig!)

The *Beacon*

Prominent among the Tory leaders seeking a counterbalance to *The Scotsman* was Walter Scott. He discussed his ideas in a letter to Lord Melville[16] dated 24 November 1819.[17] In it he refers to a letter from John Wilson Croker[18] who had written: 'Some literary Gentlemen have determined to set up a weekly paper on principles diametrically opposite to the weekly journals which are now in vogue, that is principles of morality, loyalty, respect for constituted authorities, & in short, Toryism'. Croker had written a letter to Lockhart on 18 November asking whether he or his companion contributor to *Blackwood's Magazine*, John Wilson, would be prepared to contribute to the proposed paper: 'Much of the effect of such a paper will depend on the contributors being unknown, the secret of your name shall be carefully preserved …'.[19] Scott endorsed the idea and suggested the name of *Beacon*. He anticipated the problem of finding a good editor[20] but felt that there would be no difficulty in raising funds 'but not without exposing our persons & our plans and it is astonishing what secrecy does in a matter of this kind'. In the event these predictions proved remarkably accurate. The emphasis of both Croker and Scott on the importance of concealing the names of the contributors can only be interpreted as anticipating that the contributions might be of a libellous character. Only by being anonymous could the authors be as rancorous and outspoken as the proposers hoped.

The unpleasant practice was not new. Some years before Edward Topham in his *Letters from Edinburgh* had written:

> How happy would it be for Society, if some one could always be found to avow his right to all those defamatory invectives, the allegories of abuse, which are frequently lavished on individuals by anonymous writers … but leave the guilty unknown.[21]

In discussions with Lockhart and Rae, several names were suggested for the role of editor. They seemed odd choices for mostly they were men who were in regular employment and it seemed presumptuous to think that they might be tempted. James Murray was an editor of the *London Times*; James Ballantyne, Scott's 'fat friend' and his printer was already editor and proprietor of the *Edinburgh Weekly Journal* and John Wilson, who as 'Christopher North' was the principle contributor to *Blackwood's Magazine* and Professor of Moral Philosophy at University of Edinburgh. All declined. Perhaps the most remarkable proposal was the American author and historian Washington Irving, who at that time was resident in Britain, struggling to make a living. Scott, who had met Irving and had a high regard for his writings, sent him a letter.

> You have not only the talents necessary for making a figure in literature ... and want nothing but a sphere of action in which to exercise them ... . Would you have any objection to superintend an Anti-Jacobin periodical publication which will appear weekly in Edinburgh, supported by the most respectable talent, ...The appointment of the editor (for which ample funds are provided) will be £500 a year certain, with the reasonable prospect of further advantages ... . One thing I may hint, that some of your coadjutors being young and clever men, may need a bridle rather than a spur ...[22]

Although chronically short of funds, Irving rejected this most generous offer, worth in today's values about £50,000. He replied to Scott, '... I am peculiarly unfitted for the post proposed. I have no strong political prejudices ... my whole course of life has been desultory, and I am unfitted for any periodically recurrent task'.[23] The style and fortune of the paper might have been radically different had he accepted. Whether Scott could have raised these 'ample funds' is doubtful, but he was right in believing that the success of the paper would depend on the quality of the editor.

Fifteen anonymous backers provided financial backing and the *Beacon* was launched in Edinburgh on 6 January 1821. No experienced and responsible editor was secured. A number of young lawyers, to whom the editorship had been entrusted, contributed 'the rude drollery of ... young hot-bloods'.[24]

The *Beacon's* prospectus read:

> This paper aspires to a place in the public favour, which in this city is wholly unoccupied. It appears as the Champion of our Civil Rights, and of the Government under which we enjoy them. It claims the honourable distinction of maintaining the Causes of Social Order, with the zeal which has hitherto belonged entirely to its enemies ... . No privilege worth preserving was ever maintained without a contest. We must defend our rights like men who value them. We must

repel the dangers by which they are threatened, with the energy which has distinguished our opponents ... the evils of the Free Press can only be corrected by the wise use of its advantages.

Despite these worthy objectives, the *Beacon* developed into a scurrilous rag, introducing a style of journalism which led to the fatal duel between Boswell and Stuart.

Of all these politically oriented publications – newspapers and periodicals such as the *Edinburgh Review* and *Blackwood's* – only *The Scotsman* has survived to the present day. According to Grant (1881–83), it was 'the leading journal in Scotland, and of which it may be truly said that there is no newspaper out of London, and only one or two in it, which has an influence so widely felt'.[25]

Notes

1   Mackenzie (1890): *Old Reminiscences of Glasgow*, p. 126.
2   Alexander (1822): *Letter to Sir J. Mackintosh, Knt., M.P.*, pp. 12–3.
3   Cockburn (1909): *Memorials of his time*, pp. 74–5.
4   Boswell (1871): *The Poetical Works of Sir Alexander Boswell*, p. xxxiii.
5   Cockburn (1909): *Memorials*, pp. 352–3.
6   Brougham (1871): *The Life and Times of Henry Lord Brougham*, **2**, p. 423.
7   Cockburn held Moncreiff in high regard 'I am not aware how his moral nature could have been improved. A truer friend, a more upright judge, or a more affectionate man, could not be', Cockburn (1909): *Memorials*, p. 252. Moncreiff inherited his father's baronetcy and estate of Tullibole in 1827. He appears later in this book as one of Stuart's counsel in his trial.
8   Cockburn (1909): *Memorials*, p. 355.
9   Black (1885): *Memoirs of Adam Black*, p. 66.
10   Cockburn (1909): *Memorials*, p. 434.
11   Chalmers (2010): *Andrew Duncan Senior: Physician of the Enlightenment* p 173
12   Boswell (1871), p. 220.
13   Lockhart (1819): *Peter's Letters to his Kinsfolk*, **II**, p. 204.
14   Anon (1822): *Trial 1*, Introduction.
15   Black (1885), p. 53.
16   Lord Melville, Henry Dundas, Lord Advocate for Scotland and holder of many other offices of state under the Tory administration was without question the leading government figure in Scotland.
17   Scott (1932–37): *The Letters of Sir Walter Scott*, **VI**, pp. 22–4.
18   John Wilson Croker (1780–1857) was a barrister, an Irish Member of Parliament and long serving secretary to the Admiralty. He was a resolute Tory, opposed to the Reform Bill. He wrote a number of books including an edition of Boswell's *Life of Johnson* and critical articles in the *Quarterly Review*, a magazine which he helped to found in London in 1809, as a riposte to the liberal *Edinburgh Review*. John Gibson Lockhart became editor of the *Review* from 1826 until shortly before his death in 1854.
19   Lockhart (1819), **II**, p. 194. Lockhart wrote: 'I rejoice in the privilege of writing and printing *incognito* – 'tis the finest discovery of our age'.
20   Scott (1932 37): *Letters*, **VI**, pp. 20–1, 17 November 1819.
21   Topham (1776): *Letters from Edinburgh*, **I**, p.208.
22   Scott (1932–37): *Letters*, **VI**, pp. 21–2, 17 November 1819.
23   Washington Irving letter to Scott, 20 November 1819 in Scott (1984): *Scott's familiar letters*, **2**, pp. 60–1.

24   Lockhart (1902): *Life of Sir Walter Scott*, **VI**, p. 395.
25   Grant (1881–83): *Old and New Edinburgh*, **I**, p. 283.

CHAPTER 3

The status of duelling

… in a state of highly polished society, an affront is held to be a serious injury … a duel must be fought upon it; as men have agreed to banish from their society one who puts up with an affront without fighting a duel … I could wish there was not that superfluity of refinement; but while such notions prevail, no doubt a man may lawfully fight a duel.

Samuel Johnson 10 April 1772[1]

No man can give or accept a challenge to fight with weapons, on any private difference whatever, without being guilty of wilful murder if he kills his antagonist.

Granville Sharp 1790[2]

AT THIS time disagreements between individuals were resolved in a variety of ways. Insults could be exchanged in the press or in privately circulated broadsheets. If a more physical resolution was required, the manner depended on one's social status. According to Samuel Johnson, unrefined men settled their differences with a blow, but the gentry were obliged to fight a duel – 'a man may shoot the man who invades his character, as he may shoot a man who attempts to break into his house'. James Boswell, the father of Alexander, had many discussions with Johnson over the matter of duelling. Johnson was generally in favour of it and Francis Jeffrey, Stuart's counsel, quoted Johnson's opinions on this subject at length in his defence of Stuart (see pp. 101–2). It is a strange paradox that the writings of Alexander Boswell's father should be used in the defence of his son's antagonist. James Boswell found it difficult to agree with Johnson's views although he himself challenged a Frenchman to a duel on one occasion. The matter was settled with both men apologising publicly.[3]

The etiquette of duelling was well defined. The principals asked 'friends' to act as 'seconds', who then took over the management of the affair. The seconds had great responsibility. They had to confirm that the matter was sufficiently serious to justify a duel, and that the opponents were suitably matched with regard to social status. They were obliged to try to obtain an amicable resolution. If this failed they had to choose the timing, location and the weapons, which by the nineteenth century were invariably pistols – swords had long been abandoned. They measured the site, usually twelve long paces, and supervised the loading of the weapons. One of the seconds was chosen to give the command to fire. Finally they had to give appropriate aid and support to the protagonists, which might involve fleeing the country or giving lengthy evidence in court.

The legal status of duelling was less well defined. Statutes of 1660 and 1696 had prohibited duelling. Even giving or accepting a challenge to a duel was an offence. Anyone involved in the duel whether a principal or a second or spectators who were there by design 'shall be punished by the pain of banishment and escheat of moveables'.[4] These statutes had fallen into disuse and had been ignored. Alexander Boswell's part in having these statutes removed is detailed on page 9. It is an odd coincidence that Boswell's solitary parliamentary contribution should be concerned with subject of his own death.

Although these harsh penalties had been removed, duelling remained an offence at common law as a breach of the peace. According to Lord Advocate Rae, in Scotland, 'duelling was in noways sanctioned by our law, but, on the contrary, a deadly wound committed in a duel … constituted the crime of murder',[5] although this was questioned by Lord Kames (see p. 102). In England, from time to time, the legality of duelling was debated in Parliament, but attempts to ban it outright were always outvoted.

Cockburn in his preparatory ms notes in the *Case of James Stuart* wrote:

> In no one instance of fatal duel … where … the parties had gone to the Field not with felonious intent, but in defence of honour, has a jury ever convicted anyone of murder or culpable homicide despite institutional writers laying down Homicide in duel as Murder in Common Law.

Granville Sharp (1735–1813), an ardent campaigner against social injustices such as slavery and duelling opined that:

> The indulgence allowed by the Courts to voluntary manslaughter in …duels, is indiscriminate and without foundation in law; and that impunity in such cases of voluntary manslaughter is one of the principal causes of the continuous and present increase of the base and disgraceful practice of duelling.[6]

He went on to say:

> Now the absurd and depraved notions of honour, and gentleman-like satisfaction of which I complain, could not possibly exist if every conqueror in a duel, who kills his antagonist, was sure of being hanged up as an ignominious felon, … I apprehend that the diabolical practice of settling private differences with sword and pistols is chiefly to be attributed to the want of punishment due to voluntary manslaughter,

through the mistaken concession of the Writers on Common Law, and the false mercy of Juries ...[7]

The public at large clearly regarded duelling as a right and proper way of settling a difference and in the army an officer could be court-martialled for cowardice if he failed to accept a challenge.

Several of the individuals who feature in this book, apart from Boswell and Stuart, were also involved in challenges or duels and these will be briefly described as they illustrate some of the vagaries associated with duelling.

Sir Walter Scott was closely involved, not only with the main duel but also had a part in one other and he himself was challenged (see p. 54). Scott included accounts of duels in several of his novels. The duel scene of *St Ronan's Well* is said by Lockhart to be based on the duel between Boswell and Stuart[8] but it is difficult to find any similarity between the two events.

John Scott vs John Gibson Lockhart

In 1821 Walter Scott's son-in-law, John Gibson Lockhart (Fig. 9), was involved in one of the most extraordinary duels. In 1820 *Blackwood's Magazine* published, under pseudonyms, parodies of what they called the 'Cockney School of Poetry', which included the poets Coleridge, Byron and Wordsworth. *Baldwin's London Magazine* had been founded in that year and was modelled in style of *Blackwood's*. John Scott, the editor of *Baldwin's* took particular offence at a criticism of Coleridge in *Blackwood's*. John Scott attributed the authorship (wrongly) to Lockhart whom he attacked anonymously in his *Magazine* in January 1821 Lockhart asked Jonathan Christie, an old friend from his student days in Oxford who was based in London, to enquire of Scott whether he was the author of the offending articles. Scott refused to give his answer to Christie and said that he would only respond to Lockhart in person and only if Lockhart would clarify his standing with *Blackwood's*. Lockhart hastened down to London with the intention of forcing an apology or fighting a duel. Scott acknowledged that he was the author of the articles in *London Magazine* but refused to accept Lockhart's challenge on the curious grounds that Lockhart refused to clarify his status with *Blackwood's*.

Lockhart, uncertain what to do, consulted John Wilson Croker who wrote to Walter Scott that he had advised Lockhart that John Scott's:

> ... evasions and equivocations left no alternative but the telling him ... that he was a lyer [*sic*], a coward and a scoundrel and under these agreeable epithets the Champion is satisfied to remain. The matter is now terminated and in a manner as

satisfactory as possible. Lockhart has not been even perill'd and his rascal antagonist is rolled in the mire...[9]

Walter Scott wrote to thank Croker. 'It is truly fortunate that when he had to do with so rascally an antagonist he was in the possession of your directions and sentiments.'[10]

The two protagonists then published their accounts of events, each claiming a moral victory over their opponent. Christie, as Lockhart's second, decided to publish his version which contained a very mild rebuke which John Scott interpreted as an insult and in his turn challenged Christie to a duel. Scott's first choice as his second was Horatio Smith, who declined as he despised duelling and considered that rival editors who would 'change their pens for pistols, ink for blood appeared to me ... a species of Quixotism totally inconsistent with their calling ...'. He was prepared to act as a mediator but not as a party to hostile meeting.[11] Alas this sensible advice was ignored and the duel went ahead, with Scott's alternative choice of a second acting for him.

The duel between John Scott and Christie took place on 16 February 1821. Scott was shot in the stomach and died ten days later. Christie described the incident to Walter Scott with whom he had dined in London two days before the duel:

> We met accordingly at nine o'clock at night at Chalk Farm [a popular site for duelling in London]. My first shot I fired in the air. But my Second (James Traill) perceiving that Scott took careful aim ... insisted aloud that I should give myself the usual chances for my life. For self preservation, I did so... [12]

Christie and Traill carried Scott to a neighbouring inn, his own surgeon having deserted the field, and made sure that he was well settled in bed and remained with him until his relatives arrived. Walter Scott met Christie again on the following day, just before he and Traill left for France pending the subsequent trial. He described the meeting to Lockhart.

> I offered him all sort of assistance in my power either by purse, recommendations or otherwise ... he was a little dejected about the business, but I left him much cheered, as indeed he should be, for he behaved with the utmost moderation as well as gallantry ... . Knowing how much you will suffer from the inconvenience to which your friend has been subjected, it would be cruel to say anything more about it ...[13]

At the trial Christie was acquitted of murder by the jury such as was almost invariably the case in matters of this nature.

Lockhart, whose wife Sophia (Fig. 9) had given birth to their first child two days before the duel, came in for criticism for the circumstance of his second having taken his place, and although this had happened without his knowledge, his reputation suffered. Robert Louis Stevenson was one of those who charged him with cowardice although later he withdrew has criticism.[14] Lockhart wrote to Christie when he first heard of the duel:

> You bid me to pity you. Pity me much more, who have to sustain the thought of having brought you, your dear wife and family, into such a situation as this. God grant that this man may live! All the world must agree that you acted nobly, yet all will think that you did much more than was right …[15]

James Traill tried to comfort Lockhart in a letter, 6 April 1821:

> I am really sorry to find that you still suffer yourself to be annoyed by this business … Scott behaved towards you like a mean coward … and towards Christie … like an unfeeling coward … I have a great respect for the motto '*De mortuis* etc' but in this case I must be allowed to suggest the slight alteration of '*verum*' (truth) for '*bonum*'.[16]

The *Beacon* reported the events of the duel in great detail on four occasions between 3 February and 31 March 1821. Walter Scott in a letter to Lockhart, 14 March 1821 said 'I wish the *Beacon* would let Scott's affair alone'. This comment is of interest on several accounts; firstly it indicates that Walter Scott had no editorial control over the *Beacon*, and secondly that he must have read the paper, which later he was to deny.[17] Finally it reveals that he and Lockhart must have had feelings of guilt with regard to the affair and did not want it publicised, although these articles in the *Beacon* were entirely objective and accurate and made no criticism of Lockhart, who, as a staunch Tory, had the same political leanings as the *Beacon*.

After reporting the inquest in the issue of 10 March the *Beacon* concluded:

> Last of all, it is impossible to think of this unfortunate affair, without hoping that it may produce a salutary change on the complexion of much of the periodical literature of the day.

What a hypocritical comment this was in a paper which constantly published libellous remarks much more offensive than those which led to the Scott/Christie duel!

The last reference to the duel in the *Beacon* was an advertisement appealing for subscriptions to a fund for Mr Scott's widow and two children. Lord Byron, who had been a fellow student with Scott at Aberdeen Grammar School, made an anonymous contribution of £30 to the public subscription.[18]

Blackwood's Magazine came in for much criticism for its part in the affair and for a time advised its contributors to modify their contributions to lessen offence. Blackwood, the editor, wrote to Hogg '… the Magazine is now too serious a concern to be trifled with. It has got quite above attacks and malignities …'.[19]

Walter Scott, who regarded *Blackwood's* as the 'mother of mischief', advised Lockhart to give up his association with the magazine which had landed him in so much trouble:

> You have now the best opportunity to break off with the magazine, which will otherwise remain a snare and temptation to your love of satire … I make this my most earnest entreaty to you, and as it agrees with that of all your friends and well wishers, I trust it will not be made in vain … [20]

Lockhart replied:

> I hope I need not say how cordially I enter into the hope you express, that this bloody lesson may be a sufficient & a lasting one. I can never be sufficiently grateful for the advice which kept *me* from having any hand in all these newspaper skirmishings'.[21]

He continued, however, to contribute to *Blackwood's*. Grierson[22] believes that Sir Walter could have prevented John Scott's death by intervening at an earlier stage, for he had great influence over Lockhart. Walter Scott had little sympathy for his namesake. 'It would be great hypocrisy in me to say I am sorry for John Scott. He got exactly what he was long wishing for & I think it probable the incident will diminish the licence of the periodical press so far as private character is concerned.'[23]

Later Lockhart wrote to his friend Robert Haydon, 'I was punished cruelly and irremediably in my worldly fortunes, for the outcry cut off all prospects of professional advancement from me'.[24] He did, however, accept in 1825, the editorship of the *Quarterly Review*, a Tory journal founded in London in 1809 as a counter to the influential *Edinburgh Review*, but he declined an offer from the Duke of Wellington to edit a Tory newspaper in London. He had resolved to:

> Have nothing to do wt [*sic*] it … I will not even serve the Duke [to] mix myself up wt the Newspapers … I cant afford to sacrifice the advantage which feel I have gained in these later years by abstaining altogether from partisan scribbling …[25]

Scott, who had suffered badly from his association with the *Beacon* (see Chapter 4), advised Lockhart, 'Your connection with any newspaper would be a disgrace and degradation. I would rather sell gin to the poor people and poison them in that way'.[26]

Thomas Moore vs Francis Jeffrey

The events which gave rise to the next duel were very similar to the previous one. The *Edinburgh Review*, like *Blackwood's*, was noted for its trenchant criticisms of contemporary poets. In the summer of 1806, an article in the *Review* written by its editor, Francis Jeffrey, criticised an Irish poet Thomas Moore's book *Epistles, Odes, and other Poems* on the ground of immorality. He wrote that '[i]t seems to be his aim to impose corruption upon his readers by concealing it under the mask of refinement … . Such are the demerits of this work, that we wish to see it consigned to universal reprobation'. Moore challenged Jeffrey to a duel, which took place at Chalk Farm, with Francis Horner acting as Jeffrey's second. Both men were novices in the duelling business and unaccustomed to handling pistols. Just as they were about to fire, two Bow Street Runners,[27] having been informed of the duel, suddenly appeared and arrested them. They were bound over to keep the peace. The two then considered going over to Hamburg to complete their duel, but after discussion they resolved their differences amicably. When the police examined the pistols it was reported (wrongly) that Jeffrey's contained no bullet and Moore's contained balls of paper. The press treated the episode with 'much waggery'. One commented that 'the balls of pistols, like the courage of the combatants, were found to have evaporated'. Moore was mortified by the disgrace.

Lord Byron, whose poetry had been mocked by the *Edinburgh Review* and *Blackwood's*, seized the opportunity to get his own back. *English Bards and Scotch Reviewers*, a lengthy poem in which he attacked the Scottish reviewers who had criticised his poetry, included the following verses:

> Can none remember that eventful day,
> That ever glorious, almost fatal fray,
> When Little's[28] leadless pistols met his eye,
> And Bow Street myrmidons stood laughing by?

> Health to great Jeffrey! Heaven preserve his life,
> To flourish on the fertile shores of Fife,[29]
> And guard it sacred in his future wars,
> Since authors sometimes seek the field of Mars!

And later with reference to Caledonia's goddess:

> 'My son' she cried, 'ne'er thirst for guns again,
> Resign the pistol, and resume the pen;
> O'er politics and poesy preside,
> Boast of thy country, and Britannia's guide!

And with reference to the grim Old Tolbooth Prison:

> The Tolbooth felt defrauded of her charms,
> If Jeffrey died except within her arms.

Moore initially reacted by sending a challenge to Byron who was then in Greece. The challenge was not delivered and by the time Byron returned to Britain, Moore's anger had evaporated. Byron, Moore and Jeffrey subsequently became reconciled and developed lifelong friendships even to the extent of Jeffrey offering to give Moore £500 when he suffered financial hardship. Moore became a contributor to the *Edinburgh Review* and described Jeffrey as 'the great master of the art of criticism in our day' and his 'sincerely regarded and valued friend'.[31]

At this time in Scotland duelling had become a rare event although still quite common in England. Before the Stuart/Boswell encounter only one fatal duel had taken place in Scotland in the nineteenth century, between a military surgeon Cahill and Captain Rutherford in 1811. Rutherford was killed and Cahill acquitted of murder. After the Stuart/Boswell duel only two more fatal duels took place (see pp. 153–6).

Notes

1 Boswell (1964): *Life of Johnson*, **2**, pp. 179–8.
2 Sharp (1790): *A Tract on Duelling*, p. xi.
3 Baldwick (1970): *The Duel: A history of duelling*, pp. 184–5.
4 *Encyclopaedia of the Laws of Scotland*, **V**, p. 86, section 214. Escheat of moveables – confiscation of property.
5 Anon (1822): *Trial 2*, p. 30.
6 Sharp (1790), p. ii.
7 Ibid, pp. xv–xvi.
8 Lockhart (1902): *Life of Sir Walter Scott*, **V**, p. 29, fn.
9 Scott (1932–37): *The Letters of Sir Walter Scott*, **VI**, p. 341, fn. Another footnote pp. 348–50 gives a good account of the petty and rather childish dispute between the two men. Parker (2000): *Literary Magazines and British Romanticism*, pp. 20–7 gives an excellent critique of the part played by the two rival magazines.
10 Scott (1932–37): *Letters*, **VI**, pp. 341–3.
11 Lang (1897): *The Life and Letters of John Gibson Lockhart*, **I**, p. 264.
12 Partington (1932): *Sir Walter's Post-bag*, p. 153; letter undated.
13 Scott's letter to Lockhart, London 20 February 1821 in Scott (1932–37): *Letters*, **VI**, pp. 361–2.

14   Scott (1932–37): *Letters*, **VI**, p. 350, fn.
15   Lang (1897), **I**, p. 276.
16   Scott (1932–37): *Letters*, **VI**, p. 377, fn. The complete motto is of course *De mortuis nil nisi bonum* – Concerning the dead [say] nothing unless good.
17   Lockhart (1902), **III**, p. 613 said 'Scott never even saw the journal' and Grierson (1938), pp. 195–6 said Scott 'never caught sight of it even by chance'. Both statements were certainly untrue. See Scott (1932–37) *Letters*, **VI**, p. 346 and p. 377.
18   Cronin (2010): *Paper Pellets: Culture after Waterloo*, p. 6.
19   Letter to James Hogg 18 June 1822, in Mason (2006): *Blackwood's Magazine 1817–1825*, **1**, pp. xviii–xix.
20   Scott's letter to Lockhart, 24 February 1821 in Scott (1932–37: *Letters*, **VI**, pp. 362–5.
21   Lockhart letter to Scott, 22 March 1821 in Partington (1932), p. 165
22   Grierson (1938): *Sir Walter Scott Bart: A new life*, p. 247.
23   Scott (1932–37) *Letters*, **VI**, p. 374.
24   Letter to Haydon 11 July 1838 cited in Lang (1897), **I**, p. 130.
25   Letter to Scott, 30 March 1829, Scott (1932–37): *Letters*, **XI**, p. 161, fn.
26   Letter to Lockhart, 3 April 1829, Scott (1932–37): *Letters*, **XI**, p. 162.
27   'Bow Street Runners' was the nickname given to London's first professional police force.
28   'Little' was a *nom de plume* used by Moore in *Poems of the late Thomas Little Esq.* 'Little' scans better than 'Moore' would have done in the verse.
29   This was another poetic licence; Jeffrey had no particular link with Fife.
30   Greig (1948): *Francis Jeffrey of The Edinburgh Review*, p. 8.
31   Jeffrey's speech, Anon (1822): *Trial 2*, pp. 166–7.

CHAPTER 4

The *Beacon* is extinguished

… there has existed of late a degree of violence which will be slaked, I fear, with nothing but blood; I suspect daily to hear that someone is killd.

Walter Scott, letter to Archibald Constable, 30 September 1821,
concerning the journalism of the day.

Now is the stately column broke,
The beacon-light is quench'd in smoke

Walter Scott, *Marmion Canto I*, introduction

NEWSPAPERS IN the early nineteenth century were slender publications of four to eight pages, usually published weekly and distributed by hand or posted to enrolled subscribers; they were not sold in shops. The government stamp duty on newspapers was increased to four pence a copy in 1815, making them relatively expensive and affordable only to the wealthy. The poor had to make do with broadsheets, which were issued whenever a particularly interesting local event such as a murder, duel, execution or criminal trial occurred. These were distributed by street criers and cost a half penny or a penny. When the stamp duty was reduced to one penny in 1836 and finally abolished in 1855, it became financially possible to issue newspapers on a daily basis to a wider public. *The Scotsman* for example became a daily in that year.

The printer was often the proprietor, publisher and sometimes the editor and chief reporter of a local newspaper. Articles, editorials and letters were usually published anonymously or under a pseudonym in order to protect the author from a charge of libel or a challenge to a duel, which in many instances was justified by their scurrilous nature.

The proprietor, printer and publisher of the *Beacon*, which was launched on 6 January 1821, was Duncan Stevenson, the owner of a successful printing firm in Edinburgh, but the editor was not revealed. It was published every Saturday as an eight-page paper and achieved 800 subscribers despite costing ten pence a copy.

The paper took the usual form of a contemporary weekly newspaper. The front page contained an editorial, usually criticising some aspect of the Whig cause. Inside there were reports from various countries copied from foreign papers and from London and other parts of Britain. When Parliament was in session the proceedings were detailed at length. Items of local news were reported especially if they were critical of prominent Whigs. The local Whig press was castigated, particularly the *Edinburgh Review* and *The Scotsman* newspaper. Correspondence, invariably selected for its political bias, was published under pseudonyms and many poems or songs were printed mostly of a very puerile character and mostly mocking prominent Whigs identified by the first and last letters of their name or by a nickname, coined by the paper, which would be easily recognised by the readers of the day. Thus Stuart was represented as S....t or as the *Ox*. The last page contained market reports, announcements of births, marriages and deaths and advertisements which became progressively fewer as the reputation of the paper declined.

Henry Brougham said of the *Beacon* that it was:

> Devoted to violent personal attacks, as well as political, like papers of the same kind established by the King's friends in England on the loss of their bill against the Queen. As generally happens, the party violence and the personal attacks reached a greater height, and were of longer continuance in provincial places than in the capital.[1]

Walter Scott, in 1821, wrote with uncanny prescience:

> The news from Edinburgh is very distressing, for with the usual degree of party spirit there has existed of late a degree of violence which will be slaked, I fear, with nothing but blood; I expect daily to hear that someone is killd. The Scotsman and Review have much to answer for.[2]

Occasionally the tedium of the constant political harangue was leavened by items of a more general interest such as reports from the Arctic voyages of Captain Parry in the *Discovery*, for example the method of growing mustard and cress aboard ship for the prevention of scurvy. The time occupying practice of taking snuff was commented upon:

> Every professed, inveterate and incurable snuff taker, at a moderated computation takes one pinch every 10 minutes. Every pinch, with the agreeable ceremony of blowing and wiping the nose ... consumes a minute and a half.

Shipwrecks, reports of trials, hangings and bare fist boxing matches which went to more than twenty rounds were mentioned. The completion of the Union

Canal was noted and it was reported that the proposed pillar of the statue of Viscount Melville in St Andrew Square was not to be solid but would contain a central staircase, access to which would be denied to the public. Henry Cockburn's proposal that a copy of the Parthenon should be erected on Calton Hill as the National Monument to commemorate the victorious conclusion of the Napoleonic wars was noted. (This is the only occasion that Cockburn – a Whig – was mentioned without criticism.)[3]

An interesting eye witness account of a sale of slaves in Richmond, Virginia was reported. On one day more than 100 slaves from the estate of a wealthy Scotsman were disposed of. The patter of the auctioneer was given of which this extract is a sample:

> Gentlemen, the next we offer you for sale is Billy! [A] good rough carpenter, about 38 years of age, able bodied and warranted sound; can do plantation work if required – Gentlemen, what will you give me for the rough carpenter? – Will no one give me a bid for Billy?

Eventually Billy was sold for $425. A couple with two children were sold together for $840.[4] (See also pp. 147–8.)

The exclusion of the Queen from Westminster Abbey at the coronation of George IV was described with much detail and gloating as was her chaotic funeral procession soon thereafter. An incident was recorded in which a bullock escaped and ran into a baker's shop, ascended several flights of stairs, and poked its head out of a garret window overlooking the mourners. Napoleon's death and memorial ceremonies were described.

Most of the paper, however was taken up with attacks on opposing publications or individuals. *The Scotsman* for example was:

> 13 January 1821
> Supported *principally for the private purposes of a few gentlemen, who occupy private stations at the Scots bar* ... . The real guilt of the *Scotsman's* offence lies with Mr. Cockburn, Mr James Stuart, Mr James Gibson, Mr John Murray who report their own stupid and venomous harangues in its pages ... Mr Jeffrey, who on the day he first put pen to paper for the Scotsman, sealed the irreversible sentence of his own eternal degradation ... . It is imposing on himself a supererogatory stain to give the shelter of his name to the malice, the slander, the earth-creeping insolence, and profligate stupidity of the *Scotsman*.

20 June 1821

> It is sometimes suggested to us, that we have not been sufficiently active in exposing
> the falsehoods and calumnies of this noxious publication. If we have not, it is chiefly
> from two reasons – first, that we have not been able to task ourselves with the intol-
> erable drudgery of reading it regularly; and secondly, that we have too good an
> opinion of the public to think that it can be influenced by anything which is
> conveyed through so dirty a channel.

Blackwood's Magazine which like the *Beacon*, supported the Tories, was
regarded favourably, '… it is entirely free from the stupid affectation of dignity
with which the *Edinburgh* [*Review*] and others endeavour to disguise their
dulness [*sic*]' (28 April 1821).

Among the Whigs who were particularly abused were Francis Jeffrey, James
Stuart, James Gibson and the MP Lord Archibald Hamilton. Jeffrey had the
wisdom to ignore the libellous attacks but the others reacted vigorously.

The offending article

Although Stuart was singled out for critical mention from the very first issue of
the *Beacon* on 6 January 1821, it was an item in the issue of 28 July 1821 which
provoked him to react. On this date – the Saturday following the coronation
from which Queen Caroline had been excluded – the *Beacon* reported that the
Queen, who was pilloried by the Tories and championed by the Whigs:

> … has announced her intention of soon visiting this City … . As to her receiving the
> slightest attention here from any person of respectability, it is quite out of the
> question … . We do believe that none above the rank of … Mr James Stuart would
> commit such an outrage on decency and good manners.

The next issue contained a mocking scenario of Stuart acting as one of her
Majesty's pages:

> When however he is properly powdered, and dressed in a lace silk suit, with an open
> neck and round frill, and has been taught to *walk* instead of waddling, and to keep
> his hands out of his breeches pockets, I dare say he will look the page very well.

(Stuart's appearance was often a subject of comment. He was variously
described as stout or lubberly with a face pitted with small pox.) Alas the poor
Queen died a month later so the situation was never put to trial. It is difficult

today to understand why such trivial insults should cause a violent reaction. Scott described it as, 'A very stupid joke in the *Beacon* paper against a hot-headed cold-livered crack-brained Whig, y-cleped James Stuart …'.[5]

Stuart was incensed by this slur on his social standing and on 2 August, accompanied by Mr Mansfield, he called upon Duncan Stevenson to protest about the article.[6] He demanded to know the name of the author or else Stevenson 'must abide the serious consequences of refusal'. Stevenson denied that he was the writer and referred Stuart to John Nimmo as editor, saying, 'I have no control over the management of the paper …'.[7] Nimmo was a journeyman printer on a salary of 25 shillings a week and it was absurd to take him seriously as having editorial responsibilities. Stuart refused to have any dealings with Nimmo, regarding Stevenson as personally responsible for the publication 'of the false and malignant attack which it has made upon my honour and character … . Nothing can relieve you from the *perilous predicament* in which you have voluntarily … placed yourself'.[8]

Letters between the two men were exchanged on almost a daily basis, Stuart demanding to know the name of the author with ever increasing threats, Stevenson maintaining the absurdity that he did not know, or could not find out, the names of contributors to his own paper. On 10 August Stevenson wrote:

> You have no good reason for wishing to be furnished with the author's name by me, rather than the Editor, Mr Nimmo, to whom alone it was known … . Your intended course of conduct, however plain it may be to yourself, cannot be discovered either from your Memorandum or correspondence … I presume you intend to adopt legal measures against me. I venture therefore to hope that this correspondence, so mysterious and latterly so intemperate on your part is now at an end.[9]

Stuart replied at 'One o'clock am 11.8.1821':

> At half past eleven, last night, your letter was delivered here … I therefore hold you from eleven o'clock this morning to have incurred the alternative … I decline all farther [*sic*] communication in writing with you. I have taken measures for rendering it certain that this letter shall be put in your hands before 8 o'clock this morning.

Stevenson sent a reply which Stuart refused to open and demanded that the two men should meet, accompanied by a 'friend', at the Royal Exchange Coffee House (Fig. 10). On 14 August the meeting took place, Stuart accompanied by Mr Anderson Blair and Stevenson by Captain Campbell, but Stevenson still refused – or was unable – to accede to Stuart's demands.

The horse-whipping

Parliament Square (Fig. 11) on the south side of St Giles Cathedral was a hive of great activity before the Great Fire of 1824 which destroyed much of it. In 1821 it was the legal and commercial centre of the City being surrounded by the courts, and the premises of banks, publishers, goldsmiths, wine merchants, coffee shops, etc. The North British Fire & Life Insurance Company of which Stuart was a director had its offices there and Stevenson's printing works which published the *Beacon* was located on Parliamentary Stairs which led off the Square. At any time of day it was thronged with people, it was described as the busiest and most populous nook of the Old Town. The day after the abortive meeting at the Royal Exchange, Stuart and Stevenson met in Parliament Square between 1pm and 2pm on Wednesday 15 August. This meeting was unplanned but it is not as coincidental as it sounds for both men had business premises within a hundred yards. At lunch time the Square would be teeming with its occupants visiting the various coffee houses and taverns there. Stuart must have anticipated the likelihood of a meeting for he had brought two of his staff with him. Stuart and Stevenson gave differing accounts of what happened.

According to Stuart, having observed Stevenson, he immediately called to him by name and desired him to name the writer or make an apology. Stevenson refused, whereupon Stuart gave him four or five smart strokes about the lower part of the body with a switch horse whip. Stevenson held a large bamboo cane in his hand and endeavoured repeatedly to strike at Stuart about the head and upper part of his body. He only once succeeded in hitting him in the arm and one of his fingers, but not so as to break the skin. Stevenson complained that he was not treated as a gentleman, to which Mr Stuart replied that, 'the hired instrument of an anonymous slanderer had no title to the character of a gentleman'.[10]

The *Beacon*, 18 August 1821 gave Stevensons' version:

> On Wed 15th inst Mr Stevenson was walking through Parliament Square ... accompanied by a friend ... when Mr Stuart came up and ... struck him with his whip on his left shoulder. Acting on impulse of the moment, Mr Stevenson, though not half the size of his lubberly antagonist immediately gave him a sound drubbing, and sent him a challenge by Capt. Campbell which Stuart declined accepting, alleging that Mr Stevenson was not entitled to satisfaction of that kind.

Stevenson's account was supported by a witness, Neil Maclachlan, who:

> ... observed Mr. Stuart lift his whip and strike you on the left shoulder, you returned the blow several times with your stick, until Mr Stuart seemed perfectly

47

satisfied, as he kept retreating, without making use of his whip, at the same time keeping his hands crossed in front of his head ... . A great crowd having now collected, you were taken hold of by several persons, whom I took to belong to the police ... . While you were kept back by these persons, Mr Stuart made no attempt to renew the attack, but you frequently applied to me to disengage you from those who had laid hold of you, in order that you might inflict further chastisement on Mr Stuart.[11]

Another witness, Mr R. Hardie, confirmed Maclachlan's account and added 'if you [Stevenson] had not been interrupted, you would infallibly have murdered your antagonist'.[12]

The challenge declined

Later that day (15 August 1821) Stevenson challenged Stuart to a duel. Stevenson wrote to Stuart:

In consequence of your brutal and ruffian-like attack upon me, I feel myself under the necessity of requiring that you will immediately give my friend Captain Campbell the address of any gentleman you think proper, to arrange time and place for a meeting between us.

Stuart replied that because of Stevenson's repeated refusal to comply with his demands:

... and seeing no likelihood of obtaining satisfaction ... I proceeded in the most public manner in my power to inflict the chastisement to which your conduct has so justly subjected you ... . If you feel degraded by the chastisement you have received you have yourself to blame ... as the servile instrument of a partnership of slander, you are utterly unworthy of the sort of satisfaction which it belongs only to a gentleman to demand ... I regard it the consummation of your perversity and insolence to suppose that you have any right to call upon me for reparation ... our correspondence here ceases for ever.

Stevenson responded to Stuart on 16 August:

I received yours of yesterday at a late hour last night. As you decline my challenge, I shall this day post up a placard, giving you a few of the designates you deserve such as 'Coward', 'Scoundrel' and the like.

It is really a good joke in you to pretend that you inflicted public chastisement on me. The chastisement was public enough, no doubt, but it fell on your head as you well know and as many can testify: and you would have got more of it, had my arms not been pinioned by a set of persons who have been either hired by you for the purpose, or had been prompted by their own feeling to favour your escape. Upon the whole, on looking back at what has taken place between us I cannot help considering you as one of those

Who have been beaten till they know
What wood a cudgel's of by th' blow.

He was as good as his word; large posters were printed and distributed that day.

I hereby notify to all whom it may concern, that
JAMES STUART, W.S.
IS A
Ruffian, a COWARD, and a Scoundrel
Edinburgh 16th August 1821 Dun. Stevenson

The fracas attracted a great deal of public interest which led to both men being bound over by the Sheriff to keep the peace for 12 months.[13] The *Beacon* of 18 August reported that, because of this restriction, Stevenson was transferring the control of the paper to the nebulous Nimmo. Thus the entire correspondence and memoranda, which had passed between Stuart and Stevenson, could be published in the same issue under Nimmo's name so that Stevenson could not be held responsible for any consequential breach of the peace.

Convention demanded that a duel could only take place between two gentlemen of equivalent social status. Stuart in his reply to Stevenson chose to regard him as of being of an inferior status and used this as his excuse for refusal. In fact Stevenson came from a landed family in Argyll and had established a successful printing business in Edinburgh where he had been admitted as a burgess and a guild brother. The *Beacon* noted that Stevenson was universally esteemed and respected in this City; that he was a gentleman by birth, education and connections, that he was a Deputy-Lieutenant and justice of the peace for the county of Argyll; and that he held a position in society at least equal to that James Stuart held till now.

Declining to accept a challenge to a duel on the grounds of the inferior status of the challenger was a dangerous tactic. It added a further insult and at the same time it exposed the challenged to the charge of cowardice. Others also did not accept Stuart's reason for rejecting the challenge. A letter from one of the Fife

Yeomanry (of which Stuart was an officer) published in the *Beacon* on 25 August stated that: Respecting Stuart's conduct in the affair there can be but one opinion, … that this person has *deliberately struck another – no matter whom – and then refused him satisfaction*, such conduct admits of only one explanation'. He trusted that the authorities would take appropriate reaction.

An article in the *Beacon* of 8 September stated:

> We offer him [Stuart] a boon which he prizes above everything except the safety of his carcase [*sic*], vis *a perfect impunity from our lash in the future*, if he can find a single officer of respectability and rank in the whole British Army, who will declare that he is not for ever degraded by his late conduct.

As mentioned in Chapter 1 (p. 5), it is likely that this incident contributed to Stuart's enforced resignation from his commission as Lieutenant in the Fifeshire Yeomanry Cavalry a few months later. Stuart's apparent cowardice became the theme of a number of poems, letters and comments appearing in almost all the issues of the *Beacon* until its demise. Stuart also received a large number of anonymous offensive letters.

Stuart's reputation suffered a further blow when the *Beacon* on 1 September announced that it had discovered the two men were who held Mr Stevenson's arms during the horse-whipping. They were employees of Stuart, namely Gilbert Miller, gamekeeper and James Dewar, a gardener from his country estate of Hillside in Fife. Stuart stated in a letter to the paper dated 3 September that 'his servants were there merely as witnesses and my having derived assistance from them is untrue'. The *Beacon* pointed out on 8 September that he could have used his servants and clerks based in Edinburgh, rather than bringing his servants over from Fife, to act as witnesses.

> Stuart's assertion that his servants were present, MERELY AS WITNESSES is a gross and palpable falsehood: the plain truth is, he was afraid to commit his dastardly assault without some person to assist or protect him in doing so; and as he wished to conceal his cowardice, he chose persons whose secrecy he thought could be relied on, and who were not likely to be known to the bye-standers.

The attacks on Stuart continued and he approached Sheriff Adam Duff to enquire whether there was any legal protection against them only to be told that there was none because any such measures would interfere with the liberty of the press!

Stuart's attack on the Lord Advocate

Stuart having lost his battle against Stevenson decided on a new line of attack. He had heard rumours that Sir William Rae, the Lord Advocate, had been one of the financial supporters of the *Beacon*. Stuart wrote to him on 13 September accusing him of being an obligant in a Bond for the establishment and support of the paper called the *Beacon*, and sent him copies of issues no 30, 31, 33, 34 and 35, which contained most of the attacks upon his character, and asked him if he approved of these attacks.[14]

Rae replied two days later that '... if you suppose that it was ... in contemplation ... that the publication was to become a vehicle of attack upon private character, you are much mistaken ... . With respect to the conduct of that Paper, I can safely assert, that I had no sort of share in it'. He returned the submitted papers without opening them and wrote, 'I disapprove ... of all attacks upon private character in such publications.[15]

Stuart was not satisfied with this general expression of disapproval and sent a further series of letters in which he demanded that Rae should indicate specific disapproval of the attacks on him personally. He was anxious to discover 'a gentleman [who] was connected with the publication. Your lordship is the only one known to me. You have subscribed a Bond, declaring your "earnest wish to countenance and support the *Beacon* and the principles upon which it is to be conducted" '.[16]

Rae responded to this thinly veiled threat by writing on 16 September 'I deem it fitting that I should be guided by the advice of a friend in my answer'.[17] Further letters were exchanged no less than four on the 17th before Rae finally yielded. On the 18 September he wrote that he specifically disavowed, 'all approbation and sanctions of the attacks on your character and honour contained in the numbers 30, 31, 33, 34 and 35' and allowed Stuart the right to publish the correspondence if he wished. He added a PS: 'Mr Colin Mackenzie is the friend with whom I have advised on this occasion, and, if any thing more is to be said, I have to request that it be addressed to him'.[18]

Stuart wrote to Mackenzie the same day to say that he accepted 'the separate and distinct disavowal, and it was not necessary to have mentioned your name'. Had the interference of friends been required 'my relation, Captain Alexander Gordon, RN had agreed to honour me with assistance'.[19] These references to 'friends' were of course the circumlocution by which duels were conducted. Having said that, Rae had no need to mention his friend, Stuart was in effect saying that he had accepted Rae's statement and his threat of a duel was withdrawn.

The demise of the *Beacon*

On 25 August 1821 the *Beacon* must have seen that its future was in doubt for it published an editorial which stated:

> What would become of the liberty of the news paper press in this metropolis were the light of the Beacon once put out, we leave our readers to determine. The worse than Cimmerian darkness of the Scotsman would infallibly return; and moral and political murder would again walk our streets unchallenged ... attempts to subdue the pure and honest light of the Beacon ... will instead of being extinguished by the Whigs finally consume them.

Stuart's publication of the correspondence, which revealed Rae as a backer of the *Beacon*, was the trigger which led to the demise of the paper only nine months after it was founded. Having come off worst in his battle with Stevenson, he at last achieved a victory of sorts.

While Stuart's contretemps with the *Beacon* was taking place, some of the other Whigs, offended by the *Beacon*'s squibs, sought satisfaction through the law courts. Lord Archibald Hamilton and James Gibson each instituted Actions of Damages against Stevenson for libels. Hamilton, who had been accused of cowardice, was awarded damages of 1 shilling by a jury on 19 June 1822. Anne Grant, who regarded the *Beacon* as 'a paper offered to the Scotchmen, abounding in coarse humor [*sic*]' considered the accusation against Hamilton to be justified and anticipated that '... the trial is likely to be a messy one, at least his lordship, like Falstaff, will be the cause of wit ...'.[20] Cockburn, who was Hamilton's counsel, felt that this derisory award was due to misdirection of the jury by the presiding judge, but noted that the defender had to pay £300 in costs.[21]

While collecting evidence for his case, James Gibson obtained from Sir William Rae the names of the other 14 backers, most of whom were also senior law officers, including: the Solicitor General James Wedderburn, Advocate Depute Henry Home Drummond MP for County of Stirling, John Hay Forbes Sheriff-Depute for Perth, John Hope advocate and depute to the Lord Advocate, Sir Walter Scott and Colin Mackenzie both Principal Clerks of Session and The Rt Hon. William Arbuthnot Lord Provost of Edinburgh. Gibson did rather better than Hamilton, being awarded £500 and costs against Stevenson and the financial backers of the *Beacon* on 9 December 1822. (He had sought £10,000.)

Having been shamed by the exposure, the financial backers of the *Beacon* held a meeting on 21 September and decided to withdraw their support and the paper ceased publication.

Cockburn gave credit to Gibson, whose case against the *Beacon* had not yet been heard 'His triumph in getting the *Beacon* demolished has been so great and the poor Tories seem so low and unhappy'.[22]

Sir Walter Scott, who had been a prime mover in the founding of the *Beacon*, was one of those who was 'low and unhappy'. He had not been present at the meeting of backers but was informed of the decision in a letter from Colin Mackenzie, dated 21 September 1821:

> I suppose [Rae] has informed you of the fate of the Beacon, & I trust you do not disapprove our proceeding. It was a great pity but the step was indispensable .... It was agreed that all must remain or all quit and we took it on us for the absent subscribers ... to notify the retirement of all.

In other letters, Mackenzie wrote:

> ... whatever might be thought heretofore about *responsibility* the Case is materially altered now *the public know* that Rae, you, Forbes, and myself are the *Establishers*. While responsibility was limited by our own sense of what is right, and truth to speak our sense has been slow.

He ascribed this neglect 'to individual negligence common in such cases. What is every ones business is no one's'.

Scott was not at all happy with the decision. He replied to Mackenzie, 'I cannot well brook the idea of retreating before James Gibson's summons and James Stuart's pistol tinderbox and all without asking me if I chose to retreat or no'.[23] On 27 September he wrote to William Erskine (Lord Kinnedder).

> I am terribly malcontent about the *Beacon*. I was dragged into the Bond against all remonstrances I could make and now they have allowed me no role with regard to standing or flying. *Entre nous*, our friends went into the thing like fools and have come out very like cowards. I was never so sick of a transaction in my life, though I thank God I have very little to do with it ...[24]

What a hypocritical statement this was, for Scott was one of the leading figures in its foundation. Indeed the initial discussions to launch the *Beacon* took place in his own house.

In a letter to his publisher Archibald Constable on 30 September, Scott wrote: 'So I am sad and sulky, for I think the seniors might have been mediators and not fugitives'.[25] Colin Mackenzie must have heard about Scott's 'sadness and sulkiness' for he wrote to Scott on 26 September:

I must fairly own that your being sad and sulky and very crossgrained is a very adequate reason for resolving to stay at home. I am however very sorry you should be so, and still more that such a tone of feeling should be excited by transactions in which I have had a considerable share … . I must say your letter makes me somewhat sad and considerably disappoints me as being the only Censure I have as yet heard cast on the proceedings …[26]

To Lord Melville, 7 October 1821, Scott wrote:

The happy *fifteen* [the bonds men] have the appearance of having supported a system of political warfare while their names were concealed and of renouncing it as indefensible so soon as publicity attached to it … .
I could have bit my nails for anger when I found they had made me accessory to a retreat before the summons of Mr James Giblets and the pistol-tinder-box of the other fellow.[27]

James Giblets was of course James Gibson, who, supported by the Earl of Lauderdale, threatened Scott to a duel, believing him (rightly) to be the master-mind of the *Beacon* and (wrongly) to have written some of the offending articles.[28] He withdrew his challenge on the demise of the publication and having received strong reassurances that Scott had taken no part in the writing of the articles. This is probably untrue, for a letter of Scott to James Ballantyne suggests that he did indeed supply at least one unidentified article.[29] His son-in-law, Lockhart, makes the unlikely comment that Scott never even saw the paper.[30] Ten months later Scott, still fuming, wrote to Croker, 'the hasty renunciation of the thing as if we had been doing something very atrocious put me mad all together. The fact is it is a blasted business and will continue long to have bad consequences.' In this letter Scott said of Lockhart, 'he kept himself well out of all these scrapes while considering his natural temper is something wonderful. But with assistance of my *spectacles* he saw from the beginning the Beacon was not to answer'.[31]

J. R. McCulloch, a Whig contributor to *The Scotsman*, wrote to Archibald Constable on 9 December:

Of course you must be acquainted with all the particulars respecting the demise of The Beacon. The action which Mr Gibson has brought against the Lord Advocate, the Solicitor-General, your friend Sir Walter, and other enemies … of the Press … these high personages are now defenders in an action in the Jury Court for publishing a base and false, and unfounded libel! If I were Jupiter, and had the selection of the jury, I would teach Sir Walter the expedience of sticking to his Poems and his Novels.[32]

Cockburn wrote:

> Scott's conduct cannot be thought of without the deepest sorrow. The happiness
> of the city was disturbed, persons he had long professed and truly felt friendship for
> were vilified, private feelings were lacerated; and all this he could have prevented by
> a word or a look. But instead of preventing it, he gave it his countenance.[33]

The Scotsman newspaper, which had been pilloried in almost every issue of the
Beacon, chose to ignore it as being beneath its dignity, as long as it believed that it
was being run by a printer. The exposure of influential Tory backers altered its
attitude and initiated a series of editorials and articles attacking the *Beacon* and its
supporters, particularly Sir Walter Scott and the Lord Advocate Rae. The issue of
29 September 1821 announced that: 'It is not a voluntary, and unsolicited
abandonment of those who had set up a workshop of scandal and calumny; but
a tardy, reluctant, and cowardly shrinking, from their responsibility as pecuniary
supporters of that disgraceful establishment'. In its issue of 22 September, under
a heading THE BEACON AND ITS PATRONS, it quoted Bayle:

> Those who approve the authors and dispersers of defamatory libels are as guilty as if
> they had composed them. If they do not write such libels themselves, it is merely
> because they have not the talent for writing, or because they will run no hazard.[34]
>
> …
>
> So long as printers and printers' devils were the only persons known to be connected
> with this paper, we considered it as totally undeserving of attention. But this reason
> for despising it no longer exists. The real strings by which the puppets were set in
> motion – the secret patrons and foster fathers of slander and calumny – have at
> length been discovered; and we have now to deal, not with men of straw, … but
> with high official personages, – with those who move in the society of gentlemen.

The article proceeds at length to detail the iniquities of the *Beacon*: 'Individuals in every rank of life … have been unceasingly libelled, traduced, and vilified,
in the most blackguard, brutal, and revolting terms'. It goes on to mock the
claims by the backers that they were unaware of the content of the paper which
they were supporting and 'stood safely concealed behind their hirelings'. Had it
not been for the circumstance of their disclosure 'it is difficult to say how long this
system of *subornation of slander* might have been carried on'.

Blackwood's Magazine being a Tory publication might have been expected to
sympathise with the *Beacon* but instead it joined in the criticism,[35] 'what a lump
of dulness it was! it seemed to … be got up just for the private amusement of three

or four spalpeens [Irish for layabouts] … a mangy mongrel could not have lifted his leg, in passing, without putting it out'.

Lady Morgan, who as Sydney Owenson, the Irish novelist, had been harshly criticised by John Wilson Croker in the *London Quarterly Review* got her revenge on her critics by writing a lengthy satire[36] in which she mocked inter alia the Tory bondsmen of the *Beacon*, including Walter Scott and the Lord Advocate Rae.

> But long the man of song and legal knight,
> Like giants, in their course could not rejoice;
> The bond discovered, dragged to day each name,
> They've only to divide the costs and shame.

The last issue of the *Beacon*, published on 22 September, contained the extraordinary statement that it did not attack private individuals:

> We have never, in any instance, attacked an individual who did not obtrude himself on the public … or who did not chuse [*sic*] like Gibson and others, to run his head against the Beacon itself.

With regard to the accusation that the attacks were made under a system of concealment:

> We have less concealment than any other paper in the kingdom. Our Editor avows himself to the public, and is ready to stand all the consequences of what he may publish, and if any one wishes to know the writer of anything concerning him, he has only to ask his name… . We abhor concealment and consider it as quite unworthy of the cause in which we are engaged. There never was a single anonymous sentence inserted in the Beacon.

What arrant barefaced lies! There was hardly a sentence in the paper that was not anonymous. An article in *The Examiner* summarised the Whig view of the *Beacon*.

> The 'organised system of blackguardism,' as the Scotsman has well termed it, is among the most alarming features of the times … it is a conspiracy of the pensioned prostitutes of corruption against every man what exposes the abuse of Administration, or advocates the freedom of the people. The agents of this abominable system of political warfare have the means of shielding themselves and their adherents, while they prosecute with exterminating vengeance any one who employs against them the same mode of attack … . The Beacon was established … to 'show up' to

use their own phrase, every public man who was not a supporter of Ministers … .
And yet – to the eternal degradation of the British name and character, and to the
utter disgrace of that Government by which its character and name should be digni-
fied and upheld – we find this infamous system of anonymous slander patronized in
the highest circle, and adopted as an engine of political warfare. It was in Edinburgh
the infamous system first exploded; it was in Edinburgh that its connexion with a
Government party was first fully disclosed. And of what casts were the delinquents?
… . The bondsmen … the persons under whose patronage it had been established
… turned out to be persons trusted with Magistrates of great weight and authority,
with … the Lord Advocate at their head.[37]

The authors of the libellous articles and poems in the *Beacon* were mostly
young lawyers whose names were never revealed apart from one, Douglas
Cheape.[38] Cheape was probably the real editor, although he refused to contribute
to the costs incurred by the *Beacon* in the libel case against the paper which was
won by Gibson on the grounds that 'if I do it will be held by the world that I own
myself the editor of the *Beacon* – else why should I pay costs?'[39] A broadsheet
entitled *The last Speech and Confession and Dying Declaration of the Beacon* hinted
that other contributors included the advocates William Russell, Duncan
M'Neill, Blackmore and John Hope. Another anonymous paper added the
names of William Menzies and Robert Dundas.[40] Other suggested names were
John Gibson Lockhart and his fellow author John Wilson (Christopher North)
of *Blackwood's* but there is no evidence to support these allegations. Alexander
Boswell was familiar with the paper and wrote to his friend Walter Scott soon
after the publication commenced, 'I take it for granted that you take some
interest in the *Beacon* and may know the Editors'. He suggested that it should be
more popular, that extracts from other papers should be given and that the
poetical part should be more homely: 'It strikes me the *Beacon* is rather too much
a Gentleman's paper'.[41] The style of some of the poems in the *Beacon* suggests that
Boswell may have written them but he was never identified as a contributor
although Cockburn considered this likely.[42]

The young lawyers who had contributed most of the articles felt let down
when their seniors withdrew their support for the paper. Scott wrote to J. W.
Croker on 2 July 1822:

I fear disunion between the elder and younger part of our Scottish friends very
much at this moment. The younger brethren allege they were put into the front of
fight and deserted on the first pinch and on my word I cannot say the accusation is
altogether false though I have done my best to mediate betwixt the two parties and
keep the peace if possible.[43]

No one emerged from the debacle of the paper with any credit, but the printer and publisher, Duncan Stevenson, managed to survive the furore and the libel actions against him and continued to run his business successfully, becoming printer to the University. He diversified into property development, and having suffered a number of financial setbacks, died in 1867. His printing firm, Stevenson & Co, survived into the 1960s.[44]

Broadsheets

A flurry of broadsheets greeted the demise of the *Beacon*. One suggested that the 'editor', John Nimmo, was a mythical figure, the name being a pun on the Latin word *nemo* – a nobody. In fact he was a real person who, on hearing that there was a warrant against him relating to the *Beacon*, fled the same day from Leith in a smack sailing to France where he worked as a journeyman printer for a Paris newspaper for 40 years. He died in France aged 85 in 1879.[45]

Another broadsheet entitled *The Hydra with Fifteen Heads* (Fig. 12) contains a mock confession by the *Beacon* before 'his' execution, from which the following extracts are taken:

> One of my parents ... is a *lame* poet ... I am apt to think he has had the greatest
> share in my composition. ... From my youth upward I have been guilty of
> gaming, backbiting, slandering, lying, bullying, and was never better pleased
> than in traducing and defaming ... the most worthy characters. ... I would have
> continued going on from bad to worse, had not a sudden check been put to my
> vicious career, by the persevering character and keen penetration of my invincible
> and determined foes J...s G.b..n, and his no less indefatigable and determined
> coadjutor J...s S...t.[46]

Notes

1   Brougham (1871): *The Life and Times of Henry Bougham*, **2**, p. 503.

2   Scott's letter to Archibald Constable, 30 September 1821 in Constable (1873): *Archibald Constable and his Literary Correspondents*, **3**, p. 162. This letter is reproduced also in Scott (1932–37): The *Letters of Walter Scott*, **VII**, p. 17, but in the Constable version, the two publications mentioned are *The Scotsman* and the <u>*Beacon*</u> instead of *The Scotsman* and <u>*Review*</u>.

3   Several other suggestions were made including a new church, but Cockburn's was chosen. The foundation stone was laid during the visit of George IV to Edinburgh in the following year and work was stopped in 1830, when the project ran out of funds, leaving the incomplete fragment which exists today.

4   Issue no. 17, 28 April 1821, p. 135. Slaves were not always treated with such consideration. James Stuart in *Three Years in North America* records several instances in which slaves were separated from their spouses and children at auction sales. 'They made a great crying scene!', vol. 2,

pp. 113–4. Slavery was not unknown in Scotland. The *Edinburgh Courant* of 30 August 1763, contained the following advertisement: To be disposed of, a negro woman named Peggy, about nineteen years of age, born and brought up in Charlestown, in the province of South Carolina; speaks good English; an exceeding good house-wench, and washer and dresser; and is very tender and careful of children. She has a young child, a negro boy, about a year old, which will be disposed of with the mother.

5   From a letter to Croker reproduced in Cline (1971): *The fate of Cassandra: The Newspaper War of 1821–22 and Sir Walter Scott*, p. 50.

6   The *Correspondence between James Stuart and the Printer of the Beacon* (Anon, 1821a) is contained in a bound volume and is also printed in issue no. 33 of the *Beacon*. Three editions of this printed correspondence exist – each with a slightly different content. NLS Yule 2 (7). This quotation is on p. 2.

7   Ibid, p. 4, letter 3 August 1821.

8   Ibid, pp. 7–8.

9   Ibid, pp. 14–5.

10 Ibid, p. 24.

11 Letter to Stevenson, 15 August 1821 printed in the *Beacon*, 18 August 1821.

12 Second edition of *Correspondence* (see note 6), p. 21.

13 *Scots Magazine* **IX**, November 1821, p. 484.

14 The printed correspondence entitled *Correspondence between James Stuart Esq. the younger of Dunearn and the Lord Advocate* (Anon, 1821) is contained in a bound volume: Ref. Ry 1.1.9(7) in NLS. This item is on pp.1–2.

15 Ibid, pp. 4–5.

16 Ibid, p. 6.

17 Ibid, p. 9.

18 Ibid, p. 21.

19 Ibid, p. 22.

20 Letter to Dr J. G. Cogswell, 24 June 1821 in Grant (1891): *Memoirs of an American Lady*, **2**, pp. 254–6.

21 Cockburn (1909): *Memorials of his time*, pp. 374–5.

22 Cockburn letter to Kennedy, 18 November 1821 in Cockburn (1874b): *Letters chiefly concerned with the Affairs of Scotland from Lord Cockburn to Thomas Francis Kennedy*, p. 36.

23 Letter to Colin Mackenzie, 31 September 1821 in Scott (1932–37): *Letters*, **VII**, pp. 18–20

24 Letter to William Erskine (Lord Kinedder), 27 September 1821 in Scott (1932–37): *Letters*, **VII**, pp. 11–2.

25 Constable (1873), **3**, p. 162.

26 Scott (1932–37): *Letters*, **VII**, p. 19, fn.

27 Scott (1932–37): *Letters*, **VII**, pp. 26–7.

28 Grierson (1938): *Sir Walter Scott Bart: A new life*, p. 246; Johnson (1970): *Sir Walter Scott, the Great Unknown*, pp. 773–4.

29 Scott (1932–37): *Letters*, **VII**, p. 346.

30 Lockhart (1902): *Life of Sir Walter Scott*, **VI**, pp. 394–8.

31 Letter to J. W. Croker, 2 July 1822 in Scott (1932–37) *Letters*, **VII**, pp. 204–6.

32 Constable (1873), **2**, p. 370.

33 Cockburn (1909): *Memorials*, p. 375.

34 Pierre Bayle (1647–1706) a French philosopher whose teachings had a profound influence on the Scottish Enlightenment.

35 *Blackwood's Magazine*, **XII**, December 1822, p. 709.

36 Owenson (1822): *The Mohawks: A satirical Poem with Notes*.

37 *The Examiner*, no. 744, 7 April 7 1822

38 Douglas Cheape (1797–1861). Scott wrote in his *Journal* on 14 December 1826 with regard to Cheape's application for the Chair of Civil Law: 'He deserves support having been very indifferently used in the affair of the Beacon where certain high tories shewed a great desire to leave him to the mercy of the enemy'. Cheape succeeded in becoming Professor of Civil Law at University of Edinburgh from 1827–42.

39   Cockburn letter to Kennedy, 13 February 1823 in Cockburn (1874b).
40   Earl of Rosslyn's correspondence: NAS GD 164/452/14
41   Extract from a letter from Sir Alexander Boswell to Walter Scott, 19.2.21in Scott (1932–37): *Letters*, **VI**, fn p. 346.
42   Cockburn (*c.*1822a): *Trial 3*, p. 129.
43   Scott (1932–37) *Letters*, **VII**, pp. 205–6.
44   Moss (1995): 'The curious case of Duncan Stevenson, printer to University of Edinburgh', *The Bibliotheck*, **20**, pp. 88–97.
45   Grant (1881–83): *Old and New Edinburgh*, **II**, p. 242. See also Abercromby, Parliamentary debate, 25 June 1822.
46   The lame poet is of course Sir Walter Scott. J...s G.b..n and J...s S...t are James Gibson and James Stuart.

CHAPTER 5

The saga of the *Sentinel*

You must be very cautious of letting other people know that you are such an observer and such a censor morum, as they may be apt to misunderstand and form a wrong notion of you.

James Boswell's advice to Alexander in 1794[1]

I desire it as a favour, you would often examine your poetical pieces before you commit them to the press.

Advice to Robert Fergusson from his brother Harry 1773[2]

I see you have some talent about you, but my advice is, never to use it to wound the feelings of others.

Advice to Alexander Wilson, Paisley poet and ornithologist, from his father[3]

CONCURRENTLY WITH the *Beacon* saga in Edinburgh, another similar publishing activity was brewing in the west of Scotland. The printer William Murray Borthwick (1782–1866) (Fig. 13) wrote:

> In spring of 1820 when the west of Scotland was in a very disturbed state, it occurred to me that a weekly newspaper … conducted upon loyal and constitutional principles, might have considerable effect in doing away the foolish notions, then prevalent among the lower classes. My political principles were those of a Tory.[4]

The *Clydesdale Journal* and the Lord Advocate

The *Clydesdale Journal* was launched by Borthwick in Hamilton in April 1820 with £275 of capital contributed by Lord Douglas, Mr W. E. Lockhart of Cleghorn, Mr Henry Monteith of Carstairs, Sir Henry Steuart, and 'other noblemen & gentlemen of the county who approved of its principles'. Each had contributed £25. Borthwick misappropriated some of the funds to pay off old debts which led to censure from the backers. Despite that, he managed to obtain further subscriptions of £235 when once more he ran into debt. The *Journal* had a limited circulation and a series of unsatisfactory editors. The first was William Aiton, the Sheriff substitute at Hamilton who prepared the prospectus and wrote some of the principal articles. He was succeeded by Robert Alexander, who responded to an advertisement for the post and offered to advance the sum of £300 to become a partner, but failed to produce the money and was dismissed. The next was Aiton's son who tried to take over the publication and was dismissed. Curiously Borthwick then re-engaged Robert Alexander, who had fallen on hard times. He was without a home wandering about the country.[5] Alexander had tried to start a Whig newspaper in Paisley but failed to get enough financial backing to get it launched. Alexander's political leanings seem to be determined by business opportunity rather than conviction.

Alexander's second term as editor was no more successful than his first and Borthwick was once more heavily in debt. He approached the Lord Advocate, Sir William Rae, for financial assistance, but Rae – who had supported the *Beacon* financially – was not prepared to do the same for the *Clydesdale Journal* although its politics and objectives were similar. Rae did however lend his support by signing a manifesto recommending the newspaper, which was circulated to about 200 selected individuals, with a request that they maintained secrecy about it. This manifesto, which was to land Rae in much trouble, read:

> The Clydesdale Journal was begun under the auspices of some noblemen and gentlemen of the county, and has been conducted, on the whole, to their satisfaction. The editor, unfortunately, is not himself possessed of sufficient means for carrying it on and, in addition to the subscriptions alluded to, he would require further aid, to the extent of £.
>
> Considering the present state of the country, and of this county in particular, in consequence of the great industry used in disseminating publications which have a tendency to unhinge the principles of all classes and to render the middle and lower classes discontented and unhappy, we are desirous of encouraging a periodical publication which may counteract their baneful effects; and from the experience already had of the Clydesdale Journal, we recommend it to the patronage of such gentlemen as have not contributed to, and may be disposed to aid such an undertaking.
>
> Signed William Rae and eight others.[6]

This appeal failed to produce sufficient funds and the *Clydesdale Journal*, which had made very little impact, failed. The last issue was published under the joint names of Borthwick and Alexander on 28 September 1821, just a week after the expiry of the *Beacon*.

The *Glasgow Sentinel*, a phoenix from the ashes

Robert Alexander, who had bought Borthwick's printing materials – auctioned to pay off debts – regarded this as an opportune moment to start a new newspaper in Glasgow, modelled on the *Beacon* and styled the *Glasgow Sentinel*. Despite their unhappy working relationship at the *Clydesdale Journal*, Alexander invited Borthwick to join him in partnership and the *Glasgow Sentinel* was launched on 10 October 1821, like 'a Phoenix worthy of the ashes of its parent' according to *The Scotsman*. Alexander's name now preceded Borthwick's in the title. Where the financial backing came from is unclear, but certainly none of the backers of the *Beacon* was involved.[7]

The *Sentinel* was, in format, almost identical with the *Beacon*. The introductory paragraphs in the first edition declared its Tory leanings and its intention to attack those with contrary opinions:

> Truth shall be our Beacon; for our native country we shall ever act as faithful Sentinels; and the King, the People, and the Constitution, in Church and State will be our watchword. We trust to be bold without being scurrilous; and fearless of defending without being personal … . In the cause of public justice we shall steer a straightforward course, unjostled by the crowd – untempted by the titled – unfeared by the powerful – unsilenced by the resentful.

Duncan Stevenson congratulated Robert Alexander and Borthwick: 'their first number … has produced considerable sensation here to-day: I sincerely wish you every success.' William Blackwood of *Blackwood's Magazine* 'takes leave to congratulate Mr Alexander on the first number'; he had heard a 'great deal of praise'. He offered some practical advice and placed an order.[8] Alexander Boswell became an early subscriber.

The first number of the *Sentinel* continued the attack on James Stuart by repeating the account of the Stevenson horse-whipping and Stuart's refusal to accept his challenge:

> … But, oh shame to the dishonoured blood of the house and name of Stuart, he with a meanness only discernible in low life, and in humble society, sought his personal safety in the most glaring cowardice! The blustering and the passionate

are always in the rear of danger. James Stuart was consequently posted as a coward and a poltroon. The very rabble and oyster-women of the streets of Edinburgh read the label, mused upon the circumstances, and blushed for their *patriot* ...

Robert Alexander subsequently admitted to being the author of this article, which he defended by saying that he had witnessed Stuart attack The Rt Hon. Lord Succoth 'in a style of intimidation both of language and gesture, which I thought might have precluded him from being overfastidious about the sweetness of words which were applied to him'.[9]

James Stuart's reaction

Stuart responded immediately by instituting an Action of Damages against Alexander and Borthwick for the sum of £5,000.[10] A subsequent letter published in the paper on 17 December 1821, under the pseudonym of Ignotus (Latin – unknown), commented on Stuart's action and congratulated the editor for his stand against him, comparing Stuart's behaviour to another instance in which one individual had refused to fight another and deserved the white feather 'and was deservedly stigmatized and laughed at'. Ignotus subscribed £5 towards the costs of the defence and hoped 'that there is a goodly increase before a week is over'.

Borthwick, distressed by this legal threat and the prospect of others, underwent a sudden conversion. He wrote that the *Beacon* had been discontinued because:

> ... the good taste of the Public had made the sale of the Journal very limited ... as the Beacon fell in the East, the Sentinel was sent to watch in the West ... . The Paper continued in its new form, the same tissue of weekly personal defamation that had distinguished it in its old one ... . There never was a single number of either of them, which did not contain many actionable libels.[11]

Borthwick realised that writing or publishing libels was not a good career move and decided to give up his share in the paper. On 14 November he made a bargain with Alexander to relinquish his interest in the *Sentinel* upon receiving a £20 douceur in cash and £90 in bills before 8 December. Alexander agreed to buy his share of the partnership but failed to keep up with his due payments.

The final insults

Undeterred by the threat of legal action, the *Sentinel* continued to publish articles attacking Stuart. A lengthy poem, entitled the *Whig Song*, written in a crude Scottish dialect contained the following verse:

> Ther's stot-feeder Stuart,
> Kent for that fat-cow-art,
> How glegly he kicks ony ba', man;
> And Gibson, lang chiel, man,[12]
> Whase height might serve weel, man,
> To read his ain name on a wa', man.

> Your knights o' the pen, man
> Are a' *gentlemen*, man,
> Ilk *body's* a *limb* o' the law, man;
> Tacks, bonds, precognitions,
> Bills, wills, and petitions,
> And *ought* but a *trigger* some draw, man.

It is now almost impossible to understand the meaning of this doggerel but at that time it would immediately be interpreted that Stuart was known (kent) as a fat coward (cow-art). The second verse indicates that this man (ilk body) i.e. Stuart, as a lawyer, could draw up legal documents and should have drawn a trigger as well. Henry Cockburn commenting on the apparent triviality of such articles when viewed in retrospect, observed that 'the guilt of libel must be judged of as on the day it was committed, when the insinuations were understood ... the insolence fresh, and the victim quivering'.[13]

Another letter to the editor dated 25 January 1822, signed Mark Tod (tod – Scots for fox), is a mocking account of the annual Whig dinner in Edinburgh commemorating Charles Fox. The various toasts were listed. Francis Jeffrey was the 'Croupier' (master of ceremonies), whom the *Sentinel* disliked for his unashamed support of the Whigs. It mocked Jeffrey as the person 'whom Lord Byron has celebrated for some bold exploit with Anacreon[14] Moore' (see p. 39). 'The Croupier gave the health of MR JAMES STUART ... Mr James Stuart acknowledged, in grateful terms, the honour which he had received from such a quarter. So now he has a FEATHER to stick in his cap, to bear the other company.' This was another veiled reference to the 'white feather'.[15]

Another insult, in the *Sentinel* on 20 February 1822, was an article entitled 'The late Lieutenant James Stuart'. It gave a scathing account of the incident described on pages 4–6 which forced Stuart to resign his commission with the Fife Yeomanry but prefaced the article with:

> To be dragged into a contest with any individual is an evil; but the evil is aggravated when the opponent is one not in the most blooming estimation … . We now freely and ingenuously confess our error, in having repeated, in our columns, any thing regarding Mr James Stuart for had the gift of prophetic anticipation been ours, and could we have foreseen all that the *gentleman* has done for himself, we should have left his conduct to himself as the more successful satirist.

And concluded with:

> The attempt of Lord Rector Jeffrey[16] to give a *lift* to Mr James Stuart at the Fox dinner, was defeated by the laws of gravity; he might with equal success have exerted his puissant powers to *lift* the celebrated fat ox of Dunearn.
> We noticed Mr James Stuart as an active, everywhere busy bustling Whig; – as a *publicised* character who courted notice. It was under error that we noticed him at all, and we repeat our avowal of regret.

Stuart was by now incandescent. His action for libel against the publishers had become less important than finding the author of these repeated attacks maligning him. He was determined to find out who the culprit was. Only by challenging him to a duel could he clear his name of the accusations of cowardice.

Discovery of the evidence

The opportunity came about in a curious way. When Alexander failed to pay Borthwick for his share of the partnership, despite being ordered to do so on two occasions by the magistrates, Borthwick on 14 February 1822, obtained from the Glasgow magistrates the right to have his partnership reinstated – or so he thought. The wording of the magistrates ruling is rather enigmatic:

> In respect the defender [Alexander] has failed to implement the said renewed order, Ordains the defender *within six days* … to deliver the bills with security to the pursuer [Borthwick] … *and failing his doing so, decerns* [Scottish law – decrees] *in terms of the other alternative conclusions thereof,* … [17]

Borthwick interpreted 'other alternative conclusions' as meaning that he was entitled to resume his rights as a partner, and this was endorsed by his counsel,

Henry Cockburn, who said that he could not be held to have divested himself of his property and interest.[18]

Borthwick, in his voluminous writings about the affair, never stated his reasons for wanting to resume his association with a man who had landed him with so much trouble and with the paper which he now despised. The subsequent events, however, suggest that his motive was to obtain evidence of the authors of the libels. Provided with this information, he might able to persuade Stuart to withdraw the Action of Damages against him.[19]

Borthwick, armed with the magistrates' authority, entered the *Sentinel* office in Nelson Street on 1 March 1822 and spent the entire day looking through the documents in the office. Alexander, who was in the office at the time, was 'in a very bad mood' and gave him 'personal abuse' but did not attempt to stop his searches.[20] James Todd, Alexander's lawyer, also turned up during the day but did not dispute Borthwick's right to be there. Borthwick left the office, retaining the keys of his desk and the safe, with the intention of returning the following day to continue his search.

At midnight Borthwick was roused from his sleep, arrested by a messenger-at-arms and jailed in Glasgow Jail for the non payment of a debt of £50.[21] It transpired later that Alexander had engineered his arrest by contacting an individual in Hamilton and persuading him to lay a charge against Borthwick for an outstanding debt, which was not in fact due for payment.[22] Alexander's action was transparently a device for keeping Borthwick away from the office. Borthwick immediately contacted his legal agent at Hamilton, William Henderson, and instructed him to try to get a bill of suspension and liberation from his confinement. Henderson spent several days in Edinburgh for this purpose, but the legal process proceeded very slowly. Borthwick became impatient and decided on another tack. The subsequent events are described by various witnesses in the trial of James Stuart.

On 7 March, James Stuart was approached in Outer House of Parliament Hall by two men, Henderson and William Spalding,[23] who stated that they were Borthwick's legal agents. They informed him of Borthwick's predicament and said that their client was prepared to help to identify the author of the offending articles if Stuart would withdraw the Action of Damages against him. Stuart replied that 'if you give us the documents, we shall consider ... your proposal. But we make no bargain; only, we want the author, – we don't concern ourselves with the paltry printer'.[24]

In order that Borthwick might obtain the documents, it was necessary that he should be released from jail. Stuart discussed the matter with James Gibson, his friend, fellow lawyer and fellow victim of the *Beacon* libels. Gibson believed that the process to obtain the bill of suspension and liberation was taking too long:

It was a pity to temporise in a matter of this kind, – that from the character I had heard of Alexander, he would not scruple to … destroy the manuscripts … . In my opinion, some one should go to Glasgow instantly, pay the debt, procure Mr Borthwick's liberation, and secure the papers.[25]

Gibson was prepared to pay the debt himself if need be, but was not required to do so.

On Saturday 9 March, Stuart, Henderson and Spalding travelled to Glasgow with the objective of liberating Borthwick from jail despite the lack of valid legal consent. They arrived at 11pm and stayed in the Tontine Inn. Henderson visited the prison, but at that late hour was unable to gain access. The following day Borthwick was freed on the payment of the debt of £50 by Henderson, who subsequently declared that he personally had loaned the money and that Stuart had no part in it. This is difficult to credit but no evidence to the contrary was produced during the trial.[26]

Borthwick spent the night at the Tontine Inn and at 7am the next day went to the *Sentinel* office to resume possession of his property. He was accompanied by two men to act as witnesses: Loudon Robertson, a compositor who had been sacked by Alexander some months before, and Felix Dougherty, a clerk to Henderson. What transpired in the office was to become a matter of legal debate. Was Borthwick legally entitled to re-enter the premises? Had he the right to take possession of its contents? Was any violence used in obtaining these? Robbery with violence could be a capital offence.

Accounts of the 'break in'

Borthwick gave several accounts of the recovery of documents.

His first was a declaration before the magistrates of Glasgow on 12 March 1821. In a sworn statement he said that on 1 March he spent the entire day in the *Sentinel* office leaving at 8pm, notwithstanding a good deal of personal abuse being heaped upon him by Alexander. On leaving he took the keys, except the door key which he gave to a workman. When he returned on 11 March after his release from jail, he found that new locks had been fitted to the safe and to a desk drawer, but he found the new key for the safe lying in the compartment of the desk on which he had been accustomed to write and with it he opened the safe. He declared that he had not forced open any desk, or other lockfast place, or made use of any force or violence whatever, neither did he open any desk, even with a key, for he found all the desks open.

In *Proceedings* written while in jail on 8 April 1822 his statement was similar, except that he could not get into his own desk as a new lock had been fitted and that he found the safe key in another open desk – a minor detail, but perhaps an indication that Borthwick was not being entirely frank. Surely he would have remembered whether or not his own desk was accessible.

In the *Letter to Sir William Rae* on 25 September 1823, Borthwick gave an entirely different account:

> I had no occasion [to] break open any lockfast place. [On 1 March] I took posses-
> sion of the office and property therein in virtue of authority from the magistrates of
> Glasgow ... and when I left ... I took the keys of the safe and desk with me ... until
> I returned to resume possession on the 11th. While I was absent both the safe and
> desk had been broken open by Alexander ... and I had not a lockfast place in the
> office. Alexander had both a locked drawer and iron safe, which I never interfered
> with; I only examined my own repositories and took the papers belonging to me ...

No mention this time of access to the safe or finding keys.

Alexander's account of the affair is given in his *Letter to Sir J. Mackintosh*, p. 45. He wrote that at about 7am on 11 March a boy of 11 was alone in the *Sentinel* office lighting fires when Borthwick and two others entered. Borthwick and his companions 'rummaged whatever they could lay their hands on, and heaped in two or three parcels, all the manuscripts of the Sentinel since its com-mencement, all letters, private or otherwise, they could find; the book containing the list of subscribers' names and various keys'. He makes no mention of the safe or of forced entry of desks except to comment that Borthwick was clearing a desk that had been locked the night before.

Perhaps the most reliable account of the events of that morning was that of William Miller, the 11-year-old boy who was the only occupant of the office when Borthwick arrived. He was the only individual who did not have a vested interest in the affair. He stated that he saw Borthwick trying to open the safe with a key without success. Borthwick then sent his companion, Robertson, to find a smith. Meanwhile, Borthwick found a key for the safe in a desk and had opened it. When the smith returned with Robertson his services were no longer required and he observed that in any event it would not have been possible to force the safe.[27] An apprentice, who must also have entered the office during the 'break in', said that he found Borthwick standing at a desk which he had opened. He went immediately to notify Alexander's brother, David, a clerk in the office, who arrived while Borthwick was still on the premises. David Alexander noted that a desk had been broken into. It looked as if a sharp instrument had been forced under the lid at the side of the lock.[28]

The impression from all these accounts is that Borthwick or one of his henchmen probably did force the lock of a desk but did not break into the safe. In this desk they found the key of the safe and had it open before the arrival of the smith. It is impossible to escape the conclusion that Borthwick was being devious over his versions of the affair. The basic facts are however clear. Borthwick entered the office by 7am and obtained, by fair means or foul, a quantity of papers.

The boy Miller saw Robertson departing with a bundle of papers carried in a blue handkerchief 'about the size of two hats'.[29] Borthwick also left with his pockets stuffed with papers and returned some time after with empty pockets to continue his search. David Alexander approached Borthwick and told him that he had no right to have opened the desk, stating 'this is plainly stealing'. Borthwick gave him a contemptuous look and said, 'I will knock your head among your feet, Sir'. Alexander, noting that Borthwick was much stouter, decided to avoid violence. He tried to open his own desk whereupon Borthwick forced the lid down on his fingers.[30] According to Borthwick, David Alexander 'behaved in a very outrageous manner', which prevented him from examining and selecting the papers on the premises. Borthwick then left carrying the rest of the papers and joined Stuart's party at the Tontine Inn. He left Dougherty in the office planning to return unwanted papers to him, but David Alexander together with his lawyer, James Todd, who had by then turned up, forced Dougherty out of the office and locked the door.[31]

Later that day Borthwick petitioned the Glasgow magistrates to have David and Robert Alexander and James Todd bound over to keep the peace and give him peaceable possession of his property. The next day Alexander countered by instituting proceedings to have Borthwick apprehended for breaking into the office and carrying off paper. The warrant was granted and Borthwick was arrested but the magistrates dismissed the case on hearing Borthwick's account. Whether or not Borthwick obtained the papers legally was to become a matter of great importance in the subsequent events.

Sir Alexander Boswell exposed

On receiving the papers from the *Sentinel* office, Stuart, Spalding and Henderson made a rapid survey of them and although there had been some attempts to disguise the writing, and some postmarks had been obliterated or cut out, the manuscripts showed beyond doubt that some of the libels had been written by Stuart's distant kinsman and acquaintance, Sir Alexander Boswell. Stuart, who had frequently discussed the likely authors with his friends, had never considered Boswell as a possibility. Four of the offending articles were identified as being written by Boswell these were: the *Whig Song*, the letter signed Ignotus, the article on Lieutenant James Stuart and the letter by Mark Tod.

Stuart and Spalding left the Tontine Inn for Edinburgh in a post chaise at around 9.30 that morning, carrying with them the most relevant papers, leaving Henderson and Borthwick to return the rest to Borthwick's agent, Alexander Ure, as they were unable to return them to the *Sentinel* office, having been barred from entry. Among these discards it was rumoured that there were letters which incriminated others. Lockhart wrote:

> … there is some chance of Sir William Rae being in a near scrape, some letters of his having been found – but I trust this is more malice and can scarcely imagine it possible he should *after the Beacon* have compromised himself in any such Manner. At the same time these fellows have certainly boasted in Glasgow of having received in some way or other £150 from the government and if the Advocate was the channell [*sic*] through which this bonus passed there is no saying what may be the consequence …[32]

This matter was not brought up again and was presumably gossip, but it does indicate how widely Rae's involvement with the Tory press was known or suspected.

Back in Edinburgh, Stuart invited guests to dinner in order to reveal his discovery. The guests, including John Horner[33] and brothers James and John Brougham,[34] shared his astonishment at the revelation. Spalding kept custody of the papers and divided them into five parcels which he sealed. The first contained 14 letters in the same handwriting which had been identified as Boswell's. The Edinburgh Sheriff, Adam Duff, demanded that the papers be handed over to him on several occasions but Spalding at first resisted on the advice of Cockburn, who had been retained as counsel for both Stuart and Borthwick. Finally the sheriff issued a search warrant for them and they were reluctantly handed over under the condition that if and when the parcels were opened, it should be in the presence of Spalding. Cockburn wrote with regard to Duff's obtaining the documents:

> The Lord Advocate is one of the supporters of the paper – and his scamps write in it. So here we have an Advocate who first sets up a libellous paper, and then employs the machinery of his office to get the evidence out of the hands of those who could detect his connection with it.[35]

At no time did Stuart keep the evidence in his possession. Cockburn wrote with regard to Stuart, 'in getting access to the manuscripts he had directly no concern – and the part which he did take was so scrupulously correct that he is even beyond the reach of imputation in the proceeding'.[36]

The discovery of the author of the libels was to change the destiny of three individuals: James Stuart, Sir Alexander Boswell and William Murray Borthwick. It excited a great interest in both the public and the press and intensified the ill will between Whig and Tory.

The Scotsman in an editorial of 24 August 1822, at the time of George IV's visit to Edinburgh (just four months after the duel and two months after Stuart's trial), wrote:

> Can the King ... approve of those persons who never write a paragraph in the spirit
> or with the language of a gentleman, and who for years have been labouring to
> embroil the best and ablest of his Majesty's subjects, in personal and deadly quarrels?
> Are the Whigs of Scotland to yield the palm of loyalty to the bondsmen of the
> Beacon, – the writers of manifestos for the Clydesdale Journal – the secret abettors
> of the Sentinel? ... The supposition borders upon sacrilege.

According to Adam Black, 'the history of the *Beacon* and the *Sentinel* newspapers, both set up in opposition to *The Scotsman*, is a chronicle of futile malignity'.[37]

The attacks and insults directed against Stuart continued in almost every issue of the paper right up to the time of the duel. Cockburn wrote, 'I am told that the last *Sentinel* is the most villainous that has appeared, and that poor Boswell was its author'.[38] The *Sentinel*, like the *Beacon*, lasted only a few months, the last issue being published on 22 January 1823. Although Stuart's Action of Damages against Robert Alexander and Borthwick had been abandoned, Alexander became bankrupt and sought Sanctuary for Debt at Holyrood House on 6 January 1823.[39] No record of his subsequent activities was found. He died in 1854.

Notes

1 Quoted in Brady (1984): *James Boswell, the Later Years 1769–1795*, p. 455, *censor morum –* critic of morals.
2 Letter from Harry to Robert Fergusson, 8 October 1773. Quoted in Fergusson (1970): *The Works of Robert Fergusson*.
3 Alexander Wilson, who became involved with the political agitators of the Paisley weavers, was gaoled in1792 for writing a libellous poem about a local business man. In this instance it was a Whig libelling a Tory – the opposite of the Boswell/Stuart dispute. Both sides were capable of using the same vehicle for abuse. Chalmers, J. (2003): *Audubon in Edinburgh*, pp. 11–2.
4 Borthwick (1822): *Proceedings against Wm. Murray Borthwick*.
5 Ibid, p. 3.
6 Anon (1822): *Trial 2*, Appendix D, p. 80.
7 Stuart in his Declaration of 19th March 1822 named Lord Douglas, Sir Alexander Cochrane,

Mr Elliot Lockhart and some others as the supporters of the *Sentinel*. Borthwick in a letter to *The Scotsman* on December 14 1822 named three solicitors (writers), a wine merchant, a business man and hints at several others as being the backers of the *Sentinel*. He concludes that: 'The names which I have given you, Sir, are not quite so high as those of the *Beacon* bondsmen'.

8   Anon (1822): *Trial 2*, Appendix, p.53.
9   Alexander (1822): *Letter to Sir J. Mackintosh, Knt., M.P.*, pp. 25–6.
10 *Scots Magazine*, November 1821, p. 484.
11 Borthwick's *Defence in his trial*: NAS JC 26/1822/61.
12 This is a reference to Gibson's height: 6 foot 4 inches.
13 Cockburn (1909): *Memorials of his time*, p. 357.
14 Anacreon was a Greek poet of the 6th century BC renowned for his erotic poetry.
15 The first toast was offered by the Earl of Rosslyn for 'a full, fair and free Representation in the common House of Parliament'. The full toast to James Stuart said that he was 'a gentleman whose activity and unsparing toil in the prosecution of everything that was calculated to advance the interest and political freedom of his country, deserved the approbation and respect of every well directed mind'. *Morning Chronicle*, 30 January 1822.
16 Jeffrey was elected Lord Rector by the students of Glasgow University for two terms of office.
17 Anon (1822): *Trial 2*, Appendix, pp. 97–8.
18 Anon (1822a): *Trial 3*, pp. 96–7.
19 Ibid, pp. 97–8.
20 Ibid, p. 101.
21 A creditor could by law imprison a debtor even for trifling sums. Arnot (1816): *The History of Edinburgh from the earliest accounts to the year 1780*, p. 229 details the legal process at that time and records the case of a debtor being jailed for five months for a debt of £3.
22 Cockburn, writing a year later, said 'I have seen certain letters which passed between Alexander and his agents, and a person of the name of Robertson, who was the pretended creditor at whose instance Borthwick was imprisoned, and from these it is quite plain that the debt … was not due, that these worthies knew this to be a fact, and that the whole thing was a trick in order to get him out of the office'. Letter to Kennedy, 17 June 1822 in Cockburn (1874b): *Letters chiefly concerned with the Affairs of Scotland from Lord Cockburn to Thomas Francis Kennedy*, p. 57.
23 Henderson was Borthwick's agent in Hamilton and Spalding was a clerk with Messrs Young and Ayton WS in Edinburgh.
24 Cockburn's submission in Anon (1822): *Trial 2*, p. 31 and pp. 79–8.
25 Ibid, p. 100.
26 Ibid, p. 34, p. 87 and p 98. This is not the entire story. The jailor refused to release Borthwick without legal authority. Henderson spun a tale to the town clerk of Glasgow, Mr Reddie, that Borthwick was required to give evidence at a court case in Edinburgh the next day. Believing that story Reddie gave permission for his release when the £50 was paid.
27 The smith had been sent by his employer, James Napier, whose work shop was in the High Street. James Napier's son Robert and grandson James became leading shipbuilders on the Clyde.
28 Depositions of William Miller and Alexander McGlashan to the magistrates of Glasgow.
29 Cockburn (c.1822b): *Case of Borthwick*, Parliamentary Papers, precognition of William Miller, p. 68.
30 Ibid, precognition of David Alexander, p. 72.
31 Ibid, precognition of William Borthwick, p. 100.
32 Scott (1932–37): *The Letters of Sir Walter Scott*, **VII**, pp. 113–4, fn.
33 A brother of Stuart's friends Francis and Leonard Horner.
34 James (1780–1833) and John Brougham were brothers of Henry Brougham (see note 6, Chapter 1). Both brothers gave active support to Stuart during the duel, James acting as a substitute second during the absence of Lord Rosslyn (see Chapter 6). James, like Henry, became a Whig MP in 1826. Henry arranged for him to hold two lucrative Parliamentary offices. Their friendship with Stuart was strained by Stuart's importunings (see Chapter 10).
35 Letter to John Richardson, 24 March 1822: NLS 3989.44. See also letter to Andrew Rutherfurd, 26 March 1822: NLS 9687.16.

36   Cockburn (c.1822a): *Trial 3*, pp. 82–3.
37   Black (1885): *Memoirs of Adam Black*, p. 54.
38   PS to a letter to Andrew Rutherfurd, 18 March 1822: NLS 9687.18.
39   The Holyrood Sanctuary was an area in the vicinity of Holyrood Abbey where debtors could live without fear of arrest. It dated from a charter granted by King David I in the 12th Century and continued until 1880 when imprisonment for debt was abolished. Fergusson in his poem *Auld Reekie* described this sanctuary:

  Blest place! where debtors daily run,
  To rid themselves frae jail and dun;

CHAPTER 6

The duel of Stuart and Boswell

… as a place to reside in, Edinburgh is not London. Here individuals are so generally known to each other that their motions are observed, and occupy too much attention, narrowing the mind, to remark and to censure.

Comment by Boswell's sister Euphemia[1]

We must rejoice at the consequence to which the Scottish political duel must lead, – the washing out of the foulest stain that ever disgraced and degraded the periodical literature of a country.

Article in *The Scotsman* of 6 April 1822

ON DISCOVERING the author of the libels, Stuart decided – after discussion with his friends James Gibson, James Brougham and Sir Ronald Ferguson – that he had no alternative other than to challenge Boswell to a duel. Brougham advised that he should ask Lord Rosslyn to act as his second. James St Clair-Erskine, the 2nd Earl of Rosslyn, (1762–1837)[2] had a distinguished military career as a general in the Napoleonic Wars and was a Whig member of Parliament.[3] He had extensive estates including Dysart in Fife, not far from Stuart's estate of Dunearn. Stuart was at first reluctant to involve this venerable man who had already helped him in his disputes with the Earl of Morton but he was persuaded and Ferguson, another neighbouring Fife landowner and also a retired general, approached Rosslyn who agreed. Boswell, meanwhile, was in London attending to the affairs of his younger brother James who had died on 24 February 1822.[4] His return to Edinburgh was expected on 15 March and Rosslyn paid three visits to Edinburgh during the following week in order to present his challenge. Eventually he left a letter which was handed to Boswell when he arrived home on the evening of Saturday, 23 March 1822. The letter requested an urgent meeting with the Earl.

Boswell immediately recognised the significance of the letter and before meeting with the Earl he approached John Douglas[5] at 9am on Sunday morning to ask 'the greatest favour he could possibly do him to be his "friend".'[6] On the same day he sent the following letter to Robert Maconochie in London, asking him to act as a 'friend' in the event of the duel being carried out in the south:

Edinburgh 24th March 1822

... I must now address you on a subject of a delicate nature, which I do from a confidence in your friendship.

About ten days ago Mr Stuart of Dunearn went to Glasgow, and, by the instrumentality of certain persons, one formerly a partner in the Clydesdale Journal, (now the Sentinel) broke open the editor's desk and carried off his papers, and, I understand, amongst others, some squibs in my handwriting. Last night, on my arrival, I received a letter from Lord Rosslyn that he wished me to appoint an hour as early as possible, that he might make a communication to me; this, I suppose, is in reference to some of these squibs. I do not know who the offended party may be,[7] but even if it should be Mr James Stuart himself, I shall give him a meeting. In order, however, to obviate many of those circumstances which follow such transactions, I mean that the meeting shall take place on the Continent, – say Calais; and I wish to put your friendship so far to the test, as to request you to be my friend on this occasion. I saw your brother[8] this morning, – and his Lordship seemed to think that you would acquiesce. If I had deemed it expedient to meet my man here, John Douglas would have gone out with me; but, if I should be the successful shot, I should not like the after proceedings of our Courts of Law, and therefore wish to pass beyond their jurisdiction. I know nothing of particulars yet, but write in prudent anticipation, and shall write again so soon as I know them.

I know this is perhaps the greatest favour that can be asked of any man, but, by this arrangement, you will be implicated in less trouble, and you won't mind a trip to France. If my wish is acceded to, I would propose the meeting to take place about fifteen days hence, as I wish to make a slight arrangement respecting my estate, and legalize it by going to kirk and market, so that you may write on receipt of this, and if I must go sooner than I can receive yours, it is only a letter thrown away.[9]

Monday 25 March was a day packed with activity. First the meeting with Lord Rosslyn took place. Rosslyn explained that he had come at the request of James Stuart to enquire whether Boswell was responsible for the offensive articles which had been published in the *Sentinel.* Boswell replied that as the subject was of great delicacy he would like to have a friend present and left to return with John Douglas. Rosslyn repeated his purpose to Douglas who withdrew to consult with Boswell. He returned stating the Boswell would not admit to being the author but that Stuart was in possession of the facts and must act upon it as his own judgement directed. Stuart after discussion with Rosslyn decided that the only course was to demand satisfaction, i.e. to issue a challenge for a duel. Boswell accepted the challenge but requested that two conditions be met: one that the meeting should be delayed for 14 days to allow him to arrange his affairs and the other that the meeting should take place on the Continent. Rosslyn discussed these conditions with Stuart who agreed. When communicating this to Douglas, Rosslyn asked whether there was any possibility that Sir Alexander would be prepared to admit that his squibs were simply a bad joke of which he was ashamed, in which case a duel might be avoided. Douglas indicated that there was no such hope.

Rosslyn then left to return to his Fife home in Dysart. Before he embarked on the ferry at Newhaven, Douglas caught up with him to say that Boswell had taken the advice of a legal friend and had changed his mind. He no longer thought it necessary to go the Continent and he would now like the duel to take place in Scotland. The ageing and distinguished Rosslyn expressed annoyance, feeling the matter should stand as arranged, and refused to return as it might draw public attention. He did however give Douglas permission to approach Stuart directly, which Douglas did.

Stuart resented this direct approach to himself, rather than through his second, but agreed to the change of plan. Meanwhile, Boswell changed his mind once more and decided that he could arrange his affairs within two days rather than two weeks. He had started to attend to these matters with his lawyer, his second cousin, also called Alexander Boswell.[10] He asked Douglas to approach Stuart once more that evening to see whether he would agree to an earlier meeting. Stuart refused to consider this direct approach from Boswell's second and asked James Brougham, who was a guest at his house, to act for him as a substitute second. Douglas and Brougham considered a possible date – perhaps the following Thursday – and a possible location – perhaps Berwick on Tweed where they would have the choice of conducting the duel on either the English or Scottish side of the river as might be determined.[11] Brougham agreed to discuss this with Rosslyn.

Boswell spent an evening at Sir Walter Scott's house two or three days before the duel and Scott's son-in-law, Lockhart, who was also present, described the occasion:

> That evening was, I think, the gayest I ever spent in Castle Street … poor Boswell's songs, jokes, and anecdotes had exhibited no symptoms of eclipse. It turned out that he had joined the party, whom he thus delighted, immediately after completing the last arrangements for his duel.[12]

It seems extraordinary that Boswell should be able to display such joie de vivre just after the death of his beloved brother and when his own life was under threat.

On the evening of 25 March, Boswell's lawyer called to execute settlements for him. He was still with him when, at 11pm, Boswell was disturbed by two sheriff's officers who had been sent to bring him and Stuart before the Sheriff of Midlothian to be bound over to keep peace within the county and city. A friend of Boswell's had, without his knowledge and to his great annoyance, notified the Sheriff of the pending duel in the hope his action might abort the duel. In the subsequent trial, Douglas testified that he knew which friend had notified the Sheriff. The counsel, Jeffrey, refused to permit him to name the individual but believed that he had acted without Boswell's knowledge and against his will and intention, which Douglas confirmed.[13] As he was being conveyed to the Sheriff's Office, Boswell told the officer that he might just as well allow him to escape, because no binding over could prevent a meeting; and that, if they did not settle this matter by risking life, *he and Mr Stuart could not live together in the island*.[14]

Frenetic activity

After Boswell had been bound over, the sheriff's officers turned up at Stuart's house in North Charlotte Street shortly after midnight and rang the outer bell violently. Stuart, who was still up, answered the door and was instructed to attend the sheriff's house in Charlotte Square so that he too could be bound over. (He was still subject to this penalty which he had incurred after his altercation with Stevenson.) Stuart's wife, Maria, was completely unaware of the pending duel and Stuart reassured her by saying that his arrest was something to do with the recovery of the Glasgow manuscripts, which she did know about. On the way to the Sheriff's house, Stuart called in at the nearby house in Young Street, home of John Brougham,[15] younger brother of his friends James and Henry, and asked him to come with him to sign his bail bond. When that business had been completed, Stuart suddenly realised the potential consequence of the matter. The fact that two well-known local citizens had been bound over during the night would spread like wildfire in the morning making it impossible to conduct their duel in privacy. Action had to be taken with urgency.

Stuart managed to locate James Brougham who was residing in the house of Mrs Murray, widow of Lord Henderland, in George Street and persuaded him to come to his brother John's house for a meeting. James Brougham came and concurred 'that matters would be placed in a very awkward situation for all parties next morning, when it was known, as it infallibly would be, that Sir Alexander Boswell and Mr Stuart had been bound over to keep the peace on account of a challenge'.[16] He agreed that there was no alternative other than that he should contact John Douglas and endeavour to get the duel fixed for that very morning. Douglas was not at his home in Shandwick Place, but Brougham eventually found him at 2am, at a party of Lady Saltoun's in the Royal Hotel. Brougham told him of the developments and Douglas agreed to leave the party as soon as propriety allowed so as to avoid suspicion. He went to Boswell's house[17] and roused him from sleep to hear the news. Boswell accepted the urgency of the situation and suggested that the duel should be held somewhere in Lanarkshire, where he had a lot of contacts. Douglas reported back to Brougham and after further discussion they decided that the duel should take place at 10am in Fife, to enable Rosslyn to attend as Stuart's second.

Auchtertool was selected for it was a quiet location where there was little chance of interruption and convenient for Rosslyn, being only seven miles from his home in Dysart. Auchtertool was also only a few miles from Stuart's estate of Dunearn, and from Balmuto Castle, the home of Boswell's cousin, Lord Balmuto.[18] In the event both these homes were to play important roles although this possibility did not enter into the consideration of the two seconds when selecting the site. One problem was the matter of the duelling pistols. Boswell had three pairs but they were 80 miles away at Auchinleck. He had intended to send for a pair the next day but that would be too late and Stuart had none. Brougham said there was a pair belonging to Lord Rosslyn to which Boswell would be welcome if he wished.[19] The seconds conveyed their decisions to their respective principals who both acquiesced. Boswell wanted the meeting to take place earlier than 10am but accepted that it might be difficult for the elderly Rosslyn to get there in time.

James Brougham set off immediately by horse to catch a ferry to Fife in order to inform Rosslyn of the new plan. Stuart had remained in John Brougham's house while these discussions were taking place. A bottle of claret was produced and Stuart partook of the greater share of it.[20] He then returned to his own home at 3am. Maria was still up and Stuart told her that he had to leave for Fife at 5am to attend to business before setting off for London that evening, which by chance he had in fact planned to do before the date of the duel had been brought forward. He changed out of his city clothes into the rustic garments which he wore in Fife – an old coat and waistcoat. He then wrote a note, timed at 4am, to James Gibson enclosing a packet addressed to Maria which he asked to be delivered 'if I am completely done for …'. On this packet was written: 'My Dear Maria, I return what is your own. God bless you. Yrs affectly JS'.[21] The contents of the packet were never revealed. Before 5am he called on the surgeon Robert Liston[22] (Fig. 14) who lived in George Street to ask if he would accompany him to Fife. Liston agreed to this unusual request but required some moments to get ready. While waiting, Stuart took the opportunity to collect his London mail at the post office.[23] The postal service must have been very obliging in those days.

When Liston was ready, they set off in a post chaise with Stuart's servant riding in the dicky (Fig. 15). They reached Newhalls pier (now named the Hawes pier) at South Queensferry soon after 6am. Meanwhile Boswell must have been engaged in similar preparations but these have not been documented in such detail as Stuart's are in Cockburn's extensive notes. He managed to get hold of an Edinburgh surgeon, George Wood,[24] and together with Douglas they also set off for South Queensferry at 4am, arriving at the pier just before Stuart's party which had left Edinburgh at 4.30am. Stuart and Boswell had had no personal contact since the discovery of the manuscripts and had no wish to meet each other before the duel.

The Queensferry crossing (Fig. 16) at that time was in a state of transition. Traditionally it had been operated by sail boats of various sizes; one large enough to carry the stagecoach between Edinburgh and the north. The *Queen Margaret*, a paddle steamer, had been launched the year before at Leith for the Queensferry crossing, which it could do in 15 minutes towing a variety of smaller craft, but it had not yet started its day's work. Mercifully two boats appeared at the same time – a yawl and a pinnace – allowing the two parties to travel separately. Stuart offered the other party the choice; Boswell's party took the larger yawl and arrived first at North Queensferry where they breakfasted. Stuart, in the pinnace, arranged for a signal to be sent requesting a chaise to be ready to meet them on the pier. As he looked back from the chaise, he saw to his concern the steamboat approaching North Queensferry towing a string of three or four boats. Fearing that they might be carrying individuals interested in interfering with the duel, Stuart instructed the post boy of the chaise to head off north on the road to Dunfermline, in order to mislead any followers, before changing direction to the east towards his estate of Dunearn.

Stuart left North Queensferry about 7am and arrived at his Fife residence of Hillside (Fig. 17), near Aberdour at 8am. He spent an hour writing his will which he asked Liston and his servant to sign as witnesses. He then locked the will and two packets – one containing his keys and the other money – in a drawer in the sideboard and gave Liston the key. Liston observed that Stuart scarcely had time to sit during this hour but managed to eat a good breakfast including two eggs. Stuart asked his servant to light a fire in his bedroom and to open the glass doors into the dining room if he saw the chaise returning as it gave easier access than through the lobby in case he should be carried back injured. He brought six bottles of wine up from the basement and instructed that a bottle of white wine should be opened.

Stuart and Liston left for Auchtertool at about 9am. On the way Stuart found his mind at ease in consequence of the arrangements which he had leisure to make at Hillside. Liston observed that he was more cheerful. Stuart gave Liston a memo which read:

> If I am hit, and it is wrong to take me to Edinburgh, I wish, if not risking too much, to be taken to Hillside, where every thing is comfortable, and where I will recover far sooner than any where else.
>
> If my senses remain, and I am not moribund, send as fast as possible for my wife, with all due caution. She is of all her family, that one who would the least wish me to live with a dishonoured name.
>
> I have a dislike to be over-bled.[25]

He gave Liston permission to cut off his clothes if there was need for they were of no value. During the journey Stuart said to Liston that he had no animosity to Boswell, with whom he had been long acquainted and who was his relation. He hoped if he was so unlucky as to hit him, the wound might be trifling such as his friend Captain Ayton on a similar occasion lately inflicted on his antagonist when he wounded him in the toe.[26]

Meanwhile, the Boswell party was also making its way to Auchtertool. Dr Wood recorded that during the journey to Fife, Boswell had told him the background and had said that 'it was impossible that Mr Stuart could have done otherwise than he was doing'.[27] Douglas recounted a conversation which he had during the journey. Boswell discussed with him how he should handle the duel:

> He asked me, as a friend, what advice I would give him as to firing. I answered, he was the best judge of that, and that he should consult his own feelings. He said he had no ill-will at Mr Stuart, – he had no wish to put his life in jeopardy, though in an unhappy moment he had injured him, – he bore him no ill-will; and, therefore, it was his determination to fire in the air. I expressed my approbation of his resolution to do so.[28]

Lord Rosslyn was asked in the subsequent trial whether he was aware that Boswell had determined not to fire at Stuart. He replied:

> Such an intimation given to me would necessarily have concluded all proceedings, and would have amounted, in my judgment, to a declaration on the part of Sir Alexander, that he did not mean to fight. It would have been quite impossible that I could have been a party to any proceedings after such an intimation.[29]

Boswell drank some brandy and whisky en route to steady his nerves and said to his companions, 'I have made myself a dish clout to wipe off former stains'.[30] They were the first to arrive at Auchtertool at 9.30 and Stuart arrived 10 minutes later. Stuart, who appeared calmer than Boswell, smiled on seeing the amount of equipment which Dr Wood had brought with him and declared that there must be no amputations.[31] The Earl of Rosslyn soon appeared on horseback accompanied by a Kirkcaldy doctor, Dr James Brown Johnston, whom Rosslyn had summonsed in case any of the duellists had failed to bring their own. James Brougham, who had reached Dysart at 8am with the news of the changed plans, also accompanied Rosslyn to the scene but kept in the background so as not to interfere with Rosslyn's duties as principal second.[32]

The duel is engaged

When all had gathered at Baidlin Toll Bar three-quarters of a mile to the east of Auchtertool on the road to Kirkcaldy, Rosslyn and Douglas selected a suitable site for the duel in a hollow dell adjacent to the north side of the road on the farm of Balbarton (Fig. 18). It was out of sight of the road and the farmhouse. Once more Rosslyn presented Boswell, via Douglas, with two options for avoiding a duel: either by denying that he had written the offending articles, or else by treating them as a bad joke and one of which he was ashamed, declaring that he had no serious intention of reflecting on Mr Stuart's courage or character. These options were declined and the arrangements for the duel proceeded.

Stuart asked Rosslyn whether, if he came near to Boswell, he ought not to show the usual courtesy to him as a gentleman by bowing to him. Rosslyn replied he should, however Boswell kept his distance and turned his head to avoid eye contact, preventing any exchange of civilities. At the subsequent trial Jeffrey thought that this behaviour of Boswell's was unintentional.[33] Stuart then said to Rosslyn, 'I think I ought not to take aim' to which Rosslyn agreed. Stuart was advised that he should present his side rather than his front as being a smaller target – although Stuart was so portly that it probably made little difference. Douglas' last words to Boswell were: 'Be sure to fire so as to make it appear that your shot is thrown away, for instance you may turn aside and fire your pistol into the bank ...' Rosslyn and Douglas then measured out twelve long paces and each duellist took up his position. Each antagonist was provided with one of Rosslyn's pistols, (Fig. 19) which had been charged with powder and ball by Douglas.[34] The two surgeons turned their backs on the scene in order to avoid being called as witnesses; Brougham viewed the events from a distance while looking after the horses of Rosslyn, Dr Johnston and his own.

On Rosslyn's command, 'Ready, Present, FIRE' both men fired, Boswell deliberately wide and Stuart accidentally straight and was horrified to see Boswell falling slowly to the ground. The surgeons immediately attended him and found that the bullet had entered below the right shoulder fracturing his right collar bone. There was little bleeding. Each surgeon probed the wound and removed fragments of bone but was unable to find the bullet. The bullet must have lodged near the spine for Boswell became aware that he was unable to move his limbs. Dr Johnson thought that the prognosis was favourable, but Liston felt that recovery depended on finding the bullet.[35]

Stuart flees to France

Rosslyn advised Stuart to leave the scene immediately and leave the country. Stuart took one of the waiting chaises (some accounts say that he took Boswell's in his confusion) and was driven at speed to the Burntisland ferry, stopping to collect his personal servant who had been left waiting at Hillside. To his dismay he found that the steam ferry had left five minutes before, but the superintendent procured a small fishing boat manned by six oarsmen, who rowed him to Newhaven in an hour and 20 minutes.[36] On arrival Stuart took a hackney cab to James Gibson's rooms in 8 North St Andrews Street where he arrived before 2pm in a state of great agitation. Gibson was not there and his clerk tried to calm him and lent him some money to pay the cab driver, for Stuart had locked up his money and keys at Hillside before the duel. Stuart was about to leave when Gibson arrived back. Stuart, who had been engaged in feverish and stressful activity without sleep for the previous day and a half, broke down in the presence of his friend, covered his face in his hands and burst into tears. 'He was in the most complete agony of mind.'[37] He informed Gibson that he had told Rosslyn that he would take no aim and added, 'I wish to God I had done so. I never fired a pistol on foot in my life – and only three times when with the Yeomanry on horseback. If I had taken aim I am certain I would have missed him'.[38]

Gibson reinforced Rosslyn's advice that Stuart should leave immediately for France, for if he remained in Britain he would be jailed pending trial on the charge of murder if Boswell should die. Stuart was reluctant to accept this advice. By taking part in a duel of his own instigation he had surely proved that the accusations of cowardice were unfounded. He most emphatically did not want his flight to a foreign country to be regarded in that light. He eventually agreed but only on condition that Gibson would notify the Sheriff that he was ready to stand trial whenever the date was fixed. Gibson did give this assurance to Sheriff Duff the following day and put a notice to that effect in the *Star* and *Advertiser* newspapers.

Table of events of 26 March 1822	
Time	**Activity**
midnight to 1 am	Stuart arrested and taken to sheriff to be bound over to keep the peace. Arranges meeting with James Brougham and decides that the duel must take place that morning.
1–3 am	Brougham locates John Douglas at the Royal Hotel and conveys the urgency of the situation. Douglas rouses Boswell at his residence in Princes Street and Boswell agrees with plan. Brougham and Douglas decide on Auchtertool as the location. Brougham leaves for Fife to notify Lord Rosslyn.
3–5 am	Stuart explains situation to his wife Maria; writes letters and changes into country clothing; asks Robert Liston to be his surgeon; picks up his mail at post office while Liston gets ready; collects Liston and sets off by post chaise to South Queensferry. Boswell dresses, persuades George Wood to come as his surgeon and also departs for South Queensferry with John Douglas and Wood.
5–7 am	Both parties arrive at South Queensferry about 6am and take separate sailing vessels to North Queensferry, arriving about 7am.
7–9am	Boswell has breakfast there before setting off to Auchtertool. Stuart takes a post chaise to Hillside where he arrives about 8am. He writes his will and has breakfast before setting off to Auchtertool. Brougham reaches Rosslyn's home at Dysart at 8am and both men set off to Auchtertool on horseback.
9–11 am	All parties arrive at the destination between 9.30 and 10am. The seconds agree on location for duel and supply duellists with Rosslyn's pistols. Duel takes place about 10.40 am and Boswell is wounded. Stuart leaves for Edinburgh at 10.55.
11 am–1pm	Stuart reaches Burntisland and is rowed by boat to Newhaven. Boswell is carried to Balmuto. A message is sent to his wife, and another surgeon, Professor John Thomson, in Edinburgh to come to Balmuto.
1–3 pm	Stuart reaches James Gibson's office in Edinburgh at 1.30. Gibson arrives soon after and advises Stuart to go immediately to London and thence to France. Stuart goes home to pack and pick up money and leaves for London with his servant at 2.20 pm.

A jingle gained currency at this time:

For justice stood on Stuart's side,
Though he's awa tae France tae bide,
And justice felled the Tory's Pride,
That morning at Balbarton.[39]

Stuart returned briefly to his home, no doubt to change his clothing and pack some belongings. He had left his keys at Hillside and had to get a smith to open his private desk.[40] What he said to his wife is not on record. To his horror, he learned that the Sheriff's Officers had visited his house shortly beforehand – could news of the duel have preceded his rapid return? Gibson, meanwhile, went to the bank and obtained some English notes and gold coins, which he gave to Stuart together with the unopened letter which Stuart had left for Maria. Stuart set off for London with his servant in a chaise at 2.20pm – only three hours after the duel.

The frenetic activities which took place during the previous 15 hours are summarised in the table opposite. It is hard to imagine today that so much could be achieved in such a short time without prior planning, in the absence of modern facilities of communication and transport.

Stuart reached London at 3.30pm on Thursday 28 March having been on the road for 49 hours. He sent a letter from Parliament Street Hotel to Gibson at 4.30pm:

Let me know what is said, however bad they may represent me. I would if the worst has happened avoid wounding the feelings of those that remain by allusions in the papers to the cause of the meeting. The Trial will develop the truth ... I would however do nothing, while Lord Rosslyn is in Scotland, without his sanction. My debt to him can never be paid ... [41]

He asked Gibson to retain Francis Jeffrey, James Moncreiff and Henry Cockburn as his counsel.

During his day in London, Stuart met two of his Edinburgh friends who happened to be in the city: Thomas Allan, a banker, and Sir Ronald Ferguson of Raith, who had originally approached Rosslyn to ask if he would act as Stuart's second (see p. 75). Ferguson was an MP for a Fife constituency and Stuart had acted as his agent during his election. Stuart initiated the process of obtaining a passport but did not feel that it would be safe to delay his departure until the passport was ready. Ferguson arranged with Allan, who had been planning to go to France, to collect the passport and deliver it to Stuart. Stuart left for Dover at

11pm on 28 March and arrived in Calais at 3am. Allan caught up with him on Saturday 30 March at the Hotel de Meurice, bringing with him the passport and the distressing news that Boswell had died. Stuart again burst into tears and remained for some time greatly agitated. Allan pointed out how imperiously the business had been forced upon him. True said Stuart but remember the situation of his poor wife and family.[42]

Stuart's subsequent activities are related in the next chapter.

Boswell is carried to Balmuto

Meanwhile, Boswell's attendants were dealing with his wound and making preparation for transporting him to Balmuto Castle. The occupants of a neighbouring smithy, the smith Peter Moyes – who was also in charge of the Baidlin Toll Bar – and his apprentice David Blair, improvised a stretcher from a door and assisted in the transport of Boswell; a distance of one and a half miles over a rough track (Fig. 20). All the participants in the duel, except Stuart who had already left the scene, helped, for Boswell was a big, heavily built man, over six foot. Coupled with the weight of the door, at least six people at a time must have been required for the task.

According to one report written 120 years after the event, there had been a heavy fall of snow and the hedgerows were packed. Boswell asked for water on the way and was given mouthfuls of snow from the drifts.[43] None of the contemporary accounts of the duel however, mention snow and another late description of the event states that: 'On the sunny noon-day of March 26th, 1822, when the sap was stirring in tree and grass, a duel was fought …'[44] Curiously a letter written by Cockburn on the very day of the duel comments on the unseasonable weather and gives credence to the snowy scenario:

> … this day I had to cut my way up to the bath thro' snow in many places two feet deep. I took the boys up a hill this forenoon, and diverted ourselves by rolling down little pellets of snow, and seeing them become huge masses before they reached the bottom.[45]

Cockburn's home, Bonaly Tower, is only 16 miles from the site of the duel as the crow flies.

A contemporary newspaper account reported that while he was being carried to Balmuto (Fig. 21), the party was obstructed by a stone dyke, part of which had to be pulled down to allow them to pass. Boswell was reported to have said, 'with characteristic feeling to those who were supporting him that he feared they would

Figure 1 (left)

Portrait of James Stuart by Sir Daniel Macnee.

(Courtesy of the Scottish National Portrait Gallery)

Figures 2 and 3 (below, left and below, right)

Portraits of Alexander Boswell and his wife Grisel Cuming by Sir Martin Shee from James Boswell's *Book of Company at Auchinleck 1782–1795*, Viscountess Eccles (ed.) The current location of these portraits has not been found; they were sold at auction in 1978.

(Courtesy of the Harvard College and the Hon. Simon Eccles)

Figure 4

Burn's monument at Alloway; Boswell was largely responsible for raising the funds and erecting the monument.

(John Chalmers)

Figure 5

Portrait of James Gibson.

(From B. W. Crombie's *Modern Athenians*)

Figure 6

Portrait of Walter Scott.

(From B. W. Crombie's *Modern Athenians*)

Figure 7 (above, right)
Portrait of Francis Jeffrey.
(From B. W. Crombie's *Modern Athenians*)

Figure 8 (left)
Portrait of Henry Cockburn.
(From B. W. Crombie's *Modern Athenians*)

Figure 9
John Gibson
Lockhart with
Sophia by Robert
Scott Lauder.
(Courtesy of the
National Galleries
of Scotland)

Figure 10 (above)

Royal Exchange Coffee House. The entrance to the Coffee House can be seen in the bottom left corner

(From Grant (1881–83: *Edinburgh Old and New* 1, p. 189)

Figure 11 (below)

Parliament Square Engraving (1844) by John Le Conte from an etch-ing by Thomas Dobbie of a painting (c.1794, possibly by Alexander Nasmyth and John Kay) showing the activity in the Square.

(Courtesy Edinburgh City Library)

O TEMP ORA
1 2 3 4 5 6 7 8

THE MYSTERY
‘ Let him that hath understanding

O M O R R I S!
9 10 11 12 13 14 15

OF INIQUITY.
count the number of the BEAST.’

THE HYDRA

WITH

FIFTEEN HEADS;

OR,

Jack Straw in the Suds.

THAT COLOSSUS OF DEPRAVITY, THE

BEACON,

Brought to his Doom,

WITH HIS LAST SPEECH AND EXPIRING GROAN!!!

THE BEACON having been found guilty of the most atrocious crimes against Society, aggravated by circumstances of peculiar enormity, was Sentenced, by the COUNCIL of FIFTEEN, *alias* the COWGATE ASSOCIATION, to suffer death; which Sentence was carried into execution on Saturday the 29th day of September last. As the period betwixt Condemnation and Execution was unavoidably short, the Criminal passed the interval as favourably as could have been expected from a character so depraved; in which he was materially assisted by his sincere friends and Co-parents Dr Morris and Mr Rnshall, whose exertions for a reprieve were indefatigable but unavailing. The place of execution was fixed on the spot where the crimes had been perpetrated, in order that the punishment might be more awful and impressive; and accordingly, a few minutes before ten, the criminal appeared in the Press, attended by *Jack Straw* and *the Hairgyle Lieutenant*, and was immediately thereafter removed to the place of execution. Any feelings of commiseration or pity which would have been felt at the sight of a youth brought to an untimely and ignominious

Figure 12

Broadsheet The Hydra with Fifteen Heads.

(Courtesy of the National Library of Scotland)

Figure 13 (above)

Portrait of William Murray
Borthwick, artist unknown

(Courtesy of Ann Carson)

Figure 14

Map showing route taken from Edinburgh to the duel site near Auchtertool by Stuart.
Lewis Hebert Map (1823).

(Courtesy of National Galleries of Scotland)

Figure 15
Queensferry and Newhall's Pier sketch from Summer Life on Land and Water W. W. Fyfe (1851).
(Courtesy of Edinburgh City Library)

Figure 16
Pencil drawing of Hillside by Alexander Nasmyth (1825).
(Courtesy of the National Galleries of Scotland)

Figure 17 (above)

Photograph of the likely site of the duel. The author was taken to the site by Mr Bruce Boswell of Balmuto.

(John Chalmers)

Figure 18 (below)

The flintock pistols believed to be the pair used in the duel

(Courtesy of Kirkcaldy Museum, where the pistols are held)

find him too heavy, and requested them to lay him down until the impediment was removed'.[46]

John Douglas had borrowed Lord Rosslyn's horse to give advance warning to the elderly Lord Balmuto (Fig. 22), who broke down when he received his kinsman. One of the accompanying doctors asked him to restrain himself, but Boswell, who was still conscious, rebuked the doctor for his remark. A bedroom upstairs had been prepared for his reception, but the doctors advised against carrying him upstairs. He was then carried into the library (Fig. 23) and laid on a sofa, from which a portrait of his grandfather, Lord Auchinleck, had to be removed. He repeated psalms to try to soothe himself to sleep.

In view of the importance of the victim, the two attending surgeons felt that a third opinion would be appropriate and sent to Edinburgh for Mr John Thomson, Professor of Military Surgery (Fig. 24), who arrived later that afternoon. On asking Boswell how he felt, he replied, 'I feel exactly what I am – a man with a living head and a dead body mysteriously joined together'.[47] Despite this distinguished assembly of medical talent, no treatment was possible and Boswell sank gradually from internal bleeding to die the following afternoon. Wood said, 'his mind remained entire till an hour and a half of his death'.[48] Boswell's ghost is said to haunt the Castle to this day.

A message had been sent to Lady Boswell, waiting, presumably in her Edinburgh home, with her mother, Janet Chalmers Cuming, who sent a note immediately to her grandson, James Boswell:

My Dear James

Your Father is safe. The wound is in the arm. He is at Balmuto & your Mother & Theresa [his sister] are just set off to attend him, so Mr Walker & me expect you here directly & we will tell you all the particulars which [I] cannot do in this.
God bless you my Dear James
Your affec. Grandmother

J Cuming[49]

Boswell dies

Lady Boswell and Theresa arrived that evening and remained with Boswell until he died. She is said to have requested that a portrait and an impression (presumably a death mask) be taken, but there is no record that this was done.[50] According to Lockhart she 'endured the catastrophe with wonderful resolution'. Lockhart continued in his letter to his father-in-law, Walter Scott '… it is difficult to imagine any honourable life coming to a more unworthy and disgraceful termination.[51]

Boswell's body was taken to Auchinleck. The funeral on 10 April was a splendid affair. The service took place on the lawn in front of Auchinleck House. Nearly 500 people attended, including the First Regiment of Ayrshire Yeomanry, mounted. The hearse, drawn by six horses, was followed by his son James accompanied by Lords Glenlee and Balmuto and Sir James Montgomery-Cuninghame in a coach and four. Then followed between 20 and 30 carriages containing the principal friends of the deceased and the chief gentry of the County. His body was interred in the Boswell mausoleum (Fig. 25) attached to the old Parish Church of Auchinleck. About 10,000 spectators from the surrounding villages and country gathered to watch the procession, a remarkable measure of the respect in which he was held.

Walter Scott was very distressed by the outcome of the duel and must have worried about his part in the affair by his support of the *Beacon*. In a letter he wrote: '… The sudden death of both the Boswells, and the bloody end of the last have given me great pain'.[52]

With time to reflect, Lady Boswell must have lost her composure and decided to vent her anger on James Brougham, whose role in the affair had been relatively minor as a substitute second. Too distressed to write herself, she asked her teenage elder daughter, Theresa, to write to Sir Walter Scott on 15 April 1822:

> Mamma desires me to ask you if there is no law in the land that Brougham is allowed to walk about unmolested upon the face of the earth after instigating the Agent of Murder (Douglas) to call Papa out of his bed in the dead of night to drag him to the opposite shore before another sun rose to accomplish their foul conspiracy, swearing he accompanied[53] him with the intention of acting as a second in case there should be found a spark of human nature in the flinty heart of Lord Rosslin. Mamma says does standing behind a hedge whilst his bloody purpose was perpetrating shield him from the law?[54]

Scott's reply is not recorded, but he wrote to Lord Montague on 24 April:

> The catastrophe of Sir Alexander Boswell is horrid and all for writing a foolish song. Conceive, however the degree of imprudence in writing to the villain of an editor with his own hand and under his own frank. I have a notion the fellow had been a trepan (decoy) from the beginning for he wrote me two fishing letters but I was too old a fish to rise to any fly he could cast. Poor Bozzie had determined not to shoot Stuart – why the Lord knows – in his case I would have protected my self as best I could. Boswell had asked two days to draw some settlements for his family but

Brougham dragged him out of his bed after this had been agreed to, insisting the matter should be instantly decided. Said Brougham was on the field looking on at a distance ...[55]

And in a letter to J. W. Croker on 2 July 1822:

... the man [Stuart] behaved like a blackguard & a coward ... & then tried to wash clean his dirty character with poor Boswell's blood. I cannot think what made Boswell keep such terms with him. For my part if I had been draged [sic] into the affair I would have done my best to have rid the country of him.[56]

Later Lady Boswell sent a series of rather irrational letters to Scott complaining about different aspects of the duel. She attacked Boswell's second, John Douglas, for the indecent haste with which the duel was arranged and for not interfering at the last moment. She objected specifically to Douglas' advice to reject Rosslyn's offer of a last minute accommodation:

On that fatal *morning* (the sun was not up for some hours after) when my Husband and I parted. I *besought* him if there was any opening whatever to accept it; and he said 'all that depends on *the seconds*. I trust everything to my friend John here.' This he said in the most serious, grave, and impressive manner .... Both seconds saw the monster taking aim, neither interfered ...[57]

Scott tried to persuade Lady Boswell that her husband should not have agreed to consider an accommodation:

It was surely free to him to make a choice on the occasion when his own pure and immaculate sense of honour induced him rather to expose his life to hazard than his honour to the imputation which might have attachd [sic] to the concession required. Indeed I do not see how it was possible for a man ... to have agreed to the terms offerd [sic] by Lord Rosslyn nor can I suppose his Lordship had expectation for a moment that he would do so.[58]

The duel caused widespread interest throughout Britain. The following extract from a lengthy article in a London newspaper reveals how widely the details were known in that city:

For some time past, the arguments of the friends of even temperate reform have been met by every species of abuse, both in this city and in the Scottish metropolis; ... which struck us as having hardly any other object than the provocation of a duel.

We do know that in both countries, the most gross and unwarranted slanders that could issue from the press in its most degraded and abominable form have been backed, applauded, and participated in by those whose affluent station and responsibility would have made us hope for something very different … it requires only a slight glance at the dying leaves of the Sentinel, or at the dead and putrefying ones of the Beacon, to find how dark has been the purpose, and how numerous and malignant the thrusts which have been aimed at him [Stuart]. … The calumniators have now the satisfaction of knowing that the last and consummating charge – that of coward, was altogether without foundation … .We are disposed to account poor Boswell only as the servant to a mightier source of slander; …[59]

The article concludes with the notion that some good may have resulted from the duel:

We are warm advocates for political discussion, whether spoken or printed; and as such we must rejoice at the consequence to which the Scottish political duel must lead, – the washing out of the foulest stain that ever disgraced and degraded the periodical literature of a country.

Many poems were written to commemorate Alexander Boswell's death. A representative verse reads:

Thy halls, Auchinleck! are all desolate now,
Ayr! roll on in sorrow, in solitude flow;
For low lies thy bard who so sweetly did sing –
Thy chieftain so true to his country and king.[60]

Professor Andrew Duncan, president of the Harveian Society of which Boswell was a member, wrote that:

They have been deprived of their truly amiable Poet-Laureate ... His astonishing convivial powers have, on different occasions, added to their innocent mirth, by obliging them to laugh at themselves. But he was equally capable of gratifying the finest feelings of the human heart by serious strains ... [61]

An old friend of Boswell's, William Lennox, visited the site of the duel soon after the event and found the letters 'B' and 'S' carved in the turf to mark where the duellists had stood. He too, in the fashion of the time, composed a simple poem which contained the following verses:

I strew'd the spot where the Baron fell
With the bonnie yellow gowan,
And I wish'd his departed spirit well,
While my very soul was glowing.

Ending with:

But the sons of social song and mirth,
In their orisons shall greet him;
And the sons of honour, and wit, and worth,
In a brighter world shall meet him.[62]

During the hectic four-week period between his brother's death and his own, Boswell found time to write a commemorative poem for his brother, one verse of which reads:

His was the triumph of the heart and mind:
His was the lot which few are blessed to know:
More proved, more valued – fervent, yet so kind;
He never lost one friend, nor found one foe.[63]

What a pity that the last line could not have applied to himself!

Lord Rosslyn and James Brougham realised that as Stuart's seconds they might also be arrested as accessories. They too decided to absent themselves from the scene and sought temporary refuge in Broughton Hall in Westmoreland, the home of James' brother, Henry. Henry Brougham at that time was practicing as a barrister on circuit in Lancaster. When he arrived home, he found the messenger-at-arms there in quest for his two guests for whom arrest warrants had been issued but:

> … of course I refused to give him any information as to where they were concealed – they were hidden in what is called the *Priest's Hole:* it being, moreover, quite evident that the whole proceeding was intended to give trouble, – that only Stuart was really to be tried, and the two others to be called as witnesses; which they were when Stuart was tried.[64]

Interesting, but understandable, that the future Lord Chancellor should obstruct the due process of the law in this manner.

Other Whigs, who had been libelled by Boswell in the *Sentinel*, had considered challenging Boswell to a duel. Two of these individuals – Sir Robert Ferguson and Lord Duncan – were more highly regarded than Stuart and Lockhart in a letter to Scott wrote on 28 March 1822, 'it certainly would have been less painful for Boswell and his friends had he fallen by the hand of either of these Gentlemen rather than by a hand such as this'.[65]

Notes

1   Farington (1922): *The Farington Diary*, **I**, p. 325, 25 September 1801.

2   Rosslyn was also active in politics, firstly as a Whig member of the House of Commons. He entered the House of Lords when he inherited his title as second Earl in 1805. He inherited the estates of Rosslyn to the south of Edinburgh, and Dysart beside the town of Kirkcaldy in Fife, close to Stuart's estate of Dunearn. He and Stuart were distant cousins.

3   In later life he changed to support the Tories. Cockburn wrote (*Journal*, **1**, pp. 131–2), 'Had anybody told him when he was presiding at Fox dinners, and toasting the thorough reform of the Scotch representation, that in a few years he would be opposing it, he would have rejected the prediction with horror'.

4   James Boswell (1778–1822), a Shakespearian scholar of note, lived a bachelor existence in the Middle Temple in London among a wide circle of friends. He died after an acute illness on 24th February 1822 aged 43 and is buried in the Temple Church.

5   John Douglas (1779–1856) was brother of the 6th Marquis of Queensberry, whom he succeeded as 7th Marquis in 1837. He was a prominent Whig politician becoming government whip in the House of Lords during the Whig administration of Lord Melbourne. He was the father of the 8th Marquis, remembered for formulating the Queensberry rules for boxing.

6   Cockburn (*c.*1822a): *Trial 3*, p.123.

7   John Wishart in a letter dated 30 March 1822 wrote that Boswell 'had libelled so many people that …, he could not possibly escape a duel. Lord Archibald Hamilton and Lord Duncan, who had been much calumniated … had determined to challenge him …' in Wishaw (1906): *The 'Pope' of Holland House: Selections from the correspondence of John Wishaw and his friends 1813–1840*, Lady Seymour (ed.), p. 245.

8   Alexander Maconochie, Lord Meadowbank (1777–1861) Scottish judge.

9   Anon (1822): *Trial 2*, Appendix No IX, pp. 15–6.

10   The main purpose was to attend to his will which was not completed in the time available.

11   Lord Meadowbank advised Boswell that it would best be held on the Scottish side, 'it would be better to be in the hands of a gentleman like the Lord Advocate than of an English Grand Jury'. Cockburn (*c.*1822): *Trial 3*, Precognition of Douglas, p. 101.

12   Lockhart (1902): *Life of Sir Walter Scott*, **7**, p. 29, fn. Scott also refers to the occasion in his diary entry of 21 December 1825 in Lockhart (1902), **8**, p. 153.

13   Evidence of Douglas in Anon (1822): *Trial 2*, p. 68.

14   Cockburn's defence in Anon (1822): *Trial 2*, p. 38.

15   John Waugh Brougham was a wine merchant and insurance broker. He was a joint manager of the North British Fire & Life Insurance Company of which Stuart was a director.

16   Cockburn (*c.*1822a): *Trial 3*, p. 140.

17   Boswell's address in Edinburgh is not recorded. Douglas in his evidence (Anon (1822): *Trial 2*, p. 61) refers to the family being in the house – possibly the home of Boswell's father-in-law Thomas Cumming

18   Claud Irvine Boswell, Lord Balmuto (1742–1824) was a judge in the Court of Session. His father was the brother of Lord Auchinleck, Sir Alexander's grandfather, thus he and Sir Alexander were first cousins once removed. It was said that the shock of Sir Alexander's death contributed to his own death two years later. In the latter half of the 20th century Balmuto Castle became a ruin but it has since been splendidly restored by an American descendant of the Boswell family, Harry Arthur Boswell, who bought the estate. Sir Alexander's ghost is said to still make its presence felt.

19   Evidence of John Douglas at Stuart's trial in Anon (1822): *Trial 2*, pp.61–2. Kirkcaldy Museum

has a pair of flintock duelling pistols which are believed to be those used in the duel.

20 Cockburn (c.1822a): *Trial 3*, p. 143.

21 Cockburn (c.1822a): *Trial 3*, Precognition of James Gibson, p. 9.

22 Robert Liston was arguably the leading British surgeon of his day. It is extraordinary that he was prepared to set out in the middle of the night, ignorant of the purpose, but he was a close acquaintance of Stuart. In a letter to James Brougham MP on 29 November 1832 Stuart wrote, 'Liston has long attended us, and I know him well, and intimately. I have no doubt of his being the best Operator, the best educated Surgeon, best known of the World, … . You are aware of the feuds eternal among the Edinburgh Doctors of all kinds …' Brougham Correspondence. UCL Library J.843.

23 Cockburn (c.1822a): *Trial 3*, Precognition of Liston, p. 109.

24 Boswell's choice of George Wood was not surprising. George was the son of Boswell's great friend and fellow member of the Harveian Society, the eminent surgeon Alexander (Sandy) Wood. Boswell had written a poetic epitaph for Sandy Wood on his death in 1807.

25 Anon (1822): *Trial 2*, p. 111. Bloodletting was still practiced in this country until the mid-nineteenth century. It was advocated principally for febrile illnesses. Its bizarre use in trauma was quite common and inexplicable by any logic. Stuart's request shows common sense.

26 Cockburn (c.1822a): *Trial 3*, p. 109.

27 Cockburn (c.1822a): *Trial 3*, p. 173 and Precognition of Dr Wood, p. 105.

28 Anon (1822): *Trial 2*, p. 63.

29 Anon (1822): *Trial 2*, pp. 56–7.

30 Cockburn (c.1822a): *Trial 3*, p. 174.

31 Cockburn (c.1822a): *Trial 3*, Precognition of Liston, p. 119.

32 Dr Johnston was the uncle of Sir Robert Christison (1797–1882), Professor of Medical Jurisprudence at University of Edinburgh. Christison wrote in his Journal, 8th October 1867, 'On a visit to Fife, I passed in my gig the scene of the duel between James Stewart of Dunearn and Sir Alexander Boswell, – a beautiful and most suitable hollow in a field hard by the road … Dr Johnston, was hidden by Lord Rosslyn in a corner of a wood, so that he might appear at once on being called, but see nothing, and consequently should escape being compromised as a witness.' Christison (1886): *Life of Sir Robert Christison*, 2 pp. 344–5. In the event he was called as a witness at the trial but was not questioned.

33 Anon (1822): *Trial 2*, p. 104.

34 Cockburn (c.1822a): *Trial 3*, Precognition of Douglas, p. 95.

35 Cockburn (c.1822a): *Trial 3*, pp. 170–)

36 Cockburn (c.1822a): *Trial 3*, p. 168. At that time there were two main ferries across the Firth of Forth. Both were served by the recently introduced steam boats as well as traditional sailing/rowing boats. Queensferry was the shorter crossing but a much longer road journey from Edinburgh. The Newhaven/Burntisland ferry, which started beside Edinburgh would seem to be much more convenient, particularly for Stuart, for Hillside was very close to Burntisland. Presumably Queensferry must have been more reliable as it was chosen by all the involved parties on their outward journey. Other ferries crossed from Newhaven to Kinghorn, Kirkcaldy and Pettycur in Fife.

37 Anon (1822): *Trial 2*, p. 105.

38 Cockburn (c.1822a): *Trial 3*, Precognition of James Gibson, p. 11–2.

39 Harding, A. W (1992): 'James Stuart of Dunearn', *Transactions of the Gaelic Society of Inverness 1992*, 56, p. 375.

40 Cockburn (c.1822a): *Trial 3*, Precognition of William Smith [Stuart's servant], p. 119.

41 Cockburn (c.1822a): *Trial 3*, endnote, p. 10.

42 Anon (1822): *Trial 2*, p. 121.

43 Crow (1969): *'Balmuto' Leaves from the Pages of History*. Crow obtained this information in a letter from Miss Eliza Susannah Boswell dated 7 January 1949. Miss Boswell was the last survivor of the Balmuto Boswells and had recollections of conversations with an individual who had been alive at the time of the duel. A similar account written by Crow is given in *Fife Free Press* of 31 July and 7 August 1970.

44 *The Scotsman*, 22 June 1925.

45   Letter to Andrew Rutherfurd, 26 March 1828. NLS 9687.16
46   *Morning Chronicle*, 10 April 1822
47   *Dead in Trespasses and Sins*, p. 3. Tract by J. Y. Simpson (undated) published by the Religious
     Tract Society, London. Simpson was only 11 at the time of the duel. He is recording conversa-
     tions with John Thomson, which must have taken place many years later.
48   Cockburn (*c*.1822a): *Trial 3*, Precognition of Dr Wood, p.106.
49   Houghton Library, Harvard College, Hyde 52 (19)
50   Crow (1969). Miss Eliza Boswell's letter stated that Lady Boswell did not arrive until after his
     death, which contradicts the contemporary evidence. In Boswell (1871), p. xliii Smith states that
     Lady Boswell arrived when he was still alive on the previous evening, but that his son James did
     not arrive until after his death.
51   Letter from Lockhart to Scott, 28th March 1822 in Scott (1932–37): *The Letters of Walter Scott*,
     VII, p. 113–4, fn.
52   Letter to Miss Edgeworth, 24th April 1822 in Lockhart (1902), **V**, p. 29.
53   Her knowledge of events was at fault. Brougham did not accompany Boswell, he had left Edin-
     burgh before him and crossed on a earlier ferry at Queensferry to notify Lord Rosslyn of the
     change of plan.
54   Scott (1932–37): *Letters*, **VII**, p. 112, fn.
55   Scott (1932–37): *Letters*, **VII**, p. 137.
56   Scott (1932–37): *Letters*, **VII**, p. 204.
57   Partington (1932): *Sir Walter's Post-bag*, p. 166.
58   Scott (1932–37): *Letters*, **VI**, pp. 188–91.
59   From an article in the True Briton quoted in *The Scotsman* of 6 April 1822.
60   Quoted in Boswell (1871), p. xlvi
61   Chalmers (2010): *Andrew Duncan Senior: Physician of the Enlightenment*, p. 123.
62   Boswell (1871), pp. lx–lxi
63   Boswell (1871), p. 187
64   Brougham (1871): *The Life and Times of Henry Lord Brougham*, **2**, p. 503. Brougham stated that
     Stuart also stayed at Brougham Hall during his escape but his memory was at fault – Stuart went
     straight to London. Brougham was writing his autobiography 50 years after the event.
65   Scott (1932–37): *Letters*, **VII**, fn p. 113–4.

CHAPTER 7

The trial of James Stuart

There does not occur in the annals of our country, the record of a trial which excited so general an interest in the public mind, as the trial of James Stuart. – The origin of the dispute which terminated so fatally, it is well known, was of a political nature. The parties were public men, and the strenuous supporters of that side of politics which they severally espoused, – As members of society, their characters stood high, and commanded the greatest respect in the circles in which they moved.

Introduction to *Trial I*

Duelling as the law now stands can seldom be overtaken by legal punishment ...

Henry Cockburn[1]

STUART PROCEEDED to Paris with his friend Thomas Allan and stayed at the Hotel de Londres in the Place Vêndome. He wrote to James Gibson on 5 April 1822:

I am really so distressed ... the whole accounts I have seen are erroneous, and even these favourable to me ... give not the half of my case ... . It is impossible for me to enjoy any thing here, although all are most kind.[2]

Allan noticed that Stuart was constantly depressed and said, 'that the scene on the ground was ever constantly in his mind'. Eight or ten days after arriving in Paris, Stuart reported that he had got a night's sleep for the first time. Stuart obtained an interview with the British Ambassador, Sir Charles Stuart, and undertook to keep the ambassador informed of his whereabouts in France. On 18 April he decided to return to Calais to be in more ready communication with his lawyers. Stuart hoped for an early trial, but despite the best endeavours of Gibson, the date kept being postponed. Eventually the date was set for Monday 10 June 1822 and Stuart appeared as promised.

Intense public interest

Such was the public interest that two accounts of the trial were published within two weeks of its conclusion, both anonymous and both entitled *The Trial of James Stuart*. The first was offered for sale at two shillings and six pence on 15 June 1822 just five days after the trial. It was a 43-page pamphlet compiled by a 'Member of the Court'. This will be referred to as *Trial I*.[3] The second, costing three shillings and six pence, was advertised on 22 June as the '3rd edition corrected'. It consisted of 186 pages plus appendices and was said to be taken from a shorthand account of the trial and prepared under the direction of Stuart's friends. This will be referred to as *Trial 2*.[4] The speed with which these publications were produced was remarkable considering the printing and publishing techniques of the time and reflects the public interest.

The fullest and most reliable account of the events leading up to the trial however, is contained in manuscript notes and precognitions prepared by Henry Cockburn for the guidance of himself and his fellow counsel who were to defend Stuart. These notes are bound in a volume of nearly 500 foolscap pages held in the National Library of Scotland which Cockburn entitled *Case of James Stuart*. The various accounts of the duel and the trial differ somewhat in detail. Generally I have accepted Cockburn's account where there is disagreement, for he had direct personal contact with the individuals involved. His knowledge of the minute by minute details of Stuart's movements can only have been obtained by lengthy interview. He writes on the opening page: 'This volume contains the information (beyond what was supplied by their own personal knowledge) on which Stuart's case was conducted'. It is an example of the extraordinary care and effort which Cockburn devoted to his preparation for the trial. This invaluable resource is referred to as *Trial 3*.[5]

The excitement of the occasion was reported in *The Scotsman*:

> The trial in the High Court in Edinburgh attracted enormous interest. The public feeling was wrought up to the highest pitch. The avenues to the Court were crowded from four o'clock in the morning of Monday until after the same hour on the morning of Tuesday. The anxiety of those who could not gain admission to the Court house was extreme.[6]

Another account stated that 'the officers … performed their duties so well that the crush, although great, was attended with no accident'. Stuart was admitted through the Judges robing room accompanied by his relatives the Earl of Moray, Captain Alexander Gordon, Mr Erskine of Cardross with his son and a number of friends. He was dressed in black and looked remarkably well.[7]

The presiding officer was the Hon. David Boyle, the Lord Justice Clerk. The judges were Lords Hermand, Succoth, Gillies and Pitmily. Lord Meadowbank chose not to attend as he had been involved in advising Boswell and Lord Pitmily left the court before the case was finished.[8] Several distinguished visitors were allowed to join the judges on the bench including Prince Czartoriski,[9] Lord Belhaven,[10] Lord Rosslyn and the Hon. Henry Fox.[11] This was a permitted practice at that time although the visitors took no part in the trial. Stuart's friend and distant relation, the Earl of Moray, was also entitled to this privilege but preferred to sit at the Bar with relatives, foregoing the right of peerage. Four counsel represented the Crown: Sir William Rae (Lord Advocate), James Wedderburn (Solicitor General), Duncan M'Neill (Advocate Depute) and Robert Dundas. Seven counsel appeared for Stuart including Francis Jeffrey, James Moncreiff and Henry Cockburn, undoubtedly the three most eminent advocates of the day. Jeffrey in particular was known for his persuasive eloquence and his influence on a jury. 'He flatters the vanity of men by making them believe that the best proof of their own superiority will be their coming to the conclusion which he proposed.'[12]

Sir William Rae revealed a remarkable lack of judgement in appearing as chief prosecutor considering that, by virtue of his involvement in the newspapers which contained the libels against Stuart, he was a major contributor to the events leading up to the duel. This was to become the subject of parliamentary debate and criticism after the trial (see Chapter 9).

Jury selection

In those days the presiding judge in Scottish criminal prosecutions selected the jury of 15 men from a panel of 45 submitted names. Cockburn regarded this as a 'practice utterly abhorrent to the general principles of the constitution … . Even when exercised with the utmost purity, it exposed the administration of the law to obloquy'.[13] A Whig member of Parliament, Thomas Kennedy of Dunure, introduced a bill in 1821 to have juries selected by ballot, giving instances in which the existing system had been abused, but this democratic measure was strongly opposed by the Lord Advocate, Sir William Rae and it was outvoted. He reintroduced the bill again in 1822 only to have it fail. Lord Binning had said, 'if a judge could not be trusted to select a jury, he could not be trusted in law'. The persistent Kennedy succeeded in having the bill passed in the House of Commons in 1824 only to have it defeated in the Lords by the opposition of Lord Melville. Finally in 1825 the bill was passed, this time with the support of Melville who must have had a change of heart. Cockburn, who had strongly supported his friend Kennedy throughout by frequent letters and articles in the *Review*, wrote 'This is sometimes called Lord Melville's Act; and he is certainly entitled to the praise due to him who first opposes a good measure, and then adopts it. It was Mr Kennedy's Act in every true sense'.[14]

In Stuart's trial, which took place three years before the above act was passed, the Lord Justice Clerk selected the 15 jurors, half being landowners from the adjacent counties, including three baronets – Sir Alexander Maitland Gibson, Sir John Hope and Sir James Dalyell of Binns – and half tradesmen and merchants from Edinburgh. There was no suggestion in any of the commentaries on the trial that any prejudice had been introduced in their selection, indeed Cockburn stated that Boyle 'behaved admirably' in his conduct of the trial.[15]

The indictment was read which accused Stuart of the wicked and malicious murder of Sir Alexander Boswell and of absconding and fleeing from the scene. A second charge implicated Stuart in abetting William Borthwick in the theft of documents which were in the lawful possession of Robert Alexander. Stuart pleaded not guilty.

Henry Cockburn's defence

Henry Cockburn commenced his speech in defence of Stuart by objecting to the wording of the indictment which accused Stuart of conceiving malice and ill-will to Boswell. He denied that Stuart absconded and fled from justice; he was only fleeing from those inconveniences to which suspected innocence is necessarily subjected. He drew attention to Stuart's noble inheritance and good and peaceful character. He detailed to the court the events leading up to the duel – the insults and provocations emanating from the *Beacon* and the *Sentinel* and Stuart's abortive attempts to have these suppressed by legal means. He considered the attempts by Stuart to find out the author of these attacks to be well justified. He described in detail Borthwick's efforts to recover the papers from the *Sentinel* office and emphasised that he had done so entirely within his legal rights (although that matter was still *sub judice*). He continued with the details of the identification of Boswell as author of the insults and the preparations for the subsequent duel, which he agreed was the inevitable outcome. The details of the duel were described and he emphasised that Stuart's escape to France was not a flight from justice but an avoidance of the inconvenience of jail. Cockburn concluded his address by submitting,

> ... that, instead of adding to the sufferings of him who has already borne
> so much, and who, let this case terminate as it may, is doomed to suffer so much

more, the only legal, the only moral, the only appropriate conclusion of this day's trial must be a persuasion, that he acted under the operation of a great moral necessity, and that a verdict of *Not Guilty* is the result, which will give most satisfaction both of the law and to all reasonable men.[16]

Sydney Smith read Cockburn's speech with great pleasure.[17] Sir James Mackintosh,[18] in the subsequent debate which took place in the House of Commons on 25 June 1822, said of Cockburn's address, 'It was a speech, in short, which, as a specimen of forensic eloquence, considered with reference to the peculiar difficulties with which the advocate had to contend, was unrivalled by any similar effort in ancient or modern times'. A modern reader cannot fail to agree that this description is merited. One of the 'peculiar difficulties' facing the advocate is quoted as an example of Cockburn's style.

It is another grievous misfortune in this case, and one which the gentleman at the bar feels more poignantly than any stranger can, that justice cannot be done to the living without seeming to encroach on those charities which are due to the dead. I wish I could avoid this topic too, and that we could pass through the business of the day, without casting even a shade of doubt on the memory of one whose unfortunate loss has occasioned this discussion. I am afraid that we cannot. But I trust that your Lordships will go along with me, and keep it always in remembrance, that, if we shall be obliged to charge that person with impropriety, we are most willing to ascribe it to indiscretion alone.[19]

Examination of witnesses

Much of the evidence given by the witnesses has already been detailed. Only new and hitherto unrecorded evidence will be reported in this chapter.

The first witnesses were the two seconds, Lord Rosslyn and John Douglas. They confirmed Cockburn's account of the events leading to the duel and of the duel itself which is described in Chapter 6.

During Douglas' interrogation the Lord Advocate spoke for the first time in the trial to ask a series of questions relating to the handwriting of the various offending articles. Jeffrey objected to the questions, whereupon Stuart intervened to say, 'My Lord, the more complete this investigation is, the more agreeable it will be to me; and I have to request of my counsel not to object to any questions put by the Counsel of the Crown'.[20] Jeffrey responded, 'It is not in every case I would be disposed to yield to any such request on the part of a client, but here I am disposed to allow the fullest possible investigation'.[21]

The surgeons George Wood and Robert Liston described the wound and the surgical interventions. Both had assisted in carrying Boswell to Balmuto and Wood had remained with him until his death at 3.30pm the following day.

Several witnesses from both sides were called to testify as to the author of the writing of the incriminating manuscripts including Sir Alexander's lawyer and cousin, Alexander Boswell, James Walker, the tutor of Boswell's children, Stuart's friend James Gibson and William Home Lizars, the eminent engraver and artist. All agreed that the writing of the *Whig Song*, the letter signed *Ignotus*, the article beginning *Lieutenant James Stuart* and the letter signed *Mark Tod* was that of Boswell, although they considered that attempts had been made to disguise the fact. By this time, however, this confirmation was unnecessary as Boswell had acknowledged his authorship to Douglas.

The two legal representatives of William Borthwick – William Spalding and William Henderson – were then called to testify in connection with the second part of the indictment. Spalding in lengthy cross examinations by the Lord Advocate and Cockburn described the events leading up to Borthwick's release from prison, his subsequent recovery of manuscripts from the *Sentinel* office and their delivery to Stuart at the Tontine Inn described in Chapter 5. Cockburn was persuaded that Borthwick had legal right to enter the office and obtain the papers and confirmed that Stuart also believed this to be so. William Henderson then described the efforts that he and Spalding had made to obtain Borthwick's release by means of a bill of suspension and liberation, but that the legal process was delayed. He confirmed that he had provided the funds for Borthwick's release from prison from his own funds and that Stuart had made no contribution. He produced and read out the judgement from the Glasgow magistrates which he interpreted as entitling Borthwick to resume his partnership in the *Sentinel* and consequently the right to enter the premises and recover his property.

James Gibson was next examined. He stated that he had often discussed the possible author of the libels with Stuart but the name of Sir Alexander had never arisen. On the day of the duel, Gibson had received from Stuart a letter, written at 4am, which he was asked to read to the court. It included the following: 'Be so kind, if I am completely done for, as to have the inclosed [*sic*] conveyed, … within four days after this day, not sooner than the third. Be quiet till you hear'.[22] The 'inclosed' was a packet addressed to Mrs Stuart which of course was not delivered, Stuart having survived. It would be intriguing to know its content and why it had to be delivered between the third and fourth days, but alas this is not recorded. Gibson said that he had gone to the bank to obtain funds for Stuart's exile to France.

Several witnesses were called to testify to Stuart's character and all gave favourable opinion despite, in several instances, being of a different political persuasion. Typical was that of William Erskine, Lord Kinedder, who said, 'I have been very much connected with Mr Stuart professionally, and likewise privately; and certainly, in all my lifetime, I never knew a more perfectly good-tempered, kind-hearted, amiable man, nor a safer companion'. Stuart and he differed 'very decidedly' with regard to politics but Stuart never allowed this to interfere with his cordiality.[23]

The Lord Advocate's address to the jury

No further witnesses were called and the Lord Advocate summarised the prosecution case for the jury. He regretted that the expression that Stuart had fled from justice had been used in the indictment, but pointed out that the inconvenience of Stuart's absence from the country was partly responsible for the delay of the trial. He emphasised that the evidence had clearly shown that Stuart was guilty of murder. He anticipated that Stuart's counsel might make a plea for self defence but stated that, 'a person going out deliberately to fight a duel, and killing his antagonist, cannot be allowed to state himself as in those circumstances of self-defence'.[24] He conceded that juries may think themselves entitled not to regard the law in that strict point of view and might consider themselves not so much as being in a court of law as in a court of honour, but that the juries' strict duty did not entitle them to take this view (see contrary opinion of Lord Gillies, p. 155). He made no mention of the additional charge in the indictment relating to the 'illegal recovery of the manuscripts'. That item seemed to have been dropped completely.

Jeffrey's defence speech

Mr Jeffrey then addressed the jury for the defence. His closely argued case took three hours to deliver and occupies 35 pages of text,[25] which must have tried the patience of the court in the early hours of the morning. He rejected the words of the indictment which stated that Stuart had killed Boswell 'wickedly and maliciously'. Stuart had acted from motives totally unconnected with personal animosity. Jeffrey then read to the jury the several passages from James Boswell's *Life of Johnson* in which Johnson supports the moral right of duelling including the passages, 'He ... who fights a duel, does not fight from passion against his antagonist, but out of self-defence, to avert the stigma of the world, and to prevent himself from being driven from society', and that 'a man may shed the blood of a man who invades his character, as he may shoot him who attempts to break into his house'. He quoted other authorities who held similar opinions including Dr Adam Ferguson, Professor of Moral Philosophy at University of Edinburgh.

He discussed at length the legality of duelling stating that the statute forbidding it dated back to the sixteenth century at a time when duelling was commonplace, 'when, out of mere wantonness, vanity, and folly, the lives of the most valuable citizens were sacrificed'.[26] He regarded an honourable duel as being the better alternative to assassination which prevailed in Spain and Italy. He argued that duels were now rare events and the statute was no longer reasonable. During the long reign of George III (1760–1820) there had been only about 170 duels in Great Britain and Ireland with between 60 and 70 deaths. Only about 20 to 23 trials had ensued, with no convictions except in two or three instances where there had been an abuse of the conduct of the duel. During the past 150 years not one conviction had taken place in Scotland. He quoted the opinion of Lord Kames, an eminent Scottish judge, who had written that, 'a duel, which an affront forces a man upon, for vindicating his honour, when no satisfaction is offered, is very different [from other forms of killing]. I cannot see that the person affronted is guilty of any crime'.[27]

Jeffrey said, 'it is a proud and fortunate circumstance for this country, that such an institution as a jury should exist, with power occasionally to temper the severity of that law' and the jury, 'should be allowed, by means of refusal, to guide the Legislature to the repeal of particular laws, or the enactment of new ones'.[28]

Jeffrey then described a number of similar cases in which the jury had found the accused to be not guilty.

He concluded:

I trust, therefore, that, not in violation of the law, but in dutiful observance of its spirit and clear injunctions, and rigorously giving it effect, you will find him Not Guilty ... and thus restore him untainted to that society of which he is the delight, ... and in part at least, to that peace of mind ... which I fear it is not in the power of your verdict, or of any human tribunal, ever effectually or completely to restore.[29]

The Lord Justice Clerk's charge to the jury

The Lord Justice Clerk then summarised to the jury the salient features of the trial. He drew attention to the lack of clarity in the law relating to duelling and cited instances in which juries had given verdicts contrary to the legal arguments. His conclusion was distinctly favourable to the accused:

Neither I nor any other Judge in this Court can give the slightest countenance to publications such as those which were directed against the gentleman at the bar. It is one of the greatest misfortunes and evils of the present day that we have to witness the disgraceful licence of the periodical press; and I do lament, from the bottom of my heart, that the unfortunate gentleman deceased should have had any concern with writings of this description – for it is impossible to shut your eyes against the evidence by which it is proved that Sir Alexander Boswell was engaged in these writings, and that the prisoner at the bar was the object of his attacks.

You will, therefore, keep these considerations in your view, and pronounce such verdict as the circumstances of the case shall seem to you to authorize.[30]

Not guilty – public rejoicing

The jury, without retiring, after a few moments consultation, returned the verdict of 'Not Guilty', and so concluded the trial at 5am on Tuesday morning after sitting continuously for 18 hours.[31]

The crowds which had gathered around the court remained till the end:

About one o'clock on Tuesday morning a rumour was circulated that the arraigned party was acquitted; and it was followed by the most deafening shouts of 'Stuart for ever'. These were repeated so loud without, that for some time not a word that Mr Jeffrey said was heard within.[32]

The *Edinburgh Advertiser* of 11 June 1822 gave a full account of the trial with a summary of Jeffrey's speech and concluded:

It was near five o'clock this morning when the court broke up. A considerable crowd occupied Parliament Square all day, while greatly increased at night, when the populace became extremely noisy. When the verdict was announced at the door much cheering followed, and the crowd rushed toward a chaise in the Lawn Market, with the avowed purpose of taking off the horses when Mr Stuart should make his appearance, [presumably so that they could show their approval by the gesture of pulling the chaise themselves]. Stuart, however, disappointed them by withdrawing privately. He was afterwards discovered … proceeding up St Andrews St, and the people met him in Thistle St. but at his earnest solicitation, left him to pursue his way home, after shaking hands with one of their number. He was accompanied by the Earl of Rosslyn.

The Hon. Henry Fox, who had been allowed to sit on the bench between

Lords Rosslyn and Belhaven during the trial, wrote his account of the event in his Journal:

> The trial was very long and some of it very dull indeed. Lord Rosslyn and John Douglas were the chief witnesses, and both gave their evidence with the greatest perspicuity and precision. In fact, all were so much in favour of Stewart that no doubt could be entertained of the verdict, which was not given till four in the morning. I sat it out and was rather tired. Jeffrey's speech was less good than I expected, but Cockburn's was admirable. Mr Stewart was very much affected, and was two or three times in tears. His conduct has been admirable, and he had gained a great deal by the investigation. Nothing could be more convincing than the testimonies to the benevolence and gentleness of his character. The summing up of Justice Clarke [sic] was very much in his favour, and gave a severe cut at the personalities of the newspapers, which … have produced so much bloodshed and ill-will.[33]

Cockburn was naturally delighted at the outcome and wrote to his friend Kennedy:

> Never was there such a triumph! Never were wretches so wretched as the Crown counsel that day! Never was calumny so put down! Never was truth so fully and beautifully disclosed. I told Stuart last night that he was now the most dangerous man in the world. He has got so noble a character, that if he were to cut a throat every day, nobody would believe it. He behaved beautifully, uniformly firm and calm, but made amiable by some occasional bursts of tears.[34]

To the Whig masses, the duel and Stuart's acquittal were regarded as events to be celebrated. His friend Henry Brougham wrote that, 'He was most triumphantly acquitted, on the ground of the gross provocation he had received, and of the perfect fairness of the duel'.[35] Two dance tunes were composed in 1822 to celebrate the victory, a strathspey entitled *The Duel* and *Mr Stewart's Reel. The Scotsman* of 15 June 1822 said of the trial: 'It has proved that there are honourable men at both sides; that there is justice in our Courts; that Juries can be honest, and the Bench impartial.' It goes on to praise the Lord Justice Clerk who 'was admirable and judge-like in every respect'.

Lady Boswell's reaction

Lady Boswell did not agree. She was incensed at the outcome of the trial, which she considered an act of injustice and, as she had done following the duel, she expressed her grievances in a series of letters to Walter Scott. She attacked the prosecution witnesses Douglas and Rosslyn, the counsel for the defence Henry Cockburn and particularly the Lord Justice Clerk for the way with which he had presided over the trial: 'I am so angry at the Justice Clerk who in his charge to the jury has *presumed to throw obliquy* on the *conduct* of my husband for not accepting the proposals made by Ld Rosslyn for accommodation'.[36] She wanted to insert her grievance 'in some Newspaper so that the slur thrown by the Lord Justice Clerk there should be made available for the public to judge. We must submit to the Lord Justice Clerk for our judge till Government remove him to a better place and the Almighty to another place'.[37]

Scott had difficulty in replying to these letters, for as a sheriff depute he felt bound to defend the process of the law, but at the same time he must have had feelings of guilt and remorse regarding his own involvement in the affair through his backing of the *Beacon* and his close friendship with Boswell. He was not present at the trial for he could not 'bear the mental distress which must have attended it'.[38] He advised Lady Boswell against any attempt at further intervention either legally or in the press.

This was by no means the end of the affair for aspects of the trial came up for debate in the House of Commons which will be considered in Chapter 9.

Stuart returned to his country estate at Dunearn after the trial – his first visit since he departed for France. Cockburn wrote:

> Stuart is in Fife to-day seeing his terraces and evergreens for the first time since the affair. He is delighting everyone, even my neighbour Pitmilly with the honour of his behaviour, which is uniformly modest temperate, firm and gentle.
>
> I talked to Pitmilly to-day about the proceeding of introducing Borthwick's case into Stuart's trial to create a prejudice, and then letting him out next day and giving up the charge; and even he seemed shocked.[39]

Notes

1   Cockburn (c.1822a): *Trial 3*, p. 195.
2   Anon (1822): *Trial 2*, Appendix XI.
3   Anon (1822): *Trial I*.
4   Anon (1822): *Trial 2*. William Bennet WS stated that he was responsible for the editing 'the great length of the Report and the necessity of having it expeditiously published, ... should more than justify any trifling oversight ... that may have inadvertently occurred in it', *Courant* 8 July 1822. Cockburn regarded this as being the more correct account, Cockburn, H. (1874b): *Letters chiefly concerned with the Affairs of Scotland from Lord Cockburn to Thomas Francis Kennedy*, 12 June 1822, pp. 50–1.
5   Cockburn (c.1822a): *Trial 3*.
6   *The Scotsman*, 15 June 1822
7   Anon (1822): *Trial I*, p. 3.

8   Lord Pitmilly was David Monypenny, a friend of Stuart's from his student days at University. He
     may have felt obliged to take no further part in view of his friendship. He was also a senior col-
     league and friend of Cockburn. He was Solicitor General from 1811–13.
9   Prince Adam Czartoriski 1779–1861 was a wealthy Polish nobleman, politician and anglophile.
     He seems to have had a liking for attending notable trials for he had been present at the trial of
     Warren Hastings (who was also involved in a duel).
10   Lord Belhaven 1793–1868 was a Scottish representative peer in the House of Lords, sitting in
     the Whig benches. He was Lord Lieutenant of Lanarkshire.
11   Hon. Henry Fox 1773–1840, later Baron Holland. Nephew of Charles James Fox, the Whig
     leader and himself a Whig.
12   Lockhart (1819): *Peter's Letters to his Kinsfolk*, **2**, p. 63.
13   Cockburn (1909): *Memorials of his time*, p. 361. Cockburn published two long articles in the
     Edinburgh Review **36**, pp. 174–219 and **38**, pp. 226–34 on the injustice of 'jury picking' by the
     presiding judge.
14   Cockburn (1909): *Memorials*, p. 363.
15   Ibid, p. 372
16   Anon (1822): *Trial 2*. p. 42
17   Letter to Francis Jeffrey, 22 June 1822 in Smith (1953): *Letters of Sydney Smith*, **1**, p. 390. 'I read
     Cockburn's speech with much pleasure. I admire in the strongest manner, the conduct of the
     many upright and patriotic lawyers at the Scottish bar.'
18   Sir James Mackintosh (1765–1832) was a distinguished lawyer, doctor, and historian. He was a
     Whig member of Parliament from 1813 and a supporter of Catholic emancipation and the Re-
     form Bill.
19   Anon (1822): *Trial 2*, p. 25.
20   Ibid, p. 67.
21   Cockburn (*c*.1822a): *Trial 3*, Precognition of Douglas, p. 99 and pp. 101–2.
22   Anon (1822): *Trial 2*, pp. 102–3.
23   Ibid, p. 123
24   Ibid, p. 134
25   Ibid, pp. 135–71
26   Ibid, p. 150
27   Ibid, p. 143
28   Ibid, p. 146
29   Ibid, p. 171
30   Ibid, p. 135
31   This was by no means a record. The trial of Katherine Nairn and Patrick Ogilvie in 1765 lasted
     for 22 hours without interruption and the trial of Burke and Hare, who murdered 16 subjects to
     provide bodies for Dr Knox's anatomy school, commenced on 24 December 1828 and contin-
     ued into Christmas morning.
32   Anon (1822): *Trial I*.
33   Fox (1923): *The Journal of the Hon. Henry Edward Fox 1818–1830*, p. 123.
34   Cockburn (1874b): *Letters chiefly concerned with the Affairs of Scotland from Lord Cockburn to
     Thomas Francis Kennedy*, 12 June 1822.
35   Brougham (1871): *The Life and Times of Henry Lord Brougham*, **2**, p. 503.
36   Lady Boswell to Scott, 15 June 1822, Scott (1932–37): *The Letters of Walter Scott*, **VII**, p. 188,
     fn.
37   Ibid, Lady Boswell to Scott, 21 June 1822.
38   Scott to Lady Boswell Scott, 22 June 1822, Scott (1932–37), *Letters*, **VII**, pp. 188–91.
39   Cockburn (1874b), 13 June 1822.

CHAPTER 8
The Borthwick affair

A case well worthy of being studied, in all its details, by those who wish to learn the working of the old Scotch legal system in bad times.
                    Henry Cockburn, Preface to *Case of William Murray Borthwick*

A case which had excited a greater sensation in Scotland than any thing which had occurred since the Rebellion in 1746.
                    Sir James Mackintosh, House of Commons debate 25 June 1822

It is very painful to remember these things, but truth must not be sacrificed utterly.
                    Henry Cockburn, *Memorials of his Time*, p. 376

The Dundee interlude

FOLLOWING HIS recovery of the papers from the *Sentinel* office, William Borthwick left Glasgow for Edinburgh on 12 March 1822. The next day he sent a message to his agent Alexander Ure in Glasgow instructing him to contact Loudon Robertson and request that he join him in Edinburgh. He enclosed a pound note for his expenses. Borthwick had persuaded the reluctant Robertson to take a part in the 'break-in' by promising to help him find a job and it was probably in order to fulfil his promise that he requested Robertson's company. The two men left for Dundee on 19 March, on the advice of William Spalding – for by then the news of the break-in to the *Sentinel* office had been widely published and it was felt that they should avoid the limelight. Borthwick maintained that he had important business to transact in Dundee and that he lived there quite openly, even giving his real name to the Chalmers circulating library where he borrowed books. While there, he managed to obtain a job for Robertson as compositor with the *Dundee Advertiser.*

Concurrently with the preparations for the Stuart trial, another related legal process was taking place. The Lord Advocate, Sir William Rae, had charged Stuart with two offences: one, the murder of Sir Alexander Boswell and the other of being associated with William Murray Borthwick in the unlawful procurement of papers from the offices of the *Glasgow Sentinel* which were the property of Robert Alexander. In order to prove the second part of this indictment it was clearly necessary to charge Borthwick with the same offence.

On 29 March, three days after the duel, the Lord Advocate's deputy, John Hope (Fig. 27), issued a warrant for Borthwick's arrest while acting for his chief, Rae, who was in London at the time. The indictment stated *inter alia* that Borthwick on 12 March 1822 did feloniously open by force and violence a locked desk belonging to Robert Alexander and did thereby feloniously obtain possession of the keys to the safe and other lockfast repositories which he did ransack and rummage and did wickedly and feloniously steal and theftuously abstract a great variety of letters and communications.[1]

Hope instructed the Crown agent to arrest Borthwick without delay in order to prevent his escape. It had been rumoured that he was waiting in Dundee to embark to America in a boat that was due to leave for Charleston, South Carolina in a few days, although Borthwick denied this and said repeatedly that he was there on business. His ex-partner and now arch enemy, Alexander, gave a different version. He maintained that Spalding and William Henderson had visited Borthwick in Dundee and encouraged him to go abroad. They had arranged for Mr Rentoul, an editor in Dundee, to lend him money for the journey and for Henderson to look after the family.[2] As with many of the statements made by Borthwick and Alexander it is impossible to say who is telling the truth. It seems highly improbable, however, that Borthwick would be prepared to abandon his family to whom he was devoted, particularly as he believed that he had not committed a crime.[3]

Borthwick's arrest and imprisonment

In compliance with Hope's warrant for Borthwick's arrest, on 2 April a messenger-at-arms, Patrick Mackay, was given the task of arresting him in Dundee. The warrant was brought by James Todd, Alexander's lawyer, who would be able to identify Borthwick and could assist in the arrest. The participation of Todd indicates that Alexander must have been collaborating with Hope in Borthwick's arrest. Not knowing where Borthwick was living, Mackay and Todd, stationed themselves outside the Dundee post office hoping that Borthwick would come to collect his mail. In the event Robertson, who was still living with Borthwick in lodgings, turned up in his stead. He was recognised by Todd, who asked the postmaster to whom the letter picked up by Robertson had been addressed. The postmaster very properly refused to tell. The next day the pair again attended the post office when the mail coach from the south arrived and once more Robertson turned up. This time they followed him back to his lodgings with Mrs Gray in Overgate Street and were able to arrest Borthwick as he emerged from the house. Robertson was also arrested but immediately released to enable him to act as a witness.

Although Borthwick had been charged with a felony, he bitterly resented being treated as a common felon. In particular he objected to the ignominy of being handcuffed, especially in public. While in jail, Borthwick prepared a detailed account of his arrest.[4] In this he described that:

> I was seized by a messenger at arms, accompanied by Mr James Todd, the agent of Alexander, and conveyed in irons between them to Edinburgh jail, where, at first, I was refused all communication with my agents, and am now informed that I am to be brought to trial at the instance of the Public Prosecutor, accused of abstracting papers from the Glasgow Sentinel office.[5]

In another published account he wrote:

> I was apprehended in Dundee, searched as if I had been suspected of traitorous correspondence; hand cuffed as an abandoned or convicted felon; and used in such a manner as would have drawn sympathy from the heart of a *negro slave dealer*, my wrists were shockingly lacerated.[6]

After Borthwick had published his account of his arrest, Mackay gave a rather different version. He said that Borthwick, on being arrested and jailed in Dundee, requested that he be jailed in Edinburgh to which the Dundee magistrates agreed. They left for Edinburgh at 2am on 4 April in a post chaise. Borthwick was seated between Mackay and Todd, who both carried loaded pistols. Before setting off, Borthwick had been involved in an altercation with Mackay's assistants and for that reason manacles were applied. They weighed only 9oz English and were not too small and did not hurt his wrists. If Borthwick had complained of discomfort, Mackay had a pair of fetters with him which could have been used instead. In any event the handcuffs were removed before joining the steamboat ferry to cross the Forth at Pettycur, Borthwick having given an assurance that he would make no attempt to escape.[7]

When admitted to Edinburgh's jail, Borthwick's legal advisors were refused access to him. Spalding protested, as did Henry Cockburn, who had agreed to act as counsel for Borthwick together with James Moncreiff. Both men – who were also acting for Stuart – probably offered their services *pro bono*, as they did when acting in a number of cases involving miscarriage of justice, for Borthwick certainly did not have the funds to pay their fees. It seems strange that these two prominent Whigs, should be offering their services free to a notorious Tory, but the injustice of the case was so gross as to override political affiliations and by then Borthwick was regretting his Tory associations.

Whether or not Cockburn was being paid for his time he certainly did not spare his efforts. His documents and ms notes, relating to the case, are bound in a large volume entitled *Case of William Murray Borthwick*[8] and are as comprehensive as his corresponding volume prepared for the trial of Stuart, for which he was undoubtedly paid. Bound within its pages are printed copies of the legal documents involving the dissolution and reinstatement of the partnership between Borthwick and Alexander. Another 400 pages contain a combination of ms reports, witnesses' precognitions, Cockburn's comments and appendices.

Cockburn's protest at being denied access to Borthwick was addressed to the Lord Justice General, the Lord Justice Clerk and the Lords Commissioners of the Justiciary:

> The petitioner cannot help regarding this course as highly oppressive, and he humbly submits, that it is unauthorised, and illegal … the petitioner has very little time indeed to prepare for the trial, which is to be hurried on within 15 days.[9]

Cockburn also appealed for bail. John Hope replied on 5 April that:

> The petitioner [Borthwick] was apprehended in Dundee, when about to leave the country, according to the information of the Public Prosecutor, in a ship bound for America and, under the circumstances of the case, the Public Prosecutor cannot consent to the liberation of the petitioner on bail. Borthwick is not to be examined until this evening or tomorrow – until such an examination takes place, it would be highly improper, and contrary to all law and practice, to permit the prisoner to communicate with counsel or agent … . The warrant, distinctly charges the commission of theft, and that of a very serious and aggravated nature, from lockfast places, and therefore … the case is not bailable.[10]

The Lord Justice Clerk, David Boyle, concurred.

Borthwick did undergo an examination by the sheriff, Adam Duff, later that day. He was escorted to the sheriff's office in a chaise, buckled to the sheriff's officer by a leather strap around his arm, but on his return to jail he was allowed to walk back arm in arm with the officer 'as it is customary for people to do when walking together'[11] in order to appear less conspicuous. On the day following this examination, access was allowed to legal agents, family and friends, and Borthwick was allowed some concessions including liberty to walk to the prison chapel and to have food sent down from the governor's house.

On the day of Borthwick's incarceration in Edinburgh, the bag containing his possessions, which had been seized in Dundee by Mackay, was taken by James Todd to the sheriff for examination. Todd, who had been up all night assisting in Borthwick's arrest and transfer to Edinburgh, fell asleep during the examination and snored so loudly that the sheriff demanded that he be removed to another room.[12]

Borthwick's trial postponed

Trial was fixed for 22 April 1822 at the Circuit Court in Glasgow and Borthwick was transferred to Glasgow Jail on the 18th in preparation 'as a common felon – confined among felons … and allowed nothing but jail fare, (water and a 'coggie' of meal brose once a day) and, at first, a cell so damp, as greatly to injure his health'.[13] Ninety-four witnesses were called and an assize of 45 landowners and business men from which the presiding judge was to select 15 jurors. At the last moment the date was changed to 24 April, without a reason given, to the great annoyance of the many witnesses and potential jurors who had assembled at the court.

The *Glasgow Courier*, Tuesday 23 April, reported that:

> The general belief that Borthwick's trial would come on yesterday brought a great concourse of people to the vicinity of the Court-house at an early hour, the persons assembled would have filled the Justiciary Hall ten times. The interest excited by the expectation, that this important case would come on then, was so great, that the doorkeepers were unable, without great inconvenience to the parties, to pass the jury, the counsel and prisoners' agents, who, as usual, are admitted by tickets. Under these circumstances, Baillie Craig, i.e. the acting chief magistrate, and Mr Cleland, found it necessary to attend the principal gate an hour before the opening of the court, by which order was preserved … until the Court was filled. The crowd was kept from pressing on the gate by files of horse and infantry. To everyone's chagrin and disappointment the case was deserted.

At the reconvened trial on the 24th the counsel for the Crown, John Hope, moved to desert the trial *pro loco et tempore*, i.e. put it off for some future occasion, again without giving a reason. Hope, who had refused to grant bail on 5 April, because the heinous nature of the offence precluded it, now offered Borthwick moderate bail. Henry Cockburn advised Borthwick against accepting bail on the grounds that if he did, the trial might never take place and he would be unable to clear his name. He referred to an Act of 1701 'For preventing Wrongous Imprisonment and against undue delays in Trials'[14] which limited the duration of arrest without trial. Cockburn said that, 'the days are now running, at the end of which he must unavoidably get rid to the charge one way or another. If he were to go out upon bail … he would lose the benefit of that statute'[15] and the threat of prosecution would remain for 20 years. He requested that the trial be bought forward as speedily as possible. Hope, who appeared to know nothing about the Act in question,[16] was obliged to agree to Borthwick's continued imprisonment.

Robert Alexander's intervention

Alexander was also getting impatient at the delay in bringing Borthwick to trial. On 4 May 1822 his agent, Mr R. W. Niven, wrote to the Crown Agent:

> I am now desired by my client Mr Alexander, to apply to you for the purpose of being informed, whether it is the intention of the Lord Advocate to bring Borthwick to trial at his own instance; as should he not do so, Mr Alexander wishes to indict him at his instance, without any delay.[17]

The Crown Agent replied on 6 May that 'it is not the intention of his Majesty's advocate to bring Borthwick to trial'[18] – an extraordinary decision after keeping Borthwick in jail for a month on a serious charge. Despite this statement, Borthwick was not released from jail and on 25 May it was announced that his trial was fixed for 10 June at the High Court in Edinburgh. Under the provisions of the Act of 1701, Borthwick was due to be released on 4 June and the Lord Justice Clerk, David Boyle, was obliged to liberate Borthwick from jail on that date. He then promptly recommitted him to jail at the instance of Robert Alexander, charging Borthwick with an indictment virtually identical to that with which he had originally been arrested at the instance of the Lord Advocate's depute, John Hope.

In Scotland at that time a warrant against an individual could be brought either by the Lord Advocate and his deputies, or by a private individual with the concurrence of the Lord Advocate. Private prosecutions were extremely rare for the accuser was responsible for all costs in connection with the case. Alexander had recently been jailed for bankruptcy at the instance of Borthwick!

Borthwick's trial abandoned

Borthwick was transferred back to Edinburgh Tolbooth on 6 June in preparation for his trial on the 10th, but as that date coincided with the trial of James Stuart, Borthwick's trial was adjourned for the fourth time until the 17th. On the day following Stuart's acquittal Borthwick was liberated from jail, without trial, on the authority of a letter from Alexander's lawyer, Niven, which read:

> Mr Alexander has come to the resolution not to insist in the criminal letters which he has raised against William Murray Borthwick, and I have in consequence withdrawn the warrant at Alexander's instance against him. I take the earliest opportunity of communicating this to you, that you may not bring forward witnesses, or make any preparation for the trial, the diet [sic] of which stands for Monday next.[19]

Cockburn, representing Borthwick, stated that:

> his client had been served with criminal letters, at the instance of Robert Alexander, … to stand trial before their Lordships this day for the crime of stealing certain manuscripts and documents: … that as the said Robert Alexander has abandoned his interest, descreet (Scots law – legal judgement) for expenses should be given against him.[20]

The Lords agreed and found Alexander liable for Borthwick's expenses incurred in the preparation for the trial. There is no record that Alexander did make any contribution, but in view of his financial circumstances it seems most unlikely. If Cockburn had included his own fees in the expenses, it is certain that he never received any payment from this source.[21]

Borthwick's reaction

Borthwick published his reaction to these events on the day of his release:

> Being liberated from jail without any application on my part, and without trial, by the voluntary act of my incarcerators, I now respectfully lay before the public an account of the proceedings that have been instituted against me at the instance of the Lord Advocate of Scotland, and of Robert Alexander, my late partner. The account was drawn up from day to day in the form of a narrative to be ready for the ultimate issue I all along anticipated. A copious index will be annexed of the documents referred to. All argument and reflection have been purposely avoided,

that every one may form his own judgement upon the proceedings against me – proceedings which I feel to have been harsh and oppressive in the extreme, and in which the public are not a little interested; for, if there is no remedy competent at common law either against his Majesty's Advocate or the private prosecutor, what has happened to me may be the fate of any of his Majesty's subjects ... . I have been liberated from jail, after having endured the most rigorous confinement therein for upwards of seventy days, and been exposed to every privation, and great expense in preparing for my defence in three criminal prosecutions. While my wife and family have been left without support, and my private affairs entirely ruined, my partner has been suffered to remain in possession of my property, using it as his own as an engine of oppression against me, and carrying on the same system of slander and abuse against individuals which ruined my newspaper. Time will shew whether for all these wrongs there is any redress. An action of damages against Robert Alexander alone would be hopeless, and never could produce any recompense to me for the injuries I have suffered.[22]

Borthwick's primary purpose in obtaining the manuscripts from the *Sentinel* office had been to save himself from Stuart's Action of Damages. This purpose succeeded, for although Stuart had not given Borthwick any pledge, he did hint that 'Borthwick would have no reason to regret giving him full information'[23] and the action was abandoned. In his 'Preparation for his Defence', Borthwick adopted a higher moral ground, pleading that the recovery of the papers from the *Sentinel* office,

... was not only his right, but his duty. He had been induced to become an instrument for the dissemination of libels, the true character of which can only be perceived by the disgusting task of reading them. It is strange to see it maintained in a Court of Justice, that such documents are capable of being the subject of a right of property. Having unfortunately committed this offence, he was bound in legal morality, to prevent its repetition and to atone for it, by exhibiting the evidence of the real patronage and authorship of the papers.[24]

Conspiracy theory

It would appear from the timing of events that Borthwick had been used as a pawn in the case against Stuart. It had obviously been necessary that he should be charged with the theft of the documents if the case against Stuart of being an accessory to that alleged crime was to be upheld. On the other hand, if he had come to trial and been acquitted *before* Stuart's trial, Stuart could not have been

charged with participation in a non-existent crime. That unfortunate techni-
cality, from the point of view of the prosecution, could only be avoided by
keeping Borthwick in jail, charged with the theft, but delaying his trial until
after Stuart's trial. It is difficult to escape the conclusion that the prosecutors, the
Lord Advocate Sir William Rae, his deputy John Hope, together with the
connivance and collusion of Robert Alexander had contrived this deception.
What makes this idea particularly unpleasant was the political undercurrent.
Both Rae and Hope, as staunch Tories and *Beacon* bondsmen, had a connection
with Stuart's trial quite apart from their role as prosecutors in that trial.
Cockburn was of the opinion that 'the Lord Advocate had certainly abused his
office'.[25] In a letter to Kennedy on 17 June 1822, Cockburn wrote:

> Would Borthwick have been used thus, or would Stuart have been used as he was, if
> the cases of both these persons had not been connected with the defamatory system,
> and the public prosecutor with it? The truth is that Borthwick had been imprisoned
> as a thief and Stuart tried as a murderer, merely because the former gave up papers
> which the Advocate had an interest, as a libeller, to conceal, and the latter shot the
> author of the articles by which his Lordship and Co. were accustomed to defame.[26]

Hope was later to claim that he had done his best to bring the trial of Borthwick forward but that his efforts had been frustrated by the intervention of Rae
(see p. 124).

The Scotsman newspaper which had followed Borthwick's case very closely,
commented with regard to his imprisonment without trial:

> If such things may be done, there is not a man in this country who does not hold his
> liberty by the mere tolerances of the Lord Advocate and his depute. But the whole
> matter, we are confident, must be investigated by Parliament.[27]

This prediction was fulfilled. Two major debates on the subject took place in
Parliament which are detailed in the following chapter.

Borthwick considered suing Alexander for damages but Cockburn advised
him against this as both men were bankrupt and Borthwick would not be able to
recover the ruinous fees of court. Likewise, he advised that it would be useless to
charge the Lord Advocate with malicious prosecution for his office would protect
him;[28] 'it is absolutely infamous – downrightly infamous. I hope that Brougham,
even though these be Scotch matters, won't refuse to tear that Advocate to
tatters'.[29]

Notes

1   Anon (1823): Parliamentary Papers, pp. 94–5 and pp. 98–9. Parliamentary Papers: a set of these printed papers prepared for Abercromby's second Parliamentary debate (see p. 137) is bound with Cockburn's *Case of William Murray Borthwick*.

2   Alexander (1822): *Letter to Sir J. Mackintosh, Knt., M.P.*, p. 64.

3   Walter Scott, who regarded Borthwick as an 'atrocious villain', wrote to J. W. Croker 'Entre nous it was a great pity that when he was on flight to America they did not let the fellow go[,] a sort of self-conviction which would have answerd [*sic*] their purpose as well or better than any thing that could have resulted from a trial'. Scott (1894): *The Letters of Sir Walter Scott*, **VII**, p. 206.

4   Borthwick (1822): *Proceedings against Wm. Murray Borthwick*.

5   Borthwick (1822), Preface, p. 7.

6   Borthwick (1825): *Letter to Sir William Rae, M.P.*, p. 20. In making such an issue of the handcuffs, Borthwick may have been influenced by Scott's account of the harsh treatment of a prisoner by the notorious Captain Porteous, described vividly in *Heart of Midlothian* which had recently been published. The handcuffs were too small and 'Porteous proceeded with his own hands, and by great exertion of strength, to force them till they clasped together, to the exquisite torture of the unhappy criminal'. This cruelty attracted much sympathy from the public.

7   Parliamentary Papers, p. 139.

8   Cockburn (*c.*1822b): *Case of William Murray Borthwick*.

9   Parliamentary Papers, p. 98.

10 Ibid, p. 96.

11 Ibid, p. 141.

12 Ibid, p. 140.

13 Borthwick (1822), p. 49.

14 The Statute of 1701 passed in the reign of Queen Anne, enabled an accused person to insist on his trial being carried out within a specified period of time. It only applied if he was held in prison. If he accepted bail he could no longer demand a fixed date of trial and could be left with the threat hanging over him for twenty years. Cockburn discussed the significance of the Act of 1701 in an article in the *Edinburgh Review*, **36**, pp. 174–219

15 Parliamentary Papers, pp. 134–5.

16 Borthwick (1822), pp. 18–9; Borthwick (1825), p. 51.

17 Cockburn (*c.*1822b), p. 93

18 Ibid, p. 93.

19 Letter from Alexander's agent, R. W. Niven, 12 June 1822.

20 Parliamentary Papers, p. 137.

21 He acknowledges as much in a letter to Kennedy 19 June 1822., Cockburn (1874b): *Letters chiefly concerned with the Affairs of Scotland from Lord Cockburn to Thomas Francis Kennedy*, p.54.

22 Borthwick (1822), pp. 56–7.

23 Parliamentary Papers, p. 78.

24 Ibid, p. 117.

25 Cockburn (1874a): *Journal of Henry Cockburn 1831–1854*, 1, p. 76.

26 Cockburn (1874b), p. 52. In a letter to Kennedy, 12 June 1822, Cockburn lists nine offences committed under the authority of the Lord Advocate.

27 *The Scotsman*, 15 June 1822.

28 The advocate Hugo Arnot wrote, 'The Lord Advocate may of himself form an indictment against any person, for any crime he chuses to pitch upon' and even if the prisoner was acquitted and the accusation was calumnious or malicious, he could not be charged with an action for damages or expenses. 'This is a very dangerous power to be intrusted in an individual'. Arnot (1816): *History of Edinburgh*, 1779, pp. 228–9, fn.

29 Cockburn (1874b), p. 55. Letter to Kennedy, 13 June 1822. Henry Brougham was then Lord Chancellor.

CHAPTER 9
Parliament is involved

And since you know you cannot see yourself
So well as by reflexion, I, your glass
Will modestly discover to yourself
That of yourself which yet you know not of.

Preface from Borthwick's Letter to Sir William Rae
(quote from Julius Caesar Act 1)

The people are abused – This publishing
Becomes not Britain

From Lucius' Letter to John Hope (adapted from Coriolanus Act 3)

The Parliamentary debates

BORTHWICK FOUND a champion in James Abercromby (1776–1858).[1] Abercromby (Fig. 27) was a Whig Member of Parliament, who had given notice on 2 April 1822 that he was to call the attention of Parliament to the 'Conduct of the Lord Advocate with relation to the Public Press in Scotland'. The date allotted for this debate was 25 June, 13 days after Borthwick's release from jail. Abercromby decided, without giving advance notice, to take the opportunity of adding 'and more especially into the prosecution against William Murray Borthwick' to the subject to be debated. From his intimate knowledge of events it is clear that Abercromby must have been briefed by personal contact with Borthwick.[2] In the event, adding the Borthwick case at this late stage proved to be a tactical mistake. Having two separate, although related, issues to debate gave rise to confusion and must have contributed to Members' difficulties when it came to the vote.

James Abercromby's address to the House of Commons[3]

On 25 June 1822, James Abercromby introduced the debate. He proposed to show that the Lord Advocate, Sir William Rae, and his subordinates had compromised their position by connecting themselves with the press in a way which was incompatible with the duties of their situation. He proposed to show that the Lord Advocate had abused his high authority, that the forms of the law had been perverted and perverted from bad motives. If he could prove these facts to the satisfaction of the House, he did expect that they would not allow evils of such a nature to be without a remedy. He continued by describing to the English Members the great power and patronage of the Lord Advocate.[4] He was the sole public prosecutor in Scotland. Private individuals might institute a prosecution only by consent and concurrence of the Lord Advocate. He then described in detail Rae's support of the *Beacon* and the *Clydesdale Journal* paying particular attention to the clandestine way in which his letter in support of the latter was accompanied with instruction that the letter should be destroyed or returned. He gave examples of the gross and offensive libels published in these papers and Rae's deceitful attempts to dissociate himself from them. Abercromby continued by remarking upon,

> ... the strange situation in which the learned lord was placed, in appearing as the public prosecutor of Mr. Stuart for the death of Sir A. Boswell. What must have been his feelings, whilst he conducted the trial, upon recollecting that it was the system promoted by the money and the patronage which he had given to the Sentinel and the Beacon that had compelled Mr. Stuart to resort to the vindication of his injured honour?

He then drew particular attention to the libel published in the first issue of the *Sentinel* which had caused Stuart to bring an action against Borthwick and Alexander. This article included the passage,

> ... oh, shame to the dishonoured blood of the house and name of Stuart – he, with a meanness, only discernible in low life and in humble society, sought his personal safety in the most glaring cowardice. The blustering and the passionate are always in the rear of danger. James Stuart was consequently posted as a coward and poltroon. The very rabble and oyster-women in the streets of Edinburgh read the label,[5] mused upon the circumstances, and blushed for their patriot.

Abercromby then criticised two of William Rae's deputies, Duncan M'Neill (Fig. 28)[6] and John Hope. Hope had signed a document drawn up by M'Neill in the his absence. M'Neill was advocate for the defence of Robert Alexander in connection with the Action of Damages brought against him at the instance of Stuart. This document, which was to assume such importance in the debate and subsequent correspondence, stated that:

Figure 19

Map showing the duel site and the one and a half-mile trek to Balmuto Castle taken by the stretcher party. Figure 17 shows that the distribution of trees surrounding the duel site remains virtually the same today as shown in this map of 1832. John Thomson's Atlas of Scotland (1832).

(Courtesy of the National Library of Scotland)

Figure 20

Balmuto Castle as it is today after extensive restoration in 1974–84 by the Appleton Partnership.

(© Patricia Macdonald)

Figure 21

Claud Irvine Boswell,
Lord Balmuto (1799).

(by John Kay)

Figure 22

Photograph of the room in Balmuto Castle in which Boswell died.

(Courtesy of Bruce Boswell; photo John Chalmers))

Figure 23
Robert Liston (c.1820) by Clarkson Stanfield.
(Courtesy Royal College of Surgeons of Edinburgh)

Figure 24
John Thompson, Professor of Military Surgery, by Andrew Geddes.
(Courtesy of the Royal College of Surgeons of Edinburgh)

Figure 25
The Boswell mausoleum attached to the Boswell Aisle (part of the original Auchinleck Parish Church)
(John Chalmers)

Figure 26

James Abercromby
(Baron Dunfermline)
by Thomas Phillips.

(Courtesy of Fife
Council on behalf
of Dunfermline
Common Good)

Figure 27

Portrait of John Hope.

(from B. W. Crombie's Modern Athenians)

Figure 28

Portrait of Duncan M'Neill.

(from B. W. Crombie's Modern Athenians)

Figure 29

Auchinleck House.

(John Chalmers)

Figure 30

North Charlotte Street leading off from Charlotte Square. Stuart's House, 2 North Charlotte Street, is at the right margin of this drawing. From Storer, J. & H.S. (1818). *A Graphic Historical Description of the City of Edinburgh.*

(Courtesy of the National Library of Scotland)

Figure 31

Moray Place. Stuart's home, 20 Moray Place, is the last house on the right of the picture; later the home of John Hope.

(From Grant (1881–83: *Edinburgh Old and New*, II, p. 201)

Figure 32

Avenue at Middelharnis by Hobbema.

(Courtesy of the National Gallery London)

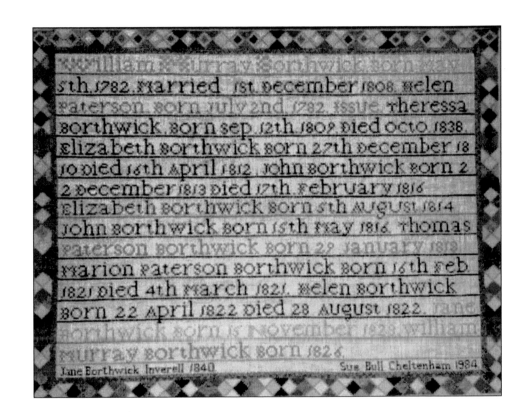

Figure 33

Sampler sewn c.1840 by Jane, Borthwick's youngest daughter, showing Borthwick's descendents.

(Courtesy of Ann Carson)

Figure 34

Gurley's memorial stone. The plaque reads:
'It is on record that Capt. Wm Gurley of Petershope, St. Vincent died at this spot on 30th October, 1824 having been fatally wounded in a pistol duel with a Mr Westall – the last to be fought in Fife'.
It was not!

(John Chalmers)

'The respondents … affirm, that the statements in the newspaper complained of are true …' and they 'offer to prove, by the evidence of persons of high character and skill in the laws and practice of honour, that the conduct of the pursuer, … was most ungentlemanly, and deserving of every condemnation'.

(signed) For Mr D. M'Neill
John Hope[7]

Abercromby could not imagine that they were ignorant of the fact that they were aggravating the offence by putting on record this sort of defence.

Abercromby then accused Rae of oppression and injustice in the case of William Murray Borthwick. He reviewed Borthwick's history as a publisher, his difficult relationship with Alexander, the events leading up to the recovery of documents and Borthwick's clearance of the charge of theft by the Glasgow magistrates. He described how Borthwick was arrested in Dundee on the authority of the Lord Advocate, who was aware that Borthwick had been found not guilty by the Glasgow magistrates:

Borthwick was arrested at Dundee, under the apprehension … that being obliged to fly from justice, he was about to proceed to America. For a man intending to go to America, it certainly did not immediately appear that the best way he could take was to proceed to the eastern coast of Scotland. Borthwick, however, was arrested, manacled, put in irons, which were too small, and produced to the unfortunate individual the greatest suffering imaginable. He was compelled in this condition to cross a public place between two men who were armed, appearing as if he were the most desperate of malefactors. Between the two persons, armed with pistols, Borthwick was conveyed into a post-chaise, and brought to Edinburgh. There he was imprisoned, and all access to him denied.

Abercromby then detailed the cancelled trials and Borthwick's eventual release without trial:

The instant … that this unhappy man became instrumental in exposing calumniators and slanderers, he was arrested at Dundee, put in irons, and treated with unusual, with unheard-of severity. A day was fixed for his trial; the learned lord and Mr. Alexander jointly proceeded against him; but when Mr Stuart was acquitted, Borthwick was set free. *Could any man, then, hesitate in saying that there had existed a strong desire to create a prejudice against Mr Stuart on his trial by these steps against Borthwick?*

Abercromby went on to detail a circumstance which had occurred during Stuart's trial. Whenever the examination of a witness was completed, Alexander's counsel (William Menzies whom he did not name) sprang up to require the witness to leave the court lest he should hear what the other witnesses might dispose, adding that otherwise they might be influenced by the evidence of these witnesses when called again to appear at Borthwick's trial the following Monday. The purpose behind these interruptions was to remind the court of Stuart's alleged involvement with Borthwick and thus to keep the prejudice alive to the last moment. '*Without investigation of such matters, there could be no real liberty, for it was impossible to conceive a more direct inroad upon it, than such a cruel persecution under the forms of law.*'

Abercromby concluded by moving, 'That a committee be appointed, for the purpose of inquiring into the conduct of the Lord Advocate, and the other law officers of the Crown in Scotland, with relation to the public press and more especially to inquire into the prosecution carried on against W. Borthwick'.

The Lord Advocate's response

The Lord Advocate believed that no man before him had been thus arraigned before the Commons.[8] He felt that in approaching this discussion, his character, credit and future happiness were at stake. For the last fortnight the press had teemed with matter obviously intended to affect the minds of Members, but he felt confident that the audience he was addressing would dismiss all such matters from their recollection, and would decide the question on its fair and honest merits. He went on to say that the powers of the Lord Advocate were not nearly as great as Abercromby had maintained.[9]

With regard to the Sentinel, he had been astonished to hear his name connected with it. So help him God, he had never seen the paper. He had no recollection of signing the letter supporting the *Clydesdale Journal*. At this point Abercromby passed over the letter, which he acknowledged showed his signature 'but he trusted that the House would give him credit for believing until he saw the paper, that he had not signed it'. He had been approached as a long resident in Lanark in his private capacity as a freeholder of the county to support a publication which seemed much needed but his support did not extend to the publication of improper articles.

He acknowledged that he had supported the *Beacon* financially but he stated boldly that the object was a just, honest and legal one and not an act of which he ought to be ashamed. The bond holders were not proprietors; they had no control, no command over the concern. Being much of his time in

London he was ignorant of its contents.[10] No evidence had been presented to the House as to the publication of any libels in that paper. The only libel which had excited public attention, was that directed against the noble lord opposite (Lord Archibald Hamilton), which had been tried within these few days and in which case the jury gave but one shilling damages when £5,000 had been sought (see p. 52). Papers were supported to promulgate the opinions held by gentlemen who differed from him in politics, and he could see no reason why those who thought as he did might not have recourse to the same system.

Rae defended his two deputies who had been criticised by Abercromby for their defence of a libel in the *Sentinel.* They were quite entitled to undertake professional practice apart from their official duties for which they were miserably paid. As to the arrest of Borthwick, he believed that there were legitimate grounds for considering that Borthwick had committed an offence and that Hope had acted appropriately. He had thought it proper to delay Borthwick's trial in Glasgow in view of the pending trial of Stuart, without attempting to justify this opinion. If Borthwick felt that he had suffered injury it was for him to apply to a court of law, where he would obtain redress. If there had been any error in the conduct of Borthwick's case, the responsibility rested with him. If he had done wrong, it was most proper and fitting that the Commons of England should condemn his conduct and the consequence must be to remove him from his present situation. If it pleased Parliament to remove him from his situation, he should console himself with the reflection that many gentlemen could be selected for the office much better qualified to perform its duties than he was.

The Home Secretary, Robert Peel, then spoke in support of Rae. He criticised Abercromby for introducing irrelevant emotive matters such as the distress of Boswell's widow and children and the duel involving the death of Mr Scott (see pp. 35–39). He should not have brought up the private legal business of Hope and M'Neill. The *Beacon's* prospectus stated the necessity of an energetic defence of the constitution: 'The evils of a free press were only to be corrected by a judicious use of its energies'. Was the Lord Advocate wrong in supporting this worthy intention when he was unaware of its slanderous attacks? Finally, Abercromby should not have raised the case of Borthwick without prior notice. If the powers of the Lord Advocate were excessive, let them have a distinct motion on that subject.

Sir James Mackintosh[11] then spoke in support of Abercromby. He said that the grave question before the House was whether the public prosecutor in Scotland had encouraged, in secret, a systematic attack on the sanctuary of private life and the laws of decency until he had been detected. It was wrong to dissociate the *Sentinel* from the *Clydesdale Journal,* when the *Sentinel* was entitled the 'late *Clydesdale Journal*' and was published by the same persons, supported by the same friends and filled with the same libels. If the House should sanction such infamous calumnies by a refusal to inquire, it would be chargeable with entailing the continuance of the system. That paper had been recommended and circulated throughout Scotland by the learned lord, and the manner in which it had been supported by his two deputies showed the animus of the proceedings. It showed the furious zeal which actuated all the parties and which appeared most strongly in the deputies of the Lord Advocate. Peel had said that the case of Borthwick was a separate question. Now, whether it were comprised in the notice or not, Mackintosh considered that the case, which had excited a greater sensation in Scotland than anything which had occurred since the rebellion in 1746, should be answered. Borthwick had been confined for 70 days, charged twice for felony and yet must have been presumed innocent for he was released without trial. He believed there was no example in the history of the law of so atrocious a proceeding. The House should inquire into so gross a case of misconduct on the part of a public officer. Justice had been perverted and he wished the House to grant inquiry: firstly that the House should know how Scotland was governed; secondly to give Rae a chance to clear his name.

After several other speakers, the House voted on Abercromby's motion. Ayes numbered 95 and Noes 120. The motion failed by 25 votes.

The Lord Advocate had survived this double pronged attack, but his reputation must have taken a knock and this was by no means the end of the matter. Cockburn said that he had a 'shabby escape by a majority of only 25'.[12] MacKenzie (1890) was of the opinion that a majority of only 25 was considered as a defeat of the strong Tory government of the day.[13] Walter Scott, a staunch friend, was on Rae's side. 'I always feard the Advocate though a man of sound sense and of remarkable personal courage as well as the most excellent intentions would feel his own situation in the House of C. too acutely to defend himself with spirit and to carry the war ... into the Quarters of the enemy'.[14]

Abercromby had used his Parliamentary privilege to the full in his attacks against Rae, Hope and M'Neill. Rae, as a Member of Parliament, had been able to defend himself in the House, but this opportunity was not available to John Hope who had been incensed by the references to him in the debate. He took the only course open to him – that of publishing his reaction in the form of a letter addressed to Abercromby. Duncan M'Neill sensibly let the matter rest, but William Menzies, the unnamed lawyer in Abercromby's address, also chose to publish a letter.

John Hope's letter

John Hope defended himself in style. On 1 July, six days after the debate, he published his 31-page *Letter to the Hon. James Abercromby*. In this letter he made many critical comments against Abercromby's conduct of the debate. In particular he defended himself against two main accusations: that he had been a party to private litigation in the defence of Alexander against Stuart and his part in the management of the Borthwick affair.

With regard to the first, Hope, at great length, tried to explain the circumstance in which he had signed a document on behalf of Mr M'Neill, who was Alexander's counsel. This document contained the arguments for the defence of Alexander and Borthwick against the libel charge of Stuart. Abercromby had implied that by signing this document Hope was acting as counsel for Alexander and that consequently it was improper for him to be acting for the prosecution in the trial of Stuart. Hope maintained that it was common practice in Scottish legal circles for one lawyer to sign a document on behalf of another who was not available, without having any knowledge of the content of the document which he was signing. He was in no way involved in the defence of Alexander. He criticised both Abercromby and Mackintosh for their ignorance of Scottish law in this matter (although both were Scots, they practised in England):

> You and Sir James Mackintosh, – English Lawyers, – think fit to make the merits of that action ... the subject of virulent invective in the House of Commons, ... the ignorance you have betrayed of the rules and practice of Scotch Courts, proves how admirably qualified you are to comment on the professional conduct of Scotch Counsel. ...
>
> Upon what grounds you and Sir James Mackintosh have proceeded in the attack which you have severally made upon me, for supposed conduct, as a counsel in a private and depending action, I have no means of exactly ascertaining. It is very possible that the wilful misrepresentation of others may have induced you to think yourselves safe in the grounds of that attack. But (whatever was the nature of your information) – that the circumstances in question have been anxiously, or at least hastily, and therefore unwarrantably, seized hold of, for the purpose of imputing my official conduct to flagitious motives, cannot be denied. Whether you truly believed the statements which you were so forward and ready to make, is a question I cannot permit myself to ask. The injustice, illiberality, and intemperance of the comments, with which these statements were accompanied, you cannot now dispute.[15]

With regard to the matter of Borthwick, Hope acknowledged that as Senior Deputy Advocate it had been his duty, because of the urgency of the case, to have Borthwick charged and arrested in the absence of the Lord Advocate. Far from delaying the conduct of the case, he had urged in the strongest and most earnest terms that the charge against Borthwick should go to a jury, at the Circuit in Glasgow in April last, *before Mr. Stuart was indicted*. He was much dissatisfied at the delay and abandonment of that case, *in consequence of instructions from the Lord Advocate*. It was unreasonable to make him responsible for the proceeding, which he had commenced, but which the Lord Advocate had interfered with; 'I was not activated by the desire to maintain the appearance of a charge against Borthwick until after Mr Stuart's trial … . He (the Lord Advocate) *finally abandoned* the prosecution which *I* instituted'. He still felt that Borthwick should have been brought to trial.

Hope pointed out that MP's enjoyed high and unquestionable impunities and it was their duty to proceed with caution, temper and forbearance in promulgating, with the privileges and authority of the situation, statements which involved the characters of others. He concluded, 'I cannot but admire the great liberality displayed in introducing charges of such a serious and grave character against the Lord Advocate and myself *without any previous communication of your intention*'.

Lucius' letter

On 6 July another letter was published entitled *Letter to John Hope Esq. containing strictures on his Letter to the Honourable James Abercromby MP*. It was signed with the pseudonym 'Lucius' but from its content and style was almost certainly written by Borthwick. He commented on every detail of Hope's letter for 21 pages. He criticised Hope for signing a document the contents of which he was ignorant. It was reasonable for others to assume that he was acting as counsel for Alexander and Borthwick in the case to which this document referred.

With reference to Hope's blaming the Lord Advocate for the delays in Borthwick's case Lucius wrote, 'It would have seemed quite as well to have kept that opinion to yourself: … Young men are often hazardous in giving opinions, which, in their maturer years, they would not have done' (Hope was 28 at the time). Despite blaming the Lord Advocate, Hope curiously had accepted the responsibility for all the aspects of the Borthwick case. Lucius comments:

> You say you are willing to bear the whole responsibility; that blame can be attached to no one but you, if you were wrong in treating Mr Borthwick in the manner you have done; in dragging that individual as a common felon in *chains* to prison; in bringing him forward for trial; in refusing to try him; in re-committing him;

refusing bail; denying his friends access to him; and after all this discharging him without trial, telling him to seek his remedy at law; still you have the confidence to assert that *this* injured man should have been tried for stealing his *own papers*, out of his *own private desk* .... You will – shelter yourself under the wings of office – a sure haven for all shipwrecked politicians, as long as the ministers can command majorities in the House of Commons.

You tell Mr Borthwick, a ruined man, to seek his remedy at law, against Alexander, or you, if he please. You well know, that from Alexander (a bankrupt) he can recover nothing, and to go to law against his Majesty's Advocate, would be madness ... . You might as well go to Rome and fight against the Pope ... Parliament alone, is the grand tribunal for granting redress to the meanest subject ... without ruining himself by incurring expenses ... . If I am not greatly mistaken, Mr Abercromby will prove such a case as will set your conduct throughout this affair in its proper light, and enable the House of Commons to do substantial justice to Mr Borthwick.[16]

Lucius added a PS:

Do you get the Scotsman on Saturday? I always do; and if you do not you should, as it would be of consequence to you. He has a capital article on the Advocate Depute today.

The Scotsman article of 6 July to which he referred is a criticism of Hope's letter to Abercromby, which the paper had published. It describes it as 'the most disgraceful publication that ever issued from the press of this city'. It refers to Hope as being young and inexperienced. It then examines Hope's letter in detail making many of the points noted by Lucius and was almost certainly written by the same hand – Borthwick?

William Menzies' letter

William Menzies, Alexander's unnamed counsel to whom Abercromby had referred in the debate, also decided to react to the criticism. He had no official standing in Stuart's trial, but was to act as prosecuting counsel in Borthwick's trial which was scheduled to be heard a week later. He too published a letter regarding Abercromby's speech.[17] He justified his request for witnesses to be removed during Stuart's trial saying that he made this request on only two occasions for witnesses who were due to give evidence at Borthwick's trial. He denied that he was aware that Borthwick's trial was going to be abandoned and declared that the

Lord Advocate had no part in that decision. He demanded to know who had given Abercromby false information. He trusted that Abercromby would make reparation by taking 'the earliest opportunity of publishing the ... facts of the case *in the same way* in which you did the misstatements of which I have so much reason to complain'.

Abercromby's duelling challenge

Abercromby, who had criticised the Scottish advocates freely under the protection of Parliamentary privilege, was provoked by the criticisms of himself contained in the letters of Hope and Menzies and reacted by letting it be known that he was proposing to challenge them to a duel.

Curiously, Abercromby's hostility was directed mainly against Menzies. The objectionable passage in his letter seems an extraordinarily mild statement to warrant the threat of a duel. It read:

> I shall be contented with saying, that in what you [in the *Courier*] put forth as a fair report of [your] speech, improper motives were, by very strong innuendo and implication, attributed to me. Such imputations I regard with the most perfect scorn, and I have now shown, that, *whoever* was the real author of them, they were altogether *unwarranted, groundless, and false.*[18]

Hope's letter had contained much more venom. J. W. Croker wrote to Scott on 8 July 1822:

> We are all in a pass here about Hope's letter. I have not yet read it, but those who have, think it not merely injudicious but as absolutely perilous. No one seems to doubt that it is a breach of privilege ... . The general opinion seems to be that the Whigs will not venture to have him to the bar, but will content themselves with pronouncing some bitter philippics against him & then condescend to pardon his offence in some contumelious way.[19]

Walter Scott replied on 12 July:

> I observe you are sadly annoyed about Hope. I cannot say I am – he shewd me his letter before publication & I pointed out to him the great chance of his being sent to Newgate [i.e. imprisoned] and also suggested addressing the letter rather to the Reporter than to the Member, but Hope a very fine fellow in point of talents and spirit declined the last mode as evasive ... . Is it then seriously to be maintaind that

a man may treat freely of the most important national concerns when they are the subject of debate in the House but that if his own character is taken away by a personal attack he is not entitled to vindicate himself.[20]

Hope and Menzies charged with breach of Parliamentary Privilege

Meanwhile, W. Courtney MP,[21] on 9 July moved a resolution to the House[22] that passages in the letters of Hope and Menzies amounted to a breach of the privileges of that House. He observed that:

> In the course of a debate, Abercromby was under the necessity of taking upon himself the disagreeable part of an accuser ... it would not be doubted that he was then discharging one of the most important functions which a member of the House could exercise. Any thing, therefore, which interfered with the free exercise of such a function, must be considered as a breach of the privileges of that House.

Courtney maintained that Hope's reaction to the words spoken by Abercromby in the conscientious discharge of his duty, were a most open and daring violation of the privileges of Parliament. 'The passages were of a nature to provoke feelings of hostility, and to bring the writer into direct personal altercation and contact with the individual to whom they were addressed.' In the interests of the House, 'they were bound to preserve their character and dignity, and to see that their most important privileges were preserved inviolate'. How could they boast of the freedom of debate, if subjected to such attacks? After some discussion in which Henry Brougham and Lord Binning took part it was ordered, 'That John Hope Esq. and Mr W. Menzies do attend this House on the 17th instant.'

It was required also that Abercromby be present.

It is probable that Courtney's motion was motivated by a desire to frustrate Abercromby's intention of challenging the two men to a duel. It must have been felt that there was a degree of urgency if a duel was to be avoided: the 17th was only eight days later and it would take two to three days to send a message to Edinburgh and three days for the recipients to travel to London. Messengers were sent immediately to notify Abercromby in London and Hope and Menzies in Edinburgh. The messenger sent to Abercromby reported back to the House that Abercromby had already left his London home the day before. He had set off on the road to Scotland accompanied by his butler. The messenger was ordered to try and catch up with him and require his return. The messengers to Edinburgh were despatched in a chaise with four horses and were provided with requisite powers for taking Mr Hope and Mr Menzies into custody and warrants instructing them to report to the House of Commons on the 17 July. The Sheriff of Edinburgh, when notified of the possible duel, bound over Hope and Menzies to keep the peace under a penalty of £5,000.[23]

Abercromby intercepted

Meanwhile Abercromby had reached the home of his Whig friend, Lord Althorp, in Northamptonshire. He sought the advice of Althorp, who agreed to act as his 'friend' in the matter and both set off together for Edinburgh. However, on reaching Ferrybridge the Parliamentary messenger caught up with them and informed Abercromby that his presence was required in the House of Commons. He abandoned his journey and returned to London. Abercromby reported to the House on the 12 July and was informed by the Speaker of the pending breach of privilege actions. The Speaker cautioned him against prosecuting any quarrel against Hope or Menzies by sending or accepting a challenge.

Cockburn wrote to Kennedy on 15 July:

I am rejoiced to learn from your letter … that Abercromby has returned to London.

The whole affair has made a great sensation here. The poor Tories seem dismayed and alarmed, and I have no doubt that the libelling system, at least in so far as it depends on his Majesty's servants, is nearly at the last gasp, and won't be soon renewed. The decided impression among sensible and liberal men as to Abercromby's last proceeding is – 1st That he ought not to have allowed himself to be drawn into a personal quarrel by almost anything that people he was obliged by public duty to arraign, could do. 2nd That if it was Menzies he was in pursuit of, he was pursuing a most unworthy antagonist. The very fact of little Menzies being selected as an object of combat by James Abercromby is an honour which has surprised all his friends, and will set him up higher than Newgate can put him down. But still pugnacity is the safe side for all gentlemen to err upon; and though we think Abercromby has helped to establish a bad precedent, that is but one feeling as to his conduct having been marked with that manliness and generosity which has all along distinguished him in these concerns. When I reflect indeed what he has done of late for Scotland, and to what risk he has exposed himself in our behalf, I know not how we can ever reward him. But if it be a reward to do good and to know that the extent of his services is equally attested by the admiration of the honest, and the terror of the base, he has it to the full … I trust that Abercromby won't let this personal affair make him think it indelicate in him to go on with Borthwick's case which would just be playing the enemy's game.[24]

Breaches repaired and duels avoided

Hope and Menzies duly turned up at the House of Commons on the 17 July 1822 to respond to the charge of breach of parliamentary privilege.[25] Hope said that he entertained the most profound respect for the House with the feeling of one who values, dearer than life, the liberty which it has secured and maintained. His letter was not published with any view of contemning the authority, or decrying the privileges of the House. His object was the vindication of his private and professional character and public conduct, and the correction of false statements. He had been charged in the debate of malicious prosecution and of wanton oppression – of having instituted a prosecution, he never intended seriously to insist – for the revolting purpose of prejudicing the cause of another person who was about to stand his trial in a case of life or death. It had been said that malignity and personal hatred had actuated his conduct. Abercromby had made no mention in the House that the Lord Advocate had overruled him and was responsible for the trial delays.

With regard to the charge that he had put his name to a document which defended the publishers of the *Sentinel* in a case of libel, he denied any knowledge of the contents of the document. He had signed the paper for one of his brother advocates without even knowing the names of the parties in the cause; signing pleadings without knowing what they were about, was a constant practice in Scottish courts. With regard to the imputation of malicious prosecution, it had been his intention, as stated in his letter, to have brought the case to a conclusion long before the trial of Stuart. He had embraced the first opportunity of endeavouring to remove the impression which these imputations and misstatements might have produced, by a contradiction and a defence as public as the way in which those imputations had been circulated throughout the country.

Sir Francis Burdett, a Whig MP, who had himself been jailed for breach of privilege, spoke up to question the right of the House to challenge an individual whose character and honour had suffered from the publication of a Parliamentary debate and who had asserted that its statements were untrue. How that could be called a breach of the privileges of the House, he was at a loss to determine.

> The power claimed by parliament was arbitrary: it was a power which would not be endured for a moment if attempted to be exercised by the king: and, therefore, its exercise was unbecoming the representatives of the people. It was a power which they ought not to exercise, even if they were the real representatives of the people, instead of being, as was notorious, the proprietors of boroughs in some instances, and the nominees of noble lords and country gentlemen in others.

Mr Brougham did not agree. The letter was a direct and substantial breach of privilege. It was a mistake to say that the letter was merely a complaint of a report of a speech said to have been spoken in that House. It was an attack upon a member and directly imputed to him as having been actuated by improper motives in the discharge of his duty. The house would be reduced to the most pitiable condition unless they opposed those who were determined to save the character of Mr. Hope, at the expense of the dignity and privileges of Parliament.

Lord Binning then spoke on behalf of his beloved friend and relative who had been brought from Scotland at a considerable expense, and with great professional inconvenience. Hope had been accused of having favoured an apparent prosecution of Borthwick, for the purpose of prejudging the case of a gentleman who was about to be put upon his trial for life or death. Good God! Was a gentleman to lie tamely under such a charge from a fear of a breach of the privileges of that House? If Mr Hope had not taken this step towards his vindication, it would have been impossible for him to have pursued his professional duties.

At the conclusion of the discussion Mr Courtney consented to withdraw his original motion, and asked the Speaker to inform Mr John Hope, '… that, under all the circumstances of the case, this House, taking into consideration the explanation given by him at the bar, and his expression of regret at his violation of its privileges, does not feel itself called upon to proceed farther in this matter'.

The case against Menzies was then considered very briefly. Abercromby had replied to his letter that he was not responsible for the newspaper reports of his speech. Menzies assumed from this that the newspaper reports had been false. He solemnly declared that he had not had the slightest idea that what he had written was a violation of the privileges of the House. It was ordered, 'That Mr Menzies, having explained his conduct to the satisfaction of this House, be excused from any farther attendance upon this House'.

The question must be asked whether there was a hidden agenda in this curious affair which occupied so much Parliamentary time. The letters of Hope and Menzies do not seem excessively objectionable in the context of many similar tirades of the time. Both men were reacting to what they considered were legitimate grievances with regard to statements made by Abercromby. Was Courtney's intervention motivated solely by a genuine regard for the rights and privileges of the House of Commons or was it a device to circumvent yet another duel resulting from the Scottish newspaper war? Whatever was his purpose, the fourth and fifth duels to be contemplated or carried out in connection with the *Beacon/Sentinel* publications, were averted.[26]

Robert Alexander's letter to Sir James Mackintosh

Robert Alexander then decided that it was his turn to give his reaction to the debate. On 12 August 1822 he published a letter of 76 pages, full of paranoia. The prolixity of the letter is indicated by the title which reads: *Letter to Sir J. Mackintosh, Knt. M.P. explanatory of the whole circumstances which led to the robbery of the Glasgow Sentinel Office; to the death of Sir Alexander Boswell Bart; to the Trial of Mr James Stuart Younger of Dunearn, and ultimately to the animadversions of the Honourable James Abercromby in the House of Commons upon the conduct of the Right Honourable the Lord Advocate and various individuals.*
Alexander said that:

> ... a more wanton attack upon private and professional reputation ... was never indulged in before the Commons of England. In these speeches, my conduct was misrepresented, and my humble character aspersed ... . The shafts, poison, and all, flew at midnight, to kill, or wound, or miss as they might; and the injury they have done cannot be calculated.

The laws of the land could afford him no redress:

> Mr Abercromby's assertions are sacred, and Mr Cockburn's venomous falsehoods pass like the deadly breath of the simoon, unpunished and unrevenged. The only shelter I can flee to is Public Opinion.

He had chosen Mackintosh rather than Abercromby as the addressee because he had a higher opinion of him than of Abercromby. He accused the Whigs of fomenting unrest, 'the political fanaticism which prevailed ... during 1819–20 was engendered and inflamed by the party ... who recognised you as their head'. He thought it exceedingly probable that the wretched person (Borthwick) whose cause had been so magnanimously espoused in the debate, will have left the kingdom before the next debate and you will be unable to expatiate upon his sufferings:

> upon the 'irons' he wore, or upon the 'firelocks' that lay beside him, or the hardships of punishing a man 'for stealing his own papers', or upon the 'damp cell' ... or upon the 'felon's fare' ... while [he] is gone where beyond the seas.

Alexander said that Rae had never subscribed either to the *Clydesdale Journal* or the *Sentinel* and that Rae's signature to the paper supporting the *Clydesdale Journal* had been forged. He claimed, without providing evidence, that Borthwick had chosen Dundee as the port of departure, as he would have been recognised if he had attempted to flee from a Clyde port. The loaded pistols were provided for the journey to Edinburgh because it had been rumoured that an attempt might be made to liberate Borthwick as they passed near Stuart's estate.

The original notice of the debate tabled on 2 April had been for a Parliamentary enquiry into the conduct of the Lord Advocate respecting the public press in Scotland. He criticised at length the last minute addition to the notice the words 'and more especially into the prosecution against William M. Borthwick'. Abercromby had obtained his information from Borthwick who had visited him in London only three days before the debate of 25 June. It gave the Lord Advocate no time to prepare his reply.

He admitted being the author of the article in the first issue of the *Sentinel* upon which Stuart had raised an Action of Damages for £5,000. 'I laughed at his empty threats, and asserted that my charges were true …'. His counsel M'Neill was of the opinion that he was able to justify the libel.

He criticised Mackintosh for praising Cockburn's speech at Stuart's trial which was full of misstatements and laboriously challenged every legal conclusion of the Glasgow magistrates regarding Borthwick's right to gain access to and remove papers from the *Sentinel* office. He disputed, with perhaps some justification, the interpretation of 'alternative conclusion' which Borthwick had accepted as giving him the right to resume the rights of partnership (see pp. 66–7).

He hinted that Stuart's funds had contributed to Borthwick's release from jail. He asserted that Borthwick had forcibly opened a desk drawer to obtain papers but made no reference to his opening the safe. He had been jailed for his unpaid debts to Borthwick on 22 June, on a charge presented by Borthwick's agent Ure but managed to obtain a bill of suspension and liberation after a few days. He objected to being called a bankrupt, but acknowledged that he had abandoned his charge against Borthwick for pecuniary reasons. The heavy expenses of the prosecution had 'thrown a shield over them'.

Parliament chose to ignore Alexander's effusion – which was much more offensive than the letters of Hope and Menzies – and there is no record that Mackintosh responded, but Borthwick did react in a letter to *The Scotsman* printed on 14 December 1822. He denied that Sir William Rae's name had been forged. He wished an opportunity of telling the public that this charge, like almost every other assertion in Alexander's letter, was 'utterly false'. The signature was genuine.

'If otherwise why does not the Lord Advocate, who is so deeply implicated, or Mr John Hope, who has not been always disinclined to commence legal proceedings, institute an action against me for forgery or fraud? ... . You will greatly oblige a very unfortunate and ill-used individual, if you allow him to enter this caveat with the public, against listening to the assertions in Alexander's letter'.

Cockburn's copy of Alexander's letter has, in Cockburn's handwriting, a note in the first page saying, 'A tissue of lies from beginning to end, HC'.

The second Parliamentary debate

As soon as the first debate was finished, Abercromby, realising the mistake that he had made by introducing Borthwick's case without preliminary notification, immediately gave notice that he was going to raise this matter again on a future occasion. Because of difficulty and delay in obtaining the relevant documents to be laid before the House, the opportunity did not arrive until a year later by which time the Parliamentary Papers relating to the Borthwick affair had been printed and tabled. These consisted of 147 pages of legal documents. One wonders how many Members took the opportunity of studying them. On 3 June 1823 Abercromby resumed his attack on the Lord Advocate.[27]

Abercromby gave the members of the House a reprise of his Borthwick speech of 25 June 1822 with greater detail. On this occasion he was careful to exclude John Hope from his assault:

> It was true that Mr. Hope avowed, in a very manly manner, the share which he had taken in the affair; but, let him stand or fall in public estimation by his conduct; he would call for no opinion of the house upon it. Under all the circumstances, and with the best consideration he could give it, he felt justified in calling for the opinion of the house upon the conduct of the Lord Advocate only.

He concluded:

> Such were the facts of Borthwick's case; but he could not avoid asserting, what unquestionably gave him pain, that there was an intimate connexion between the trial of Mr. Stuart and the proceedings against Borthwick ... it was clear, from the very terms of the indictment against Mr. Stuart that it was meant to connect his case with that of Borthwick. Statements were introduced into the indictment merely for this purpose, and which had nothing in the world to do with the charge against Mr. Stuart. No man could doubt that if the proceeding against Borthwick had been attended with success, it would most deeply have injured Mr. Stuart. It was plain that in the minds of the prosecutors of both there was an intimate connexion. Under

such circumstances, it was especially incumbent upon the learned lord to show that he had acted most carefully and deliberately, with a determination not only not to oppress an individual, but not to turn the circumstance of his confinement to the prejudice of Mr. Stuart. It was impossible to point out any course that could more effectually produce that impression, than the course that had been pursued; and *the learned lord was the most unfortunate man in the world, if all these coincidences had happened without design.*

He moved, 'that the conduct and proceedings of the Lord Advocate of Scotland in the case of William Borthwick ... were unjust and oppressive'.

Rae responded by accepting that as Lord Advocate he was responsible for all Scottish prosecutions, including those initiated by his deputies. He considered that John Hope had reasonable grounds for charging Borthwick, although when he first obtained the papers of the case, while in London on 5 August 1822, he had thought the case was not suitable for trial and countermanded Hope's arrangements. Rae totally ignored Abercromby's accusations that he had kept Borthwick in jail unjustifiably, and made no comment on the damning coincidence of Borthwick's liberation without trial immediately after Stuart's case had been concluded. He made the extraordinary statement that if Borthwick had suffered through being in prison, his sufferings were probably less than he would have suffered if he had escaped to America and lived as an outcast there. He declared that he had acted upon pure and conscientious motives. If the same circumstances were to occur again he would take the same line of conduct.

Several members contributed to the subsequent debate, one making the valid point, 'that the learned lord had totally passed by, or mistaken, the nature of the accusation.'

When the House divided, Ayes had 96 and Noes 102 votes. Although the motion was lost by six votes, the narrow margin compared with the previous years vote indicated a considerable swing of opinion against the Lord Advocate. He had survived, but with much discredit and his failure to explain or justify the timing of events left the inevitable impression that Borthwick had been used as a pawn in the greater case of Stuart with his connivance.

Borthwick's letter to Sir William Rae

As far as Parliament was concerned that was the end of the matter, but Borthwick refused to allow it to rest there. On 25 September 1823 he wrote a *Letter to Sir William Rae M.P., Lord Advocate of Scotland* but did not send it or have it published until 9 February 1825. At this later date he inserted a covering note to explain why he had not sent it earlier. It was because he entertained a hope:

> of being able to procure some recompense from his Majesty's Minister for the ruin
> and unparalleled hardships heaped upon me by you and your Deputy, John Hope
> Esq. These hopes have been futile … . May I … humbly but earnestly implore you
> to act to me as common justice requires one human being to act to another.

The remarks in his printed letter of 21 pages are so critical of the Lord
Advocate that, had the letter been delivered when first written, his hopes for
compensation from that source would certainly not have been fulfilled. He
challenged every assertion of Rae in his Parliamentary speeches in the two
debates at tiresome length. He had not forged Rae's name. He did not steal
anything for the papers were his by right. He had not forced open any desk or
interfered with the iron safe (which contradicted his own earlier statements).
The remarks respecting 'picklocks' were notoriously false (although the
evidence of others asserted that a smith had been called). 'As to your insisting
"that theft was distinctly made out," I have only to say, that if it was made out,
you are totally unfit for the situation you hold as Lord Advocate of Scotland
because you refused to try me for the crime, …'. He attacked John Hope with
particular rancour. 'He persecuted me by every means in his power. He put me
THREE different times to the expense of preparing for trial … and finally he
set me at liberty, not daring to try me.' Rae had said that there was a remedy for
false imprisonment 'but you tell me that "you are not liable" … Where then am
I to seek redress? Am I to seek it from Alexander, a man who you know is a
bankrupt, … . This is truly pitiful'.

With reference to Rae's remark that he had suffered less in prison than he
would if he had made his escape, Borthwick said that this attempt to palliate his
sufferings 'says little for either your head or your heart'. He had not absconded.
He was in Dundee on business to make enquiries about the purchase of a
newspaper. He was living quite openly and his agent had offered to produce
him at once, if he would be given bail.

Borthwick continued:

> I have now, my Lord, gone over what I consider the most material part of your grand
> defence; and you must see from what I have proven, that what has gone forth as
> your speech is gross misrepresentation, and that it has injured me in a very serious
> manner; and I call upon you and your friends for redress … I hope that when you
> have read this letter, you will, by some public act, shew me and the country that you
> regret misrepresenting me …

and concluded:

> … I have been ruined in circumstances by your Deputy's procedure, ruined in character by statements said to be your Lordship's, which I trust I have shewn to be founded in error … . I am rendered the most wretched of beings …

and signed off:

> … I have the sorrow to be Your Lordship's much injured humble servant
> W. M. Borthwick

Borthwick's letter must have fallen on stony ground. He received no apology or compensation for his wrongful imprisonment. Although his motives and actions were not always as honourable as he made out, he deserved better, for the weight of evidence indicates that he was the victim of a gross miscarriage of justice at the hands of the Lord Advocate and his deputy. An apology or compensation would have been an admission of guilt which they were not prepared to acknowledge. Cockburn, Borthwick's counsel, referring *inter alia* to 'the pretence of accusing Borthwick of theft' wrote:

> No one can have lived … in Edinburgh in my day without finding much in its public characters and transactions to be loved and admired, a great deal to be overlooked, and something to be unsparingly condemned.[28]

John Hope and Duncan M'Neill both emerged unscathed from the attacks on their conduct, Hope becoming Dean of the Faculty in 1839 and Lord Justice Clerk in 1841 (in succession to David Boyle who had presided over Stuart's trial). M'Neill became in turn Solicitor General and President of the Court of Session with the title of Lord Colonsay. Sir William Rae retained his post as Lord Advocate for Scotland during the Tory administrations until his death in 1842. The fact that he was not raised to the bench, as was customary with most Lord Advocates, may imply a degree of criticism among his legal colleagues.

At the annual Whig dinner on 26 January 1824, celebrating Fox's birthday, the health of the 'Honourable James Abercromby' was proposed to loud applause. Mention was made of his many political endeavours on behalf of the poor and his efforts toward parliamentary reform:

> But … upon no occasion did he rise so high in the estimation of his country as when he brought under the notice of Parliament the state of the public press in Scotland.

When ... no character, however inoffensive and virtuous, was secure from malignity and detraction; and when this part of the press was not only not checked by the legal authorities, but countenanced, if not supported, by them, it required a powerful arm and an undaunted spirit to drag the monster to light, if not to condign punishment.[29]

Notes

1   James Abercromby, attended the Edinburgh High School with Francis Horner and Henry Brougham. He studied law in London and was appointed a barrister in Lincoln's Inn in 1801. He became a Whig Member of Parliament from 1807 eventually becoming Speaker in 1835. On his retirement in 1839 he was made a peer as Baron Dunfermline. Throughout has parliamentary career he maintained a close interest in the affairs of Edinburgh.

2   Cockburn (1874b): *Letters chiefly concerned with the Affairs of Scotland from Lord Cockburn to Thomas Francis Kennedy*. In a letter to Kennedy, 14 June 1822, Cockburn wrote: 'There is talk of sending Borthwick and a very clever man, Henderson his agent, up to London instantly to explain everything. I hope it will be done'. Alexander in his letter to Mackintosh says that the meeting took place three days before the debate.

3   *Hansard*, 25 June 1822, vol. 7 cc1324–72. The same debate is available, with minor variations, in a separate pamphlet entitled *Proceedings in the House of Commons on Mr Abercromby's Motion for enquiring into the Conduct of the Lord Advocate and othe Law Officers, in connection with the Public Press of Scotland* (1822) Edinburgh, J. Dick & Co.

4   Cockburn described the powers of the Lord Advocate. ' The Privy council of Scotland, the Grand Jury of Scotland, the Commander-in-chief of the Forces of Scotland, – the guardian of the police of the country ... the general management of the business of Government, is devolved upon him.' He had large and undefined patronage. No one man was armed with so great power in Europe. *Edinburgh Review*, **39,** pp. 363–92. After the passing of the Reform Act in 1832, Earl Grey restricted the powers of the Lord Advocate to matters of legal importance only. Cockburn (1874a): *Journal of Henry Cockburn 1831–1854*, **I** p. 35.

5   Stevenson's poster accusing Stuart of cowardice.

6   Duncan M'Neill (1793–1874) as Advocate Depute had signed the indictment against Stuart in 1822 and took part in the trial. He acted as counsel for the proprietors of the *Beacon* in the actions raised against them by James Gibson-Craig and Lord Hamilton. He also acted for Robert Alexander, proprietor of the *Sentinel*, in the action raised against him by James Stuart.

7   Anon (1822): *Trial 2*, Appendix VI.

8   He was wrong. A previous Lord Advocate, Charles Hope, the father of Rae's deputy John Hope, was arraigned before the House in 1804 for a rather similar misjudgement, again with a political background. Cockburn (1909): *Memorials of his time*, pp. 177–8.

9   'Yet the Lord Advocate – the grand conservator of the peace in Scotland, – the high functionary vested with almost regal powers, – the public officer, who, of all others, is pledged to maintain the respectability, of all legal proceedings, – does put his name to a certificate or manifesto in favour of this obscure, scurrilous, and unprincipled journal!' Article in *The Scotsman*, 22 June 1822

10   Rae was sent a copy of each issue. Rosslyn correspondence NAS GD164/452/15

11   Sir James Mackintosh (1765–1832) was a Scottish doctor who moved to London, where he became interested in politics and qualified as a lawyer and was knighted for his legal contributions. He entered Parliament as a Whig in 1813. He wrote a number of books on the history of England. Mackintosh was one of four Whig lawyers and politicians, who feature in this book, who became Rectors of Glasgow University. He was preceded by Francis Jeffrey and succeeded by Henry Brougham and Henry Cockburn.

12   Cockburn (1909): *Memorials*, p. 374.

13   MacKenzie (1890): *Old Reminiscences of Glasgow*, p. 381.

14   Scott (1932–37) *The Letters of Sir Walter Scott,* **VII**, p. 204. Letter to J. W. Croker, 2 July 1822.
15   Ibid, p. 205. Scott wrote: 'The feeling here is that Abercromby has acted unhandsomely in con-
      founding Hope's case with the Advocate's'. With regard to Hope signing M'Neill's paper: 'This a
      courtesy which no lawyer ever thought of refusing & it is the every day practice. Hope had no
      more to do with that paper than I have and never saw a line of it ...'.
16   This refers to Abercromby's statement that he was to introduce a further debate on Borthwick's
      case.
17   Letter dated 29 June 1822 published in the *Caledonian Mercury, Courier* and *Glasgow Herald* on
      8 July 1822 and the *Morning Chronicle* on 10 July 1822.
18   Ibid.
19   Scott (1932–37), p. 209, fn. Letter from J. W. Croker, 2 July 1822. Scott and Hope were later
      to become closely associated as Governor and Deputy Governor respectively of the Scottish
      Union and Life Insurance Company.
20   From a letter to Croker quoted in Cline (1971): *The fate of Cassandra: The Newspaper War of
      1821–22 and Sir Walter Scott,* p. 49–53.
21   William Courtney (1777–1859) came from a wealthy land owning family. He was a barrister
      and an MP from 1812–26, unattached to either of the main parties but acutely aware of the
      rights of Parliament. In 1819 he successfully proposed the committal of John Hobhouse to
      Newgate prison for breach of Parliamentary privilege in a pamphlet entitled *A trifling mistake.*
22   *Hansard,* 9 July 1822, vol. 7 cc1548–58.
23   Reports in *Caledonian Mercury,* 13 July 1822 and *Glasgow Herald,* 15 July 1822.
24   Cockburn (1874b), pp. 63–4.
25   *Hansard,* 17 July 1822, vol. 7 cc1668–92.
26   The others, apart from the Boswell/Stuart duel, were James Gibson's challenge to Walter Scott
      and James Stuart's challenge to Sir William Rae.
27   *Hansard,* 3 June 1823, vol. 9 cc664–90
28   Cockburn (1909): *Memorials,* pp. 367–76.
29   Article in *The Scotsman,* 28 January 1824. Cockburn in a letter to Kennedy on 1 July 1822
      wrote: 'It is impossible to convey to you an idea of the gratefulness of the relieved people here to
      Abercromby. For his exertions ... we owe him more than we can ever repay'. See also Cockburn
      (1909): *Memorials,* p. 387.

CHAPTER 10

Epilogue

It hurts us deeply in the eyes of the world that men who are bound by their oath and by every proper consideration to conduct a faithful part in the management of the affairs of others should in order to supply their own extravagance involve many persons in heavy losses and among them those very persons whose affairs it was their duty to protect.

Secretary, WS Society, 8 August 1828

This poor man fell like myself a victim of speculation.

Sir Walter Scott, *Journal,* 9 February 1829

The law as applied to duelling is worse than a dead letter; it is partial, blind, uncertain, revolting, inoperative, and should therefore be abrogated or amended.[1]

Sir James Boswell and the Auchinleck estate

JAMES BOSWELL (1807–57) succeeded to his father's baronetcy aged 15 and as Sir James, became the 11th Laird of Auchinleck, burdened with its heavy debts. His father had spent much money on the purchase of his parliamentary seat, on ill-advised land purchases at inflated prices during the Napoleonic Wars and had personal debts of £32,000. It was many years before the debts were paid off. In 1824, his mother Grace, the daughter of a wealthy Edinburgh banker, purchased the contents of Auchinleck House from the creditors for £3,000 and gave them to her son.[2] She continued to live there until her death in 1884.

Young Sir James went to Oxford University in 1824 and returned to live the life of a country gentleman at Auchinleck. He had no pretensions to scholarship or politics but enjoyed life as a farmer and sportsman. He was a deputy lieutenant in the Ayrshire Yeomanry and a keen racehorse owner. John Frederik Herring painted his portrait with his racehorse, Constantine, a winner at Ayr in 1839. In 1830, he married his cousin Jessie Jane, the daughter of Sir James Montgomery-Cuninghame and had two daughters, Julia and Emily. He predeceased his mother, dying in 1857, aged 50. Having no son, the baronetcy was extinguished at his death.

The estate of Auchinleck had been entailed in the male line by his great-grandfather, Lord Auchinleck, but Sir James had been able to have the entail set aside because of a technical error in the original deed, which the Court of Session considered rendered it invalid.[3] This foresight enabled the estate to be passed on after his death, to his mother until her death in 1884. Thereafter it was passed on successively to Jane's older daughter Julia and on her death in 1905, to the son of the younger daughter Emily, the Hon. James Boswell Talbot de Malahide. He seldom visited the estate and the house was left unoccupied for long periods. The contents, including the library, were gradually disposed of at auction. In 1920 the estate was sold to a distant Boswell relation, Colonel John Douglas Boswell of Garrallan, who during the Second World War made the house and estate available to the Free French, Canadian and Polish forces. In 1986 the house, much damaged by age and neglect, having been unoccupied for many years, was sold by descendants of Colonel Boswell to the Landmark Trust. The Trust has since carried out extensive restoration and Auchinleck House (Fig. 29) is once more an elegant stately home accessible to the public.[4]

James Stuart

After the trial, Stuart returned to the life of a country laird at Dunearn. His reputation in the community had, if anything, been enhanced and he became increasingly involved in local affairs in Fife and Edinburgh. He won an award for his Fife oxen at the Highland Show and was appointed convenor of the judging committee. In 1825 he was elected president of the Gowks (cuckoo) Club, one of the many dining clubs which existed in Edinburgh at that time. Included among its members were six of the seven counsel who had represented Stuart at his trial – Francis Jeffrey, James Moncreiff, Henry Cockburn, John Murray, John Cuninghame and William Gibson, also Lord Gillies, one of the judges who had presided at the trial.[5] The Club met annually on All Fools' Day and at 1826 meeting the venerable Henry Mackenzie,[6] aged 81, poet laureate of the club, sent a poem to explain his absence, one verse of which reads:

> Alas! In vain your card invites
> To share your first of April rites;
> My answer must be still the same
> As when your first kind summons came,
> Half blind, half deaf, and wholly lame! –
> I would not now when turn'd fourscore
> Tax my good friends with such a bore;

With yard-long stories, often told,
Of things that passed in times of old,
When Scotland, now so vain of self,
Was rich in men, though poor in pelf;
Or, with my trumpet at my ear,
Earnest to listen, scarce to hear,
Speak, still for mutual talk unable,
Cross-purposes across the table,
And, therefore, as I am not dumb
As well as deaf, I must not come.

....

Think then dear Sir, how much I grieve
To send my answer negative:–
Yet give I pray, his kindest greeting
From your poor Laureate to the meeting:

Stuart although president at the time was absent on this occasion.

Stuart continued to serve as a convenor of the Firth of Forth Ferries Committee set up to improve the ferries from Leith and Newhaven on the south shore of the Forth to Burntisland, Kinghorn, Kirkcaldy, Dysart and Pettycur on the north shore. He was appointed to the Council of the newly founded Caledonian Horticultural Society. He continued to act as a director of the North British Fire and Life Insurance Company. In his capacity as secretary of the Edinburgh Joint Stock Water Company he arranged to buy the Pentland springs to augment the ever increasing demand for water by the city. These springs belonged to Sir Robert Liston for which £2,500 was paid. [7]

Investment in property

There is no evidence that Stuart was short of money. He invested heavily in property speculation during the years 1823–25, including the purchase of an estate of 11,000 acres in the County of Ross. An item in the *Inverness Courier* of 5 August 1824, records that:

> Mr Stuart, younger of Dunearn, while passing through Dingwall on his way to the estate of Strathconon, which he has lately purchased, happened to learn that a gentleman was confined in the jail of that town under circumstances which strongly excited his feelings. Mr Stuart immediately lodged £60 with the Magistrate of

Dingwall and secured the prisoner's enlargement. The debt was for £50. What enhanced this humane act is that Mr Stuart never heard of any of the parties concerned till his visit to Dingwall.

Perhaps Stuart recalled how Borthwick had been liberated from jail in a like manner. This extraordinary act of generosity was not an isolated event. There are records of Stuart's donations to memorials for Lord Erskine and James Watt and towards a fund for the uninsured individuals who had suffered in the great fires which destroyed large areas of the High Street and Parliament Square in 1824. His extensive land speculations, however, proved ill-advised and the financial crash of 1825–26 reduced him to bankruptcy as it did many others, including Sir Walter Scott.

Financial disaster

Rumours of Stuart's financial difficulties and of his inappropriate borrowings from the Widows' Fund must have been in circulation, for on 5 July 1828 Cockburn wrote from London to Macvey Napier,[8] librarian of the Signet Library, that those who knew Stuart would 'resort to any fancy rather than yield to the belief that one they thought so pure and firm can have imitated the paltriness of common debtors'.[9] The following day in another letter to Napier:[10]

> Pray write me a line at your leisure, saying if anything further has transpired.
> I have seen nobody who seems at all aware of what is soon to be made public ...
> I have explained it to Richardson[11] and [Leonard] Horner in order that they
> may be prepared to describe it as an ordinary retirement...but of course no
> permanent delusion of this kind can be kept up.

Eight days later on 13 July 1828, Stuart with Maria fled to Liverpool en route to America in order to escape his creditors. He wrote a letter from Liverpool on the 15th to his friend James Gibson, now Sir James Gibson-Craig, tendering his resignation as Collector of the Widows' Fund – a post which he held for 10 years. The Clerk of the WS Society, John Hamilton, alarmed by the circumstances of this precipitate resignation, immediately instituted a search for the accounts of the Widows' Fund. Stuart's cash book was recovered from his home in Moray Place which revealed that Stuart owed the Fund £4,188 (approximately £400,000 today) exclusive of a considerable sum of interest. The finances of the Fund were found to be in a state of disorder. Regular accounts had not been kept, obligatory contributions to the Fund by members of the Society had not been paid and interest due had not been collected. On 7 August 1828 John Home was instructed on to call a meeting of the Trustees without delay.[12] The Clerk wrote to Colin Mackenzie on 8 August:

> … another blow to our Society or perhaps a further purging of it – both terms are applicable. It hurts us deeply in the eyes of the world that men who are bound by their oath and by every proper consideration to conduct a faithful part in the management of the affairs of others should in order to supply their own extrava-gance involve many persons in heavy losses and among them those very persons whose affairs it was their duty to protect. … I have forgot to tell you that Jas. Stuart is the man who has gone to ruin … . The circumstance of his flying the country has a wretched appearance … [13]

William Cadell wrote in a letter to a friend on 20 August 1828:

> James Stewart of Dunearn WS who has been engaged in so many speculations in land and otherwise, sailed for America about the middle of last month without the knowledge of any persons and has left many large debts both heritable & personal, it is feared that his deficiencies will be considerable, and that some of his near Relations and Clients will suffer severely; he has long lived offensively, but says in a letter he left behind, that he never supposed himself to be insolvent, till about the middle of June … [14]

On 1 September 1828, two months after Stuart's departure to America, Cadell, as treasurer of the Bank of Scotland, obtained a sequestration order on his properties. Stuart had defaulted on repayment of £1,000 due to the Bank.

Sequestration

An accountant, Thomas Mansfield, was appointed trustee of the sequestration. He promptly prepared a list of Stuart's assets which were remarkably extensive.[15] In addition to his Dunearn estate and house at Hillside, Aberdour in Fife, his Edinburgh house, 2 North Charlotte Street (Fig. 30) with its stables and coach house, and his estate in Strathconon in Ross-shire, he had bought and now lived in the grand newly-built house, 20 Moray Place in Edinburgh's New Town (Fig. 31). He owned several flats in Hanover Street and several tenements in the Old Town which had been bought by his grandfather James Stuart, Lord Provost of Edinburgh. Another recent purchase was the mansion house of Drumsheugh, once the home of the Earl of Moray. This house with extensive grounds lay immediately to the west of his New Town properties and was due for demolition as the New Town development extended westward into the Moray Estate. He owned half an acre of land at Bruntsfield links with a mansion house and other dwellings. He had bought a number of properties around the town of Haddington in East Lothian and had extended his two estates by purchasing further land, dwellings and sporting rights including salmon fishing on the river Alness. The various properties are detailed in 88 closely-written pages.

Stuart's debt to the Widows' Fund was backed by sureties to the extent of £5,000 which had been provided by his relation, James Farquhar Gordon, his friend Sir Ronald Ferguson of Raith and his father Charles Stuart, who had died two years before. On 18 October 1828, Gordon reported to the Society that Stuart's debt to the Widows' Fund would be paid by Martinmas next, i.e. the 11 November, and that promise seems to have been fulfilled.[16] The repayment must have been made by his sureties, for the sequestration process had hardly begun. Whether or not Stuart's sister, Alison Carmichael, as executor of her father's estate, had to contribute is not on record. The earliest available accounts of the Widows' Fund, prepared by Stuart's successor, commence in 1829, the year after he resigned, and record only one debt still owed by Stuart for the sum of £34 – presumably an outstanding interest payment. This debt was cleared in the following year's account.

During his absence in America, Stuart's possessions were sold at a series of auctions. An early estimate valued his estate at £250,000 (well over £20 million today), but his friend and legal advisor, James Gibson-Craig wrote that, 'I fear that there will be a large defalcation of funds to pay the debts'.[17] The first sale, commencing 20 November 1828, consisted of the contents of 20 Moray Place. The sale of his wines and spirits followed and the house itself was sold to become a private hotel 'which combine[d] so much internal elegance and comfort with the finest local situation in Edinburgh'.[18] Curiously, 20 Moray Place was later to become the home of John Hope, who as Advocate Depute and a backer of the *Beacon*, had been much involved in the trial of Stuart. The sale of the contents of his Fife home at Hillside commenced on 10 December, the house itself having been let for the past year. The tenant had 'the privilege of using the whole walks and rides on the estate of Hillside and of shooting over it and the adjoining estate of Dunearn'.[19] The book sale from Stuart's enormous library, which commenced on 26 January 1829, lasted 14 days and was followed by a sale of his late father's library on 18 March which lasted no less than 33 days. Religious, historical and legal texts formed the bulk of these sales.

The sale of Stuart's paintings

The most valuable of these enforced sales was Stuart's collection of paintings, which started on 9 February 1829 and lasted three days. The young 5th Duke of Buccleuch, a keen collector of art works, commissioned Sir Walter Scott who had been his guardian during his minority, to buy paintings on his behalf. Scott looked over the collection on 2 February and considered that the most important painting, Hobbema's *Avenue at Middelharnis* (Fig. 32), was 'fitter for an artist's studio than a nobleman's collection ... . It is the last thing I would buy from my own taste, yet they seem to think it capital'. To the Duke he wrote: Your Grace may be reconciled to it by the figure of a shooter and a Spanish pointer who are coming down the road in quest of waterfowl. Would you like this or no?' He described other pictures to the Duke including a Watteau of three figures, a landscape by Berghem and a picture of James VI. 'There is no saying how these things may sell here, perhaps very cheap in which case I will take my chance of getting one or two for Bowhill or Langholm if not worthy of Dalkeith or Drumlanrig' (some of the Duke's homes).[20]

On the first day of the auction, Scott wrote in his *Journal*:

> At twelve I went to Stuart of Dunearn's sale of pictures. This poor man fell like myself a victim of speculation, and though I had no knowledge of him personally, and disliked him as the Causer of poor Sir Alexander Boswell's death, yet 'had he been slaughterman to all my kin', I could but pity the miserable sight of this splendid establishmen[t] broken up and his treasures of art exposed to public and unsparing sale. I wanted a picture of the Earl of Rothes for the Duke of Buccleuch, a fine Joshua [Reynolds], but Balfour of Balbirnie fancied it also and having followed it to 160 guineas [I let it go] ... . This job took me up the whole morning to little purpose.

The sale was reported in the *Edinburgh Evening Courant* of 12 February 1829. 'The collection might with truth be said to have been one of the most select and valuable ever brought to sale in Scotland; ...'. Among the old masters on offer were paintings by Guido, Murillo, Corregio, Van Dyck, Rembrandt, Cuyp, Hobbema, Ruysdael, Watteau, Brueghel and Holbein, and of the 'modern painters' were works by Reynolds, Raeburn, J. Thomson, Ewbank, Geikie and the Naysmiths. A landscape by Ruysdael sold for £36 15s and another by Jan Both, 'certainly the finest in the Collection' for which Stuart was said to have paid £700, was bought for 126 guineas. The *Wife of Rubens* by Van Dyck was sold for £57 15s and *Butcher* by Rembrandt for £34 13s. The *Great Fire of London* by Van der Poel, valued at £500, went for 30 guineas and *Noahs's*

Ark by Brueghel for 82 guineas. The Hobbema, spurned by Scott, fetched the highest price in the sale – 195 guineas.[21] A *Fête Champètre* by Watteau, for which Stuart had refused an offer of £1200, sold for 100 guineas. Sets of prints of the *Marriage-a-la-Mode* and the *Rake's Progress*, which had once belonged to Hogarth's widow, sold for 21 guineas. If the attribution to these great masters was accurate, this must have been the bargain sale of all time and would have come as a great disappointment to Stuart, for many of these paintings had been in the family for several generations and were highly regarded. Perhaps it was fortunate that he was out of the country at the time of the sale.

The sequestration process continued for several years. Creditors received dividends at intervals from 21 February 1830. In 1838, David Erskine, an uncle of Stuart's, died leaving him his estate of Carnock.[22] The will was disputed by the family who questioned Erskine's capability of making a rational settlement of his affairs. He was described as being of very eccentric habits and spent his latter years being looked after in the households of clergy. After four years of legal debate and a series of court hearings, the sequestration trustee, Thomas Mansfield, managed to obtain a compromise agreement, in May 1842, providing Stuart's sequestration fund with £4,500.[23]

Stuart's travels in North America

Stuart sailed with his wife to New York on 16 July 1822[24] and spent three years touring the eastern states, no doubt very glad to be away from it all. He seemed to enjoy his travels and on his return to Britain he wrote *Three years in North America,* published in 1833. In the Preface he wrote that, 'he had not been accustomed to write for the press, and makes no pretension to literary attainments', but in fact he wrote an entertaining travelogue which brought him a modest income. He mentions that everywhere he went people enquired about Walter Scott, Henry Brougham and Thomas Chalmers. The eloquent writings of these men must have been widely circulated in America. In the library of New Orleans he was surprised and pleased to find that the only British newspaper taken was *The Scotsman*, 'a paper which has uniformly maintained a high character, not only for talent, but for the consistency and constitutional soundness of the political opinion which it advocated.' The librarian told him that *The Scotsman* had been recommended to her as the best of the twice-a-week newspapers.[25]

The Scotsman responded to this tribute by publishing, a lengthy and generally favourable review of the book on 12 January 1833:

We have no hesitation in saying that it presents the most earnest and faithful picture of the State of North American Republic with which we are acquainted ... Mr Stuart's statements, though delivered in plain language bear the impress of truth and fidelity. He appreciates the virtues of the Americans, and is not blind to their faults. Mixing freely with men of all classes and professions, he has described American life as it presented itself to his eye, with its lights and shadows, its blemishes and beauties ...

Others gave *Three years in North America* less favourable criticism because of Stuart's tendency to compare things at home unfavourably with what he found in America. The prisons were better there. He told President Jackson, who had greeted him warmly, that education was better in the States than in Scotland. When he visited the sites of battles of the War of Independence he invariably commented that the tactics of the revolutionaries had been superior to those of the British. A particular critic was Major General Sir John Lambert, a distinguished veteran of the American War of Independence and of Waterloo, who published angry rebuttals of Stuart's opinions.

Attitudes to slavery

Slavery was a very contentious issue at that time and several of the individuals encountered in this book had strong opinions. James Boswell for example disagreed with his mentor, Samuel Johnson, who had stated that '... it may be doubted whether slavery can ever be supposed the natural condition of man.'[26] Boswell regarded the abolition movement as:

A wild and dangerous attempt ... to abolish so very important and necessary branch of commercial interest ... . To abolish a *status* which in all ages GOD has sanctioned and man has continued, would not only be robbery to an innumerable class of our fellow subjects, but it would be extreme cruelty to the African Savages, a portion of whom it saves from massacre or intolerable bondage in their own country ...[27]

On the day on which William Wilberforce first introduced the Slave Trade Bill (18 April 1793), James Boswell published a 24-page poem entitled *No Abolition of Slavery* inscribed to 'The Respectable Body of West India Planters and Merchants' in which he attempted to justify slavery in crude verse, of which the following extract is an example:

Noodles, who rave for abolition
Of the African's improved condition,

At your own cost fine projects try;
Don't rob – from pure humanity.[28]

In 1833 (the year in which the Abolition of Slavery Act was finally passed), Stuart's sister, Alison Carmichael, who had lived for several years in the West Indies, published a book *Domestic Manners and Social Condition of the White, Coloured, and Negro Population of the West Indies*. In this she robustly defended the practice of slavery and the plantation owners, than whom 'no class of men on earth [were] more calumniated'.[29] Stuart on the other hand in his *Three Years in North America,* published in the same year, roundly condemned the practice of slavery in America – as did most of his Whig friends including the ardent abolitionist, Henry Brougham. In the northern states, Stuart noted that the slaves were treated kindly. There the white population agreed that abolition would be desirable 'but no plan had yet been thought of by which so desirable an object may be attained'. A Free Black Society had been founded for the purpose of repatriating slaves to Liberia. The sum of £7.10 shillings could secure the freedom of a slave, pay his passage and give him thirty acres of fertile land. Stuart quoted President Nott of Union College in New York: 'It is as wise as merciful, to send back to Africa, as citizens, those sons of hers whom, as slaves and in chains, we have to our injury borne from thence'.[30]

Stuart was appalled by the condition of slaves in the southern states where:

Slaves were much more common, they were harshly treated, given little clothing and no bedding and were severely punished for trivial offences by whipping, wearing irons or being put in stocks. No education was offered. Their status was 'not much removed from the brute'.

He described a tragic scene:

A slave ship for New Orleans was lying in the stream, and the poor negroes, hand cuffed and pinioned were hurried off in boats, eight at a time. Here I witnessed the last farewell, – the heart-rending separation of every earthly tie. The mute and agonizing embrase [*sic*] of the husband and wife, and the convulsive grasp of the mother and child were alike torn asunder – for ever! It was a living death, – they never see or hear of each other more. Tears flowed fast, and mine with the rest.[31]

Stuart's return

Stuart returned to England in May 1831. His debts must have been enormous, for despite the sale of his possessions his creditors had still not received full payment. At first he lived in Jersey for six months, partly because the cost of living there was less than on the mainland and possibly also to avoid his creditors. However, the compelling need to find a job and earn an income obliged him to come to London, hoping that the recent establishment of a Whig government might enable him to obtain a government appointment with the help of his Whig friends. He approached the Brougham brothers, Henry and James, who had been his close friends for many years, for their help in obtaining a job. Henry had been a fellow student at University of Edinburgh and James had acted as Stuart's stopgap second at the duel. Both brothers were Whig Members of Parliament, and Henry was then in a position of influence as Lord Chancellor with the title of Baron Brougham and Vaux. Stuart hoped for a job as consul or secretary to a governor in one of the colonies. Eventually he got a tentative offer of the post of consul in the small Ionian island of Zanti. After months of anxious waiting for confirmation, while living with a relative of his wife in London, it became apparent that the job had gone to another individual without Stuart being officially notified. The Brougham brothers had done their best but other members of the ministry opposed giving employment to an undischarged bankrupt with a shady reputation.

In a long letter to Henry Brougham dated 19 November 1832,[32] Stuart vented his disappointment and anger, detailing all the broken assurances that he had been given. He felt that many of the recent appointments had been given to people less qualified than himself:

> Be so good then as to look to the Consulships filled by new men, to the Secretary-
> ships to new Governors of Colonies filled by new men, since my return, and I think
> you will find many such situations bestowed on persons, not possessing habits of
> business, and other qualification, more likely to render them useful, than those,
> which I may be supposed, or known, to have had favourable opportunities to
> acquire.

Stuart goes on to detail his desperate financial situation:

> Reflect on them [his disappointments] for a moment – and then place yourself in
> our situation, literally, without one farthing in the World, occupying here for the
> time the house of a friend and relation of my wife's, ... indebted for our daily means
> of support to the liberality of my friend Mr Cadell,[33] Bookseller in Edinburgh, who

had been giving us supplies of money for our present wants, on the faith of profits to be derived from a publication, one page of which he had not seen, written by an Individual advanced in Life, who had never previously been engaged in any literary occupation, and who is about as ignorant of the art of bookmaking, as of the art of shoemaking.

It is a strange coincidence that Robert Cadell, the publisher and bookseller who supported Stuart financially at this difficult time, was the brother of William Cadell, the banker who had commenced Stuart's sequestration. Robert Cadell acquired the copyright of Walter Scott's Waverley novels in 1827 and by the success of his publishing, played a large part in helping Scott to recover from his bankruptcy.

Stuart finds employment

In 1833 Stuart obtained a job as editor of the *Courier*, a struggling London newspaper which had changed its political leanings from Tory to Whig when the Whigs gained power in November 1830. Also in 1833 with the help of Lord Brougham, Stuart at last obtained a government job as a temporary assistant commissioner to investigate the operation of Lord Althorp's Factory Act of 1833.[34] This act was concerned with the employment of children in the woollen and cotton mills. It stipulated a minimum age of nine, and an eight-hour working day for children aged between nine and 13 with two hours schooling each day. Children over 13 were restricted to a 12-hour working day. This act was extremely unpopular with all – except perhaps the young children. The mill owners objected that it was impossible to run a factory with different grades of employees having different working hours, furthermore they did not have the facilities or teachers for the schools. The spinners objected because the child 'piecers'[35] were essential for their work. The parents of the children resented their loss of earnings and did their utmost to conceal their ages, which was not too difficult as there was no registration of births at that time. Stuart's reports in general took the side of the mill owners by emphasising their difficulties.

In 1834 Stuart, who had for many years been involved with the insurance business, was able to found the United Kingdom Life Insurance Company,[36] indicating that his finances had recovered to some extent. Despite this evidence of a turn of fortune, he publicly attacked his former friend Lord Brougham – who by then, with the return of a Tory Government, was no longer Lord Chancellor – on the grounds that he had not helped him sufficiently to find permanent employment. Brougham in a letter to a friend said:

> I *did* get one place for him in twenty-four hours after he applied to me – Factory
> Commission – I asked for four or five others. I made some point of it, and actually
> *broke* with more people about it than I ever did for any man … . So much for those
> lies. But the cause of my failure was this. I pressed Jeffrey [then Lord Advocate] for
> an office … . He refused … . He said 'He is not honest … he took away two or three
> thousand of the Widows' Fund of which he was treasurer' I … said his sureties paid
> for it, and *they* did not complain, and I again urged my suit for this unworthy
> wretch. At last, Jeffrey, pressed by my importunity, said, 'Then I must tell you that
> was not his first offence', and then disclosed a former act of embezzlement,[37] and
> told me by whom he was saved from exposure![38]

Remarkably, despite this, in 1836, Lord Brougham – who by then was thoroughly tired of Stuart and his 'false and detestable proceedings' – managed to obtain a permanent post for Stuart as one of the four factory inspectors appointed under the Factory Act, with the generous salary of £1,000 a year. Henriques (1971)[39] describes the appointment as surprising because 'he was known to the politicians who appointed him as an opinionated, jealous and irascible character, tactless, difficult to work with and biased in the conflict of interests with which he would be dealing'. Stuart's district was Scotland and the North of England where he replaced his friend Leonard Horner,[40] who had moved to Lancashire. Stuart tended to disagree with the other inspectors regarding the interpretation of the Act. As a result he fell out with Horner who wrote, 'For having been intimate with him the greater part of my life, I was very unwilling that a friendship should cease which had subsisted so long; but I did not succeed'.[41] If Stuart found abuses he tended to find fault with the spinners who engaged the children as their assistants rather than mill owners. He was reported as being superficial in his inspection of the mills and fell out with his subordinates who accused him of running his district from the London office of the *Courier* while they did all the work. Being chairman of his insurance company also demanded his presence in London. Stuart responded to the criticism by giving up the *Courier* (which promptly reverted to its original Tory loyalty) and by taking out some token prosecutions against the mill owners rather than their employees.

In 1847 the new Ten Hour Act was passed limiting the working hours of women and children under 18 to a 10-hour day. This proved equally difficult to administer and resulted in differing interpretation among the various inspectors; Stuart again falling out with his colleagues. He was then aged 74 and found it increasingly difficult to climb the 94 steps to the office in which they held their meetings, but continued to hold his post until his death at his home in Notting Hill in London on 3 November 1849.

According to Henriques:

> Stuart administered an act intended to protect working class children in such a way as to indicate to their parents that in the dispute between capital and labour the government was entirely on the masters' side. With a few more men such as he in key places the nineteenth century might well have become an epoch of revolution instead of a period which saw the peaceful development of constitutional bureaucracy.[42]

Stuart at death appears as a rather sad figure. He had lost his extensive properties, his beloved library and paintings. He had fallen out with many of his old friends. Perhaps saddest of all is that this hitherto ardent Whig spent his last years trying to frustrate the operation of a piece of liberal legislation designed to improve the lot of women and children in the workplace. An obituary read:

> His too great sensibility, his impetuosity, and his obstinate adherence to the opinions and steps he had either avowed or taken, sometimes hurried Mr. Stuart into difficulties and embarrassments which more dispassionate men, would have avoided.[43]

William Murray Borthwick

In 1822, at the age of 40, William Borthwick had to restart his life and livelihood. The actions of Rae and Hope had left him penniless and embittered by his failure to get any compensation or apology for his maltreatment. A descendant, Ann Carson, has tried to follow up his life and has published her research on a website[44] from which much of the following account has been derived.

By 1823 the family had moved to Edinburgh and was living at 6 Brown Street where Borthwick appears to have worked both as a printer and a spirit dealer. He was still at that address on 9 February 1825, when he wrote his second letter to Sir William Rae appealing for recompense from 'his Majesty's Ministers for the ruin and unparalleled hardships heaped upon me by you and your deputy John Hope Esq.'.[45] In the 1828/29 Post Office Directory a W. M. Borthwick appeared as a coach proprietor at 25 Princes Street. If it was the same Borthwick, his business activities must have prospered. No further information has been discovered until 5 June 1833 when he emigrated to Australia on the *Lady East* accompanied by his wife Helen and their six surviving children aged from six to 22. They arrived at Sydney on 15 November after a five-month voyage.

Borthwick appears to have given up his career as a printer and publisher in Australia in favour of farming. He worked as a farm hand for some years before acquiring his own property; one of the first 'squatter's runs' near the pioneering township of Inverell in New South Wales. As a squatter he would have to build his own house and fence his land. Attacks from the dispossessed aborigines and bushrangers were not uncommon. It must have been a hard life for the family, but they appear to have made a success of it. They built a home called Auburn Vale in which William and Helen spent their last years, Helen dying in 1865 and William the following year aged 84. He left an estate of £600 which was distributed among his children.

Of all the individuals involved directly or indirectly with the duel, Borthwick appears to have endured the greatest hardships. He emerges as one of the most interesting characters; his writings show him to be literate and familiar with the works of Shakespeare. Had he avoided the mistake of getting involved in libellous publications he might well have become a successful newspaper proprietor. He showed great resilience in being able to recover from the injustice of his imprisonment and had the adaptability to adopt a completely new and successful career in Australia where he has left many descendants (Fig. 33).

Subsequent duels in Scotland

Only two more fatal duels took place in Scotland – both in Fife and both curiously linked with the Boswell/Stuart duel in the involvement of some of the participants. The penultimate duel[46] was between Captain William Gurley aged 41, a half-pay army officer and owner of an estate in St Vincents, and John Brunskill Waistell aged 25, a lace salesman from London. Waistell owed Gurley £70, having lost a wager in connection with the St Leger race of 1824, which was won by the horse Jerry. Waistell refused, or was unable, to pay his debt and after an argument with Gurley during which Gurley struck him violently with a poker, a duel became inevitable. Both men were resident in Edinburgh at the time and the duel was arranged by their respective seconds to take place at 8am on 30 October 1824 at the back of Salisbury Crags on Hunter's Bog, near St Anthony's Well.[47]

As with the Boswell/Stuart duel, the law interfered and the arrival of the police aborted the event. It was decided to reconvene in Fife later the same day, and both parties accompanied by their seconds and medical attendants crossed Queensferry together at midday. Gurley's surgeon was Robert Liston, who had been Stuart's attendant. Waistell was attended by Dr. Alexander George Home. A secluded site was chosen not far from North Queensferry.

Each contestant had his pair of pistols, Gurley's were the newly invented 'detonators' or percussion pistols and Waistell's were the traditional flintlocks. The percussion pistols were thought to be more reliable and fired more quickly than the flintlocks but Gurley refused to allow Waistell to borrow one of his and each used his own.[48] It was agreed that the duellists should fire on the count of three called by one of the seconds. Observers noted that Waistell fired prematurely after the count of two, and Gurley fell to the ground without firing. He was shot through the chest and died immediately. Waistell then turned a second pistol on himself, however Dr Home managed to wrest it from him. Waistell then fled from the scene. A warrant for his arrest on the charge of murder was issued on 31 October, but Waistell had disappeared without trace. He was presumed to have gone abroad and no trial took place.

A stone was erected in memory of William Gurley at the site of the duel and can still be seen (Fig. 34). In 1987 a brass plaque was added by the North Queensferry Community Council. It reads:

> It is on record that Capt. Wm Gurley of Petershope, St. Vincent died at this spot on 30th October, 1824 having been fatally wounded in a pistol duel with a Mr Westall [*sic*] – the last to be fought in Fife.

It was not however the last. The last in Fife – and Scotland – took place on 23 August 1826.[49] The protagonists were George Morgan, a Kirkcaldy bank agent, and David Landale, a linen merchant, who was in financial difficulties with the bank. Morgan indiscreetly gossiped about Landale's affairs and when Landale came to hear about it, an angry exchange of letters took place. Finally, Morgan impetuously struck Landale with his umbrella – a challenge to a duel. It took place near the farm of Cardenbarns, in the parish of Auchterderran in Fife, and resulted in Landale killing Morgan. Morgan's medical attendant was Dr James Johnston, who had turned up at the duel of Boswell and Stuart. In the subsequent trial, Landale was defended by Jeffrey and Cockburn, two of the advocates who had defended Stuart, and once again they were successful in obtaining an acquittal.[50]

Landale's business subsequently prospered and he became Provost of Kirkcaldy. A reconciliation between the duelling families seems to have taken place, for 25 years after the duel, one of Landale's daughters married a nephew of Morgan. Descendants of both families set up together a company of brokers in India called Landale & Morgan which survived until the 1950s.[51]

The percussion pistols used in this duel are on display in the Kirkcaldy

Museum. The accompanying legend states that these pistols were also the ones used in the Gurley/Waistell duel although the account of that duel states that Gurley alone used a percussion pistol having refused to allow his opponent to use the other of the pair.[52]

In the preface to his extensive notes on the trial of Landale, Cockburn praised the presiding judge, Lord Gillies, for his address to the jury in which he allowed them to consider all aspects of the case and not to be swayed by the fact that killing someone in a duel was legally regarded as murder. Gillies came in for much criticism for this advice from the legal profession, but Cockburn liked its pragmatism.

> I can't say that the <u>Law</u> of this doctrine seems to me to be very intelligible, but there was great merit in stating any doctrine that was consistent with the common sense of the world … . Very reasonable, but very illegal.[53]

Cockburn was not the first to comment on the arbitrary nature of the judgements in such matters. In 1813 the *Edinburgh Review* had reported that:

> There are cases of total discrepancy between the laws and manners of the country; but there the letter of the law yields to the spirit of the times. Thus, a duel, where one is killed, is a capital offence ... yet this law is a mere dead letter; for what with the unwillingness of prosecutors – the connivance, first of police-officers, then of judges – the feeling of juries ... no instance is known of the law being executed upon any person for being engaged in a duel, fought in what is called a fair manner.[54]

By the mid-nineteenth century, duelling was losing its public appeal. According to the *Edinburgh Review* in 1842:

> Hitherto there has been a foolish notion, and false pride, in considering it unbecoming to apologize or retract until the adversary's fire was received; but common sense and humanity are now beginning to discover, that there is more of manliness in at once acknowledging an error, than in waiting to admit it at the pistol's mouth … . It is to the honour of the younger public men of the day, that none of them of any note ... have been engaged in a duel. For the past 12 years they have preserved their honour, their courage, and their conscience unsullied, without this vulgar appeal.[55]

In 1843, an event occurred which effectively marked the end of duelling in this country. An army officer, Col. Fawcett, was killed in a duel with another officer and the Government decided that, because of the manner of his death, his widow should not receive a pension. This established a precedent which was hotly debated in the House of Commons. Sir Robert Peel, now Prime Minister, was unyielding. He confirmed the decision regarding the pension and anticipated that further legislation regarding the legal status of duelling was unnecessary, which, in the event, proved to be the case. Although the matter of the pension applied only to army personnel, public opinion was by then turning against duelling and Col. Fawcett's duel was the last fatal duel between two Britons to take place in Britain.

The effect of the Reform Act

The undercurrent theme of this book has been the struggle of the masses to obtain some power and representation in Parliament. Cockburn had written that 'the shires and groups of boroughs returning the 45 [Scottish] members to the House of Commons were practically so many nomination seats under the control of Government'.[56] Charles James Fox had described the Scottish electoral system as 'a state of representation so monstrous and absurd, so ridiculous and so revolting, that it is good for nothing except perhaps to be placed by the side of the English, in order to set off our defective system by the comparison of one still more defective'.[57] In 1831 there was a general election and Francis Jeffrey was persuaded by public petition to stand for Edinburgh against Robert Adam Dundas. The self-elected Town Council of 33 Tory members automatically elected anyone connected with the all-powerful Dundas family. Adam Black reckoned that if the public had been given a vote, 19 out of 20 would have voted for Jeffrey. An angry reaction resulted and a mob hounded the Lord Provost to shelter in a shop. Only Jeffrey managed to curb the wrath of the citizens who unyoked the horses of his carriage and drew him home.[58] He subsequently obtained his Parliamentary seat in Perth.

The passing of the Scottish Reform Act in 1832[59] marked a resounding success for the Whigs. Francis Jeffrey and Henry Cockburn were chiefly responsible for drawing up the Act which increased the number of Scottish members of Parliament from 45 to 53 and increased the franchise from 5,000 to 65,000.

Cockburn was credited with being:

> One of a circle of enterprising and able men, who ... conceived, and in thirty years executed the idea of emancipating Scotland from a thraldom more intolerant, and a servility more despicable, than ever enslaved a country calling itself free ... after living to see its cause triumphant and to reap themselves the rewards of its triumph, they left her at their death as free in politics and in intellect, ... as any nation on the globe.[60]

It is perhaps fitting to conclude with another passage from Cockburn.[60]

He describes the enthusiasm with which the citizens of Edinburgh welcomed their first opportunity to exercise their right to vote in the election of December 1832, when Edinburgh had for the first time two members to elect and an electorate of 5,000 instead of just the City Council members. There were three candidates; two Whigs – Francis Jeffrey, proposed by Sir James Gibson-Craig, and James Abercromby, proposed by Adam Black the publisher, and one Tory – Forbes Hunter Blair, proposed by Francis Walker WS. Jeffrey and Abercromby proceeded to Merchants' Hall in a procession of carriages. Theirs had four horses and men and beasts wore blue and buff cockades.

> From the Merchants' Hall, ... we walked in procession, with banners and music, to the Hustings at the [Mercat] Cross. I don't know that I ever felt so strangely as on first getting up to the platform and beholding the sea of heads around. There must have been from 10,000 to 15,000 people there, exclusive of all who crowded the windows and roofs. ... Each of the three candidates spoke for himself. Not one word of what was said by or for Blair was allowed to be heard. The other speeches were as well listened to as they could be in such a crowd. I never saw a public show of hands before, nor was I ever more struck than at the effect of men's hands being twice as numerous as their heads. It makes a flash. The show for the two popular men was electrical .... Everything was quite peaceable and orderly. What a dream did it seem to meet with the Reformers of 1793 and of the Pantheon Meeting on these hustings![60]

Jeffrey and Abercromby were elected by a wide margin – what a contrast this election was from that of the year before, and intriguing that the two, who had played such a large part in the passing of the Act, should be among the first to benefit from its provisions. The Scottish Reform Act abolished the Tory dominance in Scotland until 1900. This was the threshold of a more peaceful and prosperous age. The intense interest aroused by the Stuart/Boswell duel by the subsequent trials and Parliamentary debates may have contributed. One observer commented that the injustices suffered by Borthwick exposed in the Parliamentary debates, 'helped on apace the measure of Reform looming in the distance'.[62]

Notes

1   *Edinburgh Review*, **75** (1842), p. 444. Review of Mellingen, J. G. (1841): *The History of Duelling.*

2   Buchanan (1975): *The Treasure of Auchinleck. The Story of the Boswell Papers*, pp. 204–6.

3   In the deed of entail, the first five letters (namely, 'irred,') in the word 'irredeemably,' in the clause fettering the right of sale, were written on an erasure, of which no notice was contained in

the testing clause. In consequence, the judges of the Court of Session declared that the entail was defective and was thus set aside.

4   The history of Auchinleck House is contained in an excellent booklet *Auchinleck House* published by the Landmark Trust (2001), Constance Barrett (ed.).

5   Cockburn, Harry A. (1910) An account of the Friday Club … with notes on certain other social clubs in Edinburgh, *Book of the Old Edinburgh Club* **3** p. 172.

6   Henry Mackenzie 1745–1831. An Edinburgh advocate, best remembered as the author of the novel A *Man of Feeling.*

7   In 1819 the Edinburgh Joint Stock Water Company took over the responsibility for Edinburgh's water supply from the Town Council. Chronic shortage of water required additional resources from Pentland springs beyond the existing Comiston and Swanston supply. Sir Robert Liston (1742–1836), who had been the British Ambassador to Washington, owned the estate of Millburn at the east end of the Pentlands. (Not to be confused with the surgeon of the same name who acted as Stuart's medical attendant at the duel.)

8   Macvey Napier was not only Librarian of the Signet Library from 1805–37 but also editor of the *Edinburgh Review* from 1829–37.

9   Quoted in Miller, K. (1975): *Cockburn's Millennium* (Duckworth: London), p. 247.

10   British Library. Add 34613 folio 408–408v.

11   John Richardson an Edinburgh lawyer who had settled in London. According to Cockburn 'No Scotchman in London ever stood higher in professional and personal character'. He was a close friend of Walter Scott and wrote a biography of him.

12   WS Society Letter Book, I, p. 355. John Home was presumably the Secretary of the Widows' Fund.

13   WS Society Letter Book, I, pp. 356–7 Colin Mackenzie was deputy keeper of the Signet.

14   Letter in National Archives of Scotland GD 180/685. William Cadell was treasurer of the Bank of Scotland. He was the brother of Robert Cadell, the publisher, who helped Walter Scott recover from his bankruptcy by publishing popular cheap editions of the Waverley novels.

15   Act Confirming and Decreet Adjudging the real and personal estates of James Stuart in favour of Thomas Mansfield Trustee NAS CS43/159 and NAS DI 8/338. Petition to Lords Ordinary by Thomas Mansfield Trustee re sequestrated estate of James Stewart of Dunearn WS and Banker of Moray Place. Sequestration Order. 1 September 1828, pp. 1–55.

16   WS Society Letter Book, I, p. 386.

17   Ibid, p. 400.

18   Advertisement in *The Scotsman,* 22 August 1829

19   Advertisement in *The Scotsman,* 16 August 1828

20   Scott (1932–37): *The Letters of Sir Walter Scott,* **XI**, 3 February 1829, pp. 121–2. In a later letter to the Duke on 14 February 1829 Scott wrote that, 'The Watteau of three figures sold for £15. Cheap enough but its authenticity is doubted'.

21   Of the named paintings I have been able to trace the present location of three: the Van Dyck portrait of Isabella Brandt, the *Wife of Rubens,* is in the National Gallery of Art in Washington; Brueghel's *Noah's Ark* is in the Getty Museum in Los Angeles and Hobbema's *Avenue at Middelharnis* is in the National Gallery in London.

22   David Erskine and Stuart's mother were children of the Revd John Erskine, Minister of Greyfriars Kirk.

23   Letter Book on Stuart's Sequestration. National Archive of Scotland GD 282/8/7.

24   Stuart travelled on one of the packets which left Liverpool three times a month for New York. He recorded that the outward fare was 35 guineas and the return journey only 30 guineas because the prevailing wind caused the outward journey to take, on average, 40 days while the return took only 25.

25   Stuart (1833), **2**, p. 246. *The Scotsman* had become a twice-weekly paper in 1823.

26   Boswell (1964), **3**, p. 202.

27   Brady (1984), pp. 165–6.

28   Quoted in McFarland, p. 59.

29   From *Domestic Manners* **1**, p. 16 cited in Williamson, K. (2008): *International Journal of Scottish Literature,* Issue **4**.

30   Stuart (1833): *Three years in North America*, **2**, p. 95.

31   Ibid, p. 111.

32   Letter from James Stuart to Henry Brougham, 19 November 1832. No J842 in the Brougham Correspondence. UCL Library.

33   Robert Cadell (1789–1849) published Stuart's *Three years in North America* in the following year. It was moderately successful and repaid Cadell's faith and friendship. Cadell, who had been in partnership with Archibald Constable, acquired the copyright of Walter Scott's Waverley Novels after Constable's bankruptcy in 1826. As a result he became very wealthy and helped Scott's recovery from his bankruptcy.

34   Henriques, U. R. Q. (1971): 'An early factory inspector, James Stuart of Dunearn', *Scottish Historical Review* **50**, pp. 18–46.

35   The piecers were children who repaired broken threads in awkward situations.

36   The United Kingdom Life Insurance Company later became part of the North British Mercantile Insurance Company of which Stuart had been a founding director.

37   Brougham letter to an unknown correspondent, Tuesday, November 1834. Cited in Aspinall (1973): *Politics and the Press c. 1780–1850*, p. 243.

38   No record of this former act of embezzlement has been found.

39   Henriques (1971), p. 27.

40   Leonard Horner (1785–1864) was the younger brother of Francis (see Chapter 1), who became a distinguished geologist. He was an active Whig, interested in education. He founded the Edinburgh School of Arts which was the start of what is now the Heriot Watt University, and was one of the founders along with Walter Scott and Henry Cockburn of the Edinburgh Academy. He was appointed as one of the Commissioners to supervise the Factories Act in 1833 and continued in that office until 1856.

41   Letter to Cornewall Lewis, 28 October 1849, cited in Henriques (1971), p. 44.

42   Henriques (1971), p. 46.

43   *Gentleman's Magazine,* new series, **XXXII**, 1849, p. 659.

44   The web site has evolved and improved over the years; first consulted in 2001: http://freepages.genealogy.rootsweb.ancestry.com/~anncarson/Borthwick/wmbinverell.htm [accessed March 2014].

45   Borthwick, W. M. (1825): *Letter to Sir William Rae, M.P., Lord Advocate of Scotland*, p. 1.

46   Leggett (1998): *Scotland's Penultimate Duel* gives an excellent account.

47   Walter Scott in *Heart of Midlothian*, Chapter 11, wrote that, 'This sequestered dell, as well as other places of the open pasturage of the King's Park, was ... often the resort of the gallants of the time [1736] who had affairs of honour to discuss with the sword'.

48   Leggett (1998), pp. 38–9.

49   *The Scotsman,* 22 June 1925, 'Two Fife Duels'.

50   The speeches of Cockburn and Jeffrey as quoted in Landale (2005) are, not surprisingly, very similar to those which they delivered at Stuart's trial.

51   Landale (2005): *Duel. A true story of death and honour*, p. 276.

52   The matter of the pistols is confusing. Landale (2005), pp. 111–2 and Cockburn (*c.*1826): *Case of David Landale* state that Landale purchased the percussion pistols the day before the duel from the shop of John Thompson in Edinburgh. Thompson informed him that one of these had killed Gurley in the earlier duel. Leggett (1998), pp. 38–9 indicates that the Waistell pistol which killed Gurley was a flintlock.

53   Cockburn (*c.*1826), preface, ms file Adv 9.1.2 NLS.

54   *Edinburgh Review,* **22** (1813), p. 74. Review of George, J. (1812): *A Treatise on the Offence of Libel.*

55   *Edinburgh Review* **75** (1842), pp. 443–4.

56   Cockburn (1852): *Life of Lord Jeffrey*, p. 64.

57   Thorne (1986): *History of Parliament: The House of Commons 1790–1820*, III, xxxiii, p. 730.

58   Black (1885): *Memoirs of Adam Black*, p. 80.

59   The act was passed concurrently with the Reform Act 1832, which applied to England and Wales.

60   *Edinburgh Review* **105** (1857), p. 219.

61   Cockburn (1874a): *Journal of Henry Cockburn 1831–1854*, **I**, pp. 40–1.
62   In 1793 the Tory government conducted the vicious 'Sedition Trials' to suppress any movement for reform in the wake of Thomas Paine's Rights of Man and the French Revolution.
63   MacKenzie (1890): *Old Reminiscences of Glasgow*, p. 381.

Bibliography

Abbreviations

NLS – National Library of Scotland
NAS – National Archives of Scotland

Alexander, R. (1822): *Letter to Sir J. Mackintosh, Knt., M.P., explanatory of the whole circumstances which led to the robbery of the Glasgow Sentinel Office; to the death of Sir Alexander Boswell Bart., to the Trial of Mr James Stuart and ultimately to the animadversions of the Hon James Abercromby in the House of Commons upon the conduct of the Right Honourable the Lord Advocate and various individuals* (Glasgow: printed in the Sentinel Office).

Anon (1821a): *Correspondence between James Stuart Esq and the Printer of the Beacon.* Three editions of this printed correspondence exist, each with a slightly different content. NLS Yule 2 (7).

Anon (1821b): *Correspondence between James Stuart Esq. the younger of Dunearn and the Lord Advocate is contained in a bound* volume. NLS Yule 2 (7).

Anon (1822): *The Trial of James Stuart Esq. Younger of Dunearn, before the High Court of Justiciary on Monday 10th day of June 1822* (Edinburgh: J Dick and Co.). Referred to in the text and notes as Trial 1.

Anon (1822): *The Trial of James Stuart, Esq. Younger of Dunearn, before the High Court of Justiciary at Edinburgh on Monday, June 10, 1822*, 3rd edition (Edinburgh: Archibald Constable & Co.). Referred to in the text and notes as Trial 2.

Anon (1822): *Proceedings in the House of Commons on Mr Abercromby's Motion for enquiring into the Conduct of the Lord Advocate and othe Law Officers, in connection with the Public Press of Scotland* (Edinburgh: J. Dick & Co.).

Anon (n.d.): Broadsheet, *Unfortunate Duel.* NLS, L C Folio 73(33).

Anon (1823): Parliamentary Papers. *Papers respecting the Case of William Murray Borthwick, Robert Alexander and others,* ordered by House of Commons.

Anon (1909): *The North British and Mercantile Company. Centenary 1809–1909.*

Arnot, H. (1816): *The History of Edinburgh from the earliest accounts to the year 1780* (Edinburgh: Thomas Turnbull).

Aspinall, A. (1973): *Politics and the Press c. 1780–1850* (Brighton: Harvester Press). Reprint of first edition of 1949.

Aspinall, A. (2005): *Lord Brougham and the Whig Party* (Stroud: Nonsuch Publishing).

Baldwick, R. (1970): *The Duel: A history of duelling* (London: Spring Books).

Black, A. (1885): *Memoirs of Adam Black*, A. Nicolson (ed.) (Edinburgh: Adam and Charles Black).

Borthwick, W. M. (1822): *Proceedings against William Murray Borthwick, at the instance of His Majestys Advocate, and of Robert Alexander, styling himself editor and proprietor of the Glasgow Sentinel newspaper. With an appendix of documents, and a preface* (Edinburgh). NLS Yule 2 (7).

Borthwick, W. M. (1825): *Letter to Sir William Rae M.P., Lord Advocate of Scotland* (Edinburgh: G. Mudie & Co.). Printed copy of letter of 25 September 1823.

Boswell, A. (1810): *Edinburgh or, the Ancient Royalty; A Sketch of Former Manners, with Notes* (Edinburgh; printed for Manners & Miller by J. Johnstone).

Boswell, A. (1871): *The Poetical Works of Sir Alexander Boswell, now first collected and edited, with memoir*, R. H. Smith (ed.) (Glasgow: Maurice Ogle & Co.).

Boswell, J. (1964): *Life of Johnson*, 6 vols, 2nd edition, G. B.Hill (ed.), revised by L. F. Powell, (Oxford: Clarendon Press).

Boswell, J. (1990): *The Journal of James Boswell 1761–1798*, selected by J. Wain (London: Heinemann).

Boswell, J. (1995): *James Boswell's Book of Company at Auchinleck 1782–1795*, Mary, Viscountess Eccles and G. Turnbull (ed.). Presented to the Roxburghe Club.

Brady, F. (1984): *James Boswell, the Later Years 1769–1795* (London: Heinemann).

Brodie, I. (2004): *Steamers of the Forth*, vol. 1 (Catrine: Stenlake Publishing).

Brougham, H. (1871): *The Life and Times of Henry Lord Brougham written by himself*, 3 vols (Edinburgh: Blackwood).

Buchan, J. (1932): *Sir Walter Scott* (London: Cassell & Co.).

Buchanan, D. (1975): *The Treasure of Auchinleck. The Story of the Boswell Papers* (London: Heinemann).

Byron, Lord (1824): *English Bards and Scotch Reviewers, a Satire* (Glasgow: James Starke). A new edition with a life of the author.

Carmichael, A. (1833): *Domestic Manners and Social Condition of the White, Coloured, and Negro Population of the West Indies*, 2 vols (London: Whittaker, Treacher and Co.).

Carson, Ann (2001): William Murray Borthwick at: http://freepages.genealogy.rootsweb. ancestry.com/~anncarson/Borthwick/ wmbinverell.htm [accessed March 2014].

Chalmers, J. (2010): *Andrew Duncan Senior, Physician of the Enlightenment* (Edinburgh: NMSE Publishing).

Chambers, R. (1875): *A Biographical Dictionary of Eminent Scotsmen* (Edinburgh: Blackie & Son).

Christison, R. (1886): *Life of Sir Robert Christison*, 2 vols (edited by his sons) (Edinburgh: Wm Blackwood).

Cline, C. L. (1971): *The fate of Cassandra: The Newspaper War of 1821–22 and Sir Walter Scott* (University of Texas, Austin).

Cockburn, H. A. (1910): An account of the Friday Club ... with notes on certain other social clubs in Edinburgh, *Book of the Old Edinburgh Club*, 3.

Cockburn, H. (c.1822a [undated]): *Case of James Stuart*. Volume of ms notes amounting to about 400 irregularly numbered pages relating to the trial of James Stuart. Referred to in the text and notes as Trial 3. NLS, Adv 9.1.1.

Cockburn, H. (c.1822b [undated]): *Case of William Murray Borthwick*. A bound volume containing Parliamentary Papers (see Anon (1823) and ms notes amounting to about 500 pages. NLS, Adv 9.1.4.

Cockburn, H. (c.1826): *Case of David Landale*. Volume of undated ms notes and printed pamphlet. NLS, Adv 9.1.2.

Cockburn, H. (1852): *Life of Lord Jeffrey*, 2 vols (Edinburgh: Adam & Charles Black).

Cockburn, H. (1874a): *Journal of Henry Cockburn 1831–1854*, 2 vols (Edinburgh: Edmonston and Douglas).

Cockburn, H. (1874b): *Letters chiefly concerned with the Affairs of Scotland from Lord Cockburn to Thomas Francis Kennedy* (London: Wm. Ridgway).

Cockburn, H. (1909): *Memorials of his time* (Edinburgh: T. N. Foulis). First published in 1856.

Conolly, M. F. (1866): *Biographical Dictionary of Eminent Men of Fife* (Cupar: John C. Orr).

Constable, T. (1873): *Archibald Constable and his Literary Correspondents*, 3 vols (Edinburgh: Constable).

Corson, J. C. (1979): *Notes and Index to Sir Herbert Grierson's Edition of the Letters of Sir Walter Scott* (Oxford: Clarendon Press).

Croker, J. W. (1887): *The Croker Papers 1808–1857*, 2nd edition, L. J. Jenning (ed.(London: B.T. Batford).

Crombie, B. W. (1882): *Modern Athenians* (Edinburgh: Adam and Charles Black).

Cronin. R. (2010): *Paper Pellets: Culture after Waterloo* (Oxford: OUP).

Crow, W. S. (1969): *'Balmuto' Leaves from the Pages of History*. Typewritten ms NLS 6.2199.

Farington, J. (1922): *The Farington Diary*, 8 vols, Greig, J. (ed.(London: Hutchison & Co.).

Fergusson, R. (1970): *The Works of Robert Fergusson*, James Thin (ed.(Mercat Press).

Fox, H. E. (1923): *The Journal of the Hon. Henry Edward Fox 1818–1830*, Earl of Ilchester (ed.) (London: Thorton Butterworth Ltd).

Fyfe, W. W. (1851): *Summer Life on Land and Water at South Queensferry* (Edinburgh: Oliver and Boyd).

Grant, A. (1891): *Memoirs of an American Lady* (New York: Dodd Mead and Co.)

Grant, J. (1881–83): *Old and New Edinburgh*, 3 vols (London: Cassell & Co.).

Greig, J. A. (1948): *Francis Jeffrey of The Edinburgh Review* (Edinburgh: Oliver & Boyd).

Grierson, Sir H. (1938): *Sir Walter Scott Bart: A new life* (London: Constable).

Hale-White, W. (1930): 'The medical Boswells', *Proc. Roy. Soc. Med.* **23**, pp. 281–84.

Harding, A. W. (1992): 'James Stuart of Dunearn', *Transactions of the Gaelic Society of*

Inverness **56**, pp. 365–76.

Henriques, U. R. Q. (1971): 'An early factory inspector, James Stuart of Dunearn', *Scottish Historical Review* **50**, pp. 18–46.

Hinks, J. (ed.) (2009): *Periodicals and Publishers: The Newspaper and Journal Trade 1740–1914* (Oak Knoll Press & British Library).

Hope, J. (1822): *Letter to the Hon. James Abercromby MP by John Hope Esq.* (Edinburgh: Wm. Blackwood).

Hunt, G. (2008): *The Duel* (London: B Tauris).

Johnson, E. (1970): *Sir Walter Scott, the Great Unknown* (London: Hamish Hamilton).

Kay, J. (1837–38): *A series of original Portraits and Caricature Etchings with Biographical Sketches and Illustrative Anecdotes*, 2 vols. Text by James Paterson et. al. (Edinburgh: Hugh Paton).

Landale, J. (2005): *Duel. A true story of death and honour* (Edinburgh: Canongate).

Lang, A. (1897): *The Life and Letters of John Gibson Lockhart*, 2 vols (London: John Nimmo).

Leggett, J. M. (1998): *Scotland's Penultimate Duel* (Kinloch Rannoch: Crossmount House).

Lockhart, J. G. (1902): *Life of Sir Walter Scott*, 8 vols (Edinburgh: T & A Constable). First published 1837–38.

Lockhart, J. G. (1819): *Peter's Letters to his Kinsfolk*, 2nd ed., 3 vols (Edinburgh: Blackwood).

Lockhead, M. (1954): *John Gibson Lockhart* (London: John Murray).

'Lucius' (1822): *Letter to John Hope Esq. containing strictures on his Letter to the Honourable James Abercromby MP* (Edinburgh: James Huie).

Lustig, I. S. (ed.) (1981): *Boswell: The Applause of the Jury 1782–1785* (London: Heinemann).

Lustig, I. S. (ed.) (1986): *Boswell: The English Experiment 1785–1789* (London: Heinemann).

McFarland, R. E. (1972): *New Rambler*, cxii, pp. 55–64.

Mack, D. S. (ed.) (1972): *James Hogg: Memoirs of the author's life and familiar anecdotes of Sir Walter Scott* (Edinburgh: Scottish Academic Press).

MacKenzie, P. (1890): *Old Reminiscences of Glasgow* (Glasgow: Forrester).

Marr, A. (2004): *My Trade: A short history of British Journalism* (London: Macmillan).

Mason, N. (ed.) (2006): *Blackwood's Magazine 1817–1825*, 6 vols (London: Pickering and Chatto).

Moss, M. (1995): 'The curious case of Duncan

Stevenson, printer to Edinburgh University', *The Bibliotheck* **20**, pp. 88–97.

Mudie, R. (1825): *The Modern Athens* (London).

Omond, G. W. T. (1883): *The Advocates of Scotland* (Edinburgh: David Douglas).

Owenson, S. (1822): *The Mohawks: A satirical Poem with Notes* (London: Colburn).

Parker, M. (2000): *Literary Magazines and British Romanticism* (Cambridge: CUP).

Partington, W. (1932): *Sir Walter's Post-bag* (London: John Murray).

Porritt, E. (1903): *The unreformed House of Commons, Parliamentary Representation before 1832*, 2 vols (Cambridge: CUP).

Reed, J. W. & Pottle, F. A. (1977): *Boswell, Laird of Auchinleck 1778–1782* (New York: McGraw-Hill Book Co.).

Scott, W. (1894): *Scott's familiar letters*, 2 vols, D. Douglas (ed.) (Edinburgh).

Scott, W, (1932–37): *The Letters of Sir Walter Scott*, 12 vols, H. J. C. Grierson (London: Constable).

Scott, W. (1972): *The Journal of Sir Walter Scott*, W. E. K. Anderson (ed.) (Oxford: Clarendon Press).

Sharp, G. (1790): *A Tract on Duelling*, 2nd ed. (London: B. White & Son and C. Dilly).

Sisman, A. (2000): *Boswell's Presumptuous Task* (London: Hamilton).

Smith, S, (1953): *Letters of Sydney Smith*, 2 vols, Nowell C. Smith (ed.) (Oxford: Clarendon Press).

Storer, J. & H. S. (1818): *A Graphic Historical Description of the City of Edinburgh* (London).

Storer, J. & H. S. (1820): *Views of Edinburgh and its Vicinity*, 2 vols (Edinburgh: A Constable and Co.).

Stuart, J. and others (1822): *Correspondence between James Stuart Younger of Dunearn and The Earl Morton, Lord Lieutenant, County of Fife relative to Mr Stuart's resignation of his Commission in the Royal Fifeshire Yeomanry Cavalry* (Edinburgh).

Stuart, J. (1822): *Declaration to the Sheriff of Edinburgh, relative to certain papers carried off from the Sentinel office Glasgow. 19th day of March 1822.*

Stuart, J. (1833): *Three years in North America* (Edinburgh: Cadell).

Thorne, R. G. (1986): *History of Parliament: The House of Commons 1790–1820*, **III** (London: Secker and Warburg).

Thomson, H. W. (1931): *A Scottish Man of Feeling* (Oxford: Oxford University Press).

Topham, E. (1776): *Letters from Edinburgh: written in the years 1774 and 1775 : con-*

taining some observations on the diversions, customs, manners, and laws, of the Scotch nation, during a six months residence in Edinburgh (London: Printed for J. Dodsley).

Weir, J. G. (1927–28): 'The case of the *Beacon* and the *Sentinel*', in *Sir Walter Scott Quarterly*, **I**, pp. 194–201.

Wilding, N. & Laundy, P. (1972): *An Encyclopaedia of Parliament*, 4th ed. (London: Casell).

Wishaw, J. (1906): *The 'Pope' of Holland House: Selections from the correspondence of John Wishaw and his friends 1813–1840*, Lady Seymour (ed) (London).

Index